DEADLY GREED

DEADLY
GREED

The Riveting True
Story of the Stuart
Murder Case That
Rocked Boston and
Shocked the Nation

Joe Sharkey

PRENTICE
HALL
PRESS

NEW YORK   LONDON   TORONTO   SYDNEY   TOKYO   SINGAPORE

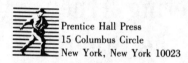Prentice Hall Press
15 Columbus Circle
New York, New York 10023

PRENTICE HALL PRESS and colophon are registered trademarks of Simon & Schuster Inc.

Library of Congress Cataloging-in-Publication Data

Sharkey, Joe.
    Deadly greed : The riveting true story of the Stuart murder case that rocked Boston and shocked the nation / Joe Sharkey.
        p.   cm.
      ISBN 0-13-584178-X
      1. Murder—Massachusetts—Boston—Case studies.
2. Stuart, Charles, 1959–. 3. Stuart, Carol. I. Title.
    HV6534.B6S53 1991
364.1′523′0974461—dc20   90-22968
                                                                          CIP

Designed by Richard Oriolo

Manufactured in the United States of America

10 9 8 7 6 5 4 3 2 1

First Edition

For Carrie

ACKNOWLEDGMENTS

I would like to thank Cynthia Hacinli for her research assistance and sharp insight during an important phase of the work on this book. Also, David Barboza provided valuable help, as did R. Andrew Pierce, who expertly led the way through genealogical records in Boston.

I also am grateful to my editor, Marilyn J. Abraham, for her perceptive guidance. Thanks also to Bridie and Ken Maguire for their kindnesses to a stranger, and to Caroline and Christopher, again.

As always, my wife, Nancy Albaugh Sharkey, illuminated the possibilities.

CONTENTS

'Put off that mask of burning gold
With emerald eyes.'
'Oh no, my dear, you make so bold
To find if hearts be wild and wise,
And yet not cold.'

'I would but find what's there to find,
Love or deceit.'
'It was the mask engaged your mind,
And after set your heart to beat,
Not what's behind.'

'But lest you are my enemy,
I must enquire,'
'Oh no, my dear, let all that be;
What matter, so there is but fire
In you, in me?'

—Yeats

O N E

The Hub

The Stuart case should have been a very simple story, as straight-forward as yesterday's police log. It occurs often enough that the headline might take only four words:

MAN KILLS WIFE, SELF

For that is what happened, though not in the usual time frame. It was a most basic kind of murder, and when the keepers of crime statistics file it away, it will go under the heading "Domestic Violence." Most female homicide victims are killed by their husbands or lovers; violence is a vocational hazard in many domestic relationships. Most of the time, the murderer then kills himself as well. When he does not commit suicide, the killer commonly blames someone else for the crime, often after wounding himself to underscore his innocence.

It should have been no surprise, what actually transpired on

1

that dark, lonely street in Boston on the night of October 23, 1989. A man, of whom the standard psychological profile of the wife abuser fit like the expensive suits he wore, shot his pregnant wife to death, and blamed someone else. Later, when it became clear that the jig, as they used to say in the movies, was up, the murderer jumped off a bridge and killed himself.

Yet it became the biggest news story of the year in Boston, and reverberated for months across the nation. That people like the Stuarts would become victims of random violence reinforced our national fears of urban life, and then came the shock of the terrible hoax.

Some say this story could only have itself played out in Boston. To this day, it is a big city with small-town perspectives—for better or worse. Everyone has a place; there is a place for everyone. And everyone knows it. A city so full of itself that its headline writers routinely refer to it as the "Hub," and have for more than one hundred years, since the poet Oliver Wendell Holmes wrote: "All I claim for Boston is that it is the thinking center of the continent, and therefore for the planet . . . the hub of the solar system." It is also a metropolitan area so provincial in outlook that its best-known newspaper, the *Globe,* could without subsequent embarrassment print this bold headline across its front page on the day after President Kennedy was assassinated in 1963:

John Fitzgerald Kennedy, Born in Brookline, Massachusetts,
Shot and Killed in Dallas, Texas, at Age of 46

Twenty-five years later, the state that launched President Kennedy, the only state to vote against Nixon in 1972, was pilloried by George Bush in the 1988 presidential election with his campaign's strikingly effective use of images of Boston's polluted harbor and the state's most famous parolee, Willie Horton. Boston is a city many people in America love to loathe. And yet Boston, good and bad, has been an elemental part of our national makeup for three hundred and fifty years.

While there are elements of this story that have a particular local resonance, there are clear echoes in every part of this country. Revere Beach, Massachusetts, could just as well be Asbury Park, New Jersey; Venice Beach, California; Warren, Michigan; Columbus, Georgia; Austin, Texas; Birmingham, Alabama; or any town where people work hard for their share of the American dream.

This is a tragedy that has its roots in what has defined not only Boston but the nation as well: the struggle for turf. But as tragedies must, this has to do first with human beings, three of whom came together one night at the end of the 1980s in a metaphor for an era.

TWO

Chuck

A few minutes before one o'clock on a warm afternoon in the final summer of the 1980s—and Chuck Stuart, as usual, was a young man in a big hurry. Frowning, he jerked his left forearm front-and-center to consult his gold LaSalle watch, which flashed in the sunlight on Newbury Street as he quickened his pace to make up for the time he had just lost taking a phone call from a wealthy customer who was worried that her fur coat would not be repaired, cleaned, and ready when she came to get it.

That would be sometime in early November, Chuck thought with the sort of annoyance that lately had come to characterize his attitude toward the fur business in general and his career in particular. Though he had earned one hundred and forty thousand dollars the previous year, the climate in the industry had turned decidedly chilly and he was not at all happy. He had just received his annual bonus, and it was considerably less than what he thought it should have

4

been, considering his obvious contributions to the bottom line. Disgusted, Chuck had already decided that he had had it with the fur business and everything associated with it, from the wealthy old fools who had nothing better to do than chart the seasonal migration of their minks from closet to vault and back, to his bosses, two demanding Hungarians who had inherited the fur business from their father and had lately made it clear to their general manager that, as valued an employee as he might be, he was never going to become their equity partner.

Characteristically, Chuck brooded rather than making his discontent clear to his employers, whom he then instinctively blamed for not sensing what he believed should be a patently obvious change in his attitude. To hell with the pelt peddlers, Chuck thought. He had long known he was worth every penny they paid him, and then some, and now he strongly believed that he could do better elsewhere, preferably as his own boss at last. With the fur business on the ropes all over the country, Edward F. Kakas and Sons, Boston's best-known furrier, had nevertheless been holding its own—largely, he thought, because of his own considerable talents as general manager. Not only could Chuck ably supervise the day-to-day operations of a six-day-a-week business with fifty employees but he could sell, too. Chuck could sell anything: He could sell corkscrews at an Alcoholics Anonymous meeting—that's how good he was. At Kakas, a fair portion of his success came from an ability to sell expensive fur coats to women—usually young women, but sometimes old ones, too—who were not the traditional well-heeled customers of the trade and for whom the purchase of a fur had the fiscal gravity of the purchase of a new car.

Six feet three inches tall, ruggedly handsome, with a twinkle in his eye and a homey Irish charm that he could turn on (and off) in a flash, Chuck conveyed an attractive and, it transpired, lucrative image that amazed and delighted the Kakas brothers, two strikingly blond middle-aged furriers who liked to make magazine ads with their equally blond wives, all of them swathed in full-length minks and sables, usually posed amid the quiet elegance of the landmark Back Bay store which their great-grandfather had founded to cater to the carriage trade that congregated at the tony Ritz-Carlton Hotel a block up Newbury Street at the foot of the Public Garden.

Deep in his brooding, Chuck saw himself as a proud descendant of that retailing line, a master salesman whose skills caused him to be singlehandedly responsible, among other feats, for the anomalous appearance of the occasional mink coat or collar on the streets of such rabbit-pelt strongholds as South Boston and Revere Beach. With its quality antique Persian carpets on marble floors, its hand-carved wood moldings smelling faintly of lemon oil, its ferocious-looking and famous stuffed polar bear on guard with its yellow fangs bared at the foot of its showroom staircase, Kakas Furs appealed to every notion of finery that impelled Chuck in his drive out of Revere. Working there as an executive gave him a sense of pride and, more importantly, of belonging. On more than one occasion, Jay Kakas, the brother who worked most closely with Chuck, was amazed to come into the store unexpectedly before opening time and find Chuck with his sleeves rolled up running an electric buffer across the floor to give it added gloss before the first customer walked in off Newbury Street. The first time this happened, it was immediately clear to Kakas that his young general manager was doing janitorial work not to impress the boss, but rather out of the same remarkable sense of pride that had radiated from him since the first day he walked in looking for a job with the classified ad for management trainee in his hand and a spit-shine on his shoes. From that day, Kakas knew that he had found the kind of worker most employers only dream of: The kid was bright, conscientious, astonishingly detail-oriented, personable, eager to learn, easy to teach, savvy—and amazingly aggressive as a salesman.

The customers loved him, Kakas soon learned—not only the well-heeled suburban matrons who were the core clientele, as their mothers had been before them but also the young people who started showing up in greater numbers with their Gold Visas to buy from Chuck, who also managed to entice as fur customers young professional males with their sharp eyes for labels and their need to impress with their attire. The kid was a completely natural salesman, Kakas thought with a sense of admiration that he believed was being expressed with the salary he paid him. Chuck kept personal files on all of the clientele; at Christmas and on their birthdays, each of Chuck's customers received a card from Kakas with a personal note in Chuck's handwriting. Quite often, a casual customer would be astonished, a year or more after her last visit to the store, to have Chuck ask about a spouse or a child by name. Furthermore, Chuck knew how to keep the revenue flowing after a sale: A good portion of Kakas business came from storing and maintaining customers' expensive furs and other fine garments, and even people who were otherwise inclined to put off for a year or two some small but costly repair job often found themselves agreeing to do it now, at the behest of the earnest young general manager who made such a good case for immediate action.

Frequently, Jay Kakas described Chuck as being "like a son to me." And Chuck, who wished that he had received more attention from his own father, responded in a glow of anticipation. Invested with the admiration and trust that would be bestowed on a favorite son, he assumed the rest. In his own mind, Chuck expected to become a partner in the family business, and he was both shocked and furious when his tightly tuned perceptiveness told him in the summer of 1989 that this was not to be.

Otherwise, on this hot July afternoon, Chuck would have had good reason to glance with soaring satisfaction at his reflection in the windows of the expensive shops on Newbury Street as he hurried past with the well-cut coat of his tailored suit casually flung over his shoulder, on his way to get a forty-dollar haircut.

But that was not the case. Despite his good looks, his remarkable career success to date and his obvious future potential; despite the fact that he was married to an attractive and appealing woman, a lawyer who was smart and deeply loving and happily pregnant with their first child; despite the quarter-million-dollar house in the suburbs with the free-form pool and hot tub out back, Chuck Stuart, in this fateful summer before his thirtieth birthday, felt the cold hand of desperation on his broad shoulder.

Not only was the job wrong. So was the wife. And in the waning years of the eighties, as he faced the chilling reality of turning thirty on his next birthday, Chuck Stuart, full of the possibilities of himself, knew that the time for making major adjustments was running out. For a bright and ambitious young man of proven ability, the future wasn't in someone else's business. *Entrepreneur* was more than the name of a magazine Chuck subscribed to and read avidly the moment he found it in the mailbox each month. It was what he planned to be, and with his thirtieth birthday approaching, he believed he had to move quickly to the next rung on his ladder to the top of the heap.

Halfway up the block, Chuck met the impassive stares of the attractive young people sitting with practiced poise at the tables of the sidewalk cafe. In the small world of Newbury Street, which had become Boston's most self-consciously fashionable thoroughfare during the years that are known as the Reagan era, appraisal was an end in itself; people at the cafes sat not facing each other across the tables, but outward, toward the sidewalk, as if at a theater, absorbed in the procedure of evaluation, searching for the ratifying reflection of themselves. This was the world, a long way from the gritty seashore town where he grew up, in which Chuck now moved: the well-swept sidewalks shaded by the green awnings of Brooks Brothers, the elegant Ritz-Carlton Hotel, the pleasingly clothed men and women who shopped across the street at Burberry's.

But something was amiss and he was savvy enough to acknowledge the vibrations. Lately, he had begun to sense that what little toehold he did have in the good life might wash away under his feet, like sand with an ebb tide. The upturned faces at the sidewalk tables were smug with a self-absorption that had its name in any number of acronyms that had come to be pejoratives, such as "dinks" ("double income, no kids") and the dreaded "yuppies." But to Chuck, these were not fighting words: Recently, they had been aspirations; now they were hard-won high ground, to defend at all costs.

Approaching one of the ages at which a man needs to take stock, Chuck had managed to overcome, through sheer determination, major personal obstacles that had become so clear to him in his late twenties. In a status-conscious metropolitan area where one was judged relentlessly by race, ethnicity, educational credentials, and even speech inflection, he had covered his tracks fairly well. Married to a woman with a law degree, but himself lacking a suitable education or a plausible excuse (he had barely graduated from a high-school-level vocational-technical school), he invented one. Most people who knew him outside of Revere, his hometown on the coast just above Boston, actually believed that he had been forced to withdraw from Brown University when a severe playing injury to his knee caused him to lose a full football scholarship. To those who knew him only casually, Chuck went further, claiming to be a graduate of Brown.

As he moved along in his career, and tried to keep pace with his wife's, he had worked diligently to smooth over the rough edges, even to the extent of buying an expensive package of cassette tapes advertised on the radio as a way to expand his vocabulary and improve (Chuck now would have said "augment") his social status. For months, he recited the lessons on his daily commute. As he progressed, he even began tape-recording his responses, working to lower his vocal pitch to a more authoritative level, and to smooth over his flat North Shore working-class accent and polish it to the neutral, urbane pattern known to linguists as Network Standard.

Given all of this effort, he had been approaching the benchmark age of thirty genuinely eager to get on with Phase Two of the gentrification of Charles Michael Stuart, Jr., as an individual of taste and import who knows something about life. And then, without real notice, his wife Carol had pulled the rug out from under him, announcing first that she was unexpectedly pregnant and second that she intended with the birth of the baby to leave her forty-thousand-dollar-a-year job as a tax lawyer actually to realize the modest ambition she had written to accompany her photograph in her 1977 high-school yearbook: "to raise a happy family." But where this might have caused another to focus on just the problems, Chuck now believed he had begun to see the possibilities.

On Newbury Street, just below Arlington, he scowled into the display window of the Carriage Square Maternity and Baby Boutique, one door down from where the Cartier doorman was rocking on his heels in the heat. Again, he checked his watch, aggravated to be late for his one-o'clock appointment. A stickler for punctuality in himself and others, he had called just before he left the store to tell his hair stylist, Bill Zecco, that he would not be on time.

"I'm going to be about fifteen minutes late," Chuck said on the phone, sounding rushed, as he usually did. "How does that affect your schedule? Do you still want me to come? Should I reschedule?"

"Not to worry, Charles," Bill told him. "Take your time."

With so many people on vacation at the Cape and elsewhere, and with business noticeably off as the first bumps of the recession rattled New England, Bill didn't have appointments stacked up. But even if he had, he would have fit Chuck in; he genuinely liked the man, not least because of just the sort of courtesy that had prompted Chuck to call. Usually, the swankier the shop was, the more some

customers treated a hairdresser like a shoe-shine boy. But not
Charles, which is the name Chuck preferred to be called by his hair
stylist.

It was not a long walk from Kakas's wood-paneled shop to the
hair stylist's at The Spa at The Heritage, a fitness salon on Arlington
Street just across from the Public Garden. Chuck was there within
ten minutes. Waiting in the well-appointed reception lounge, Bill
ushered him in.

"So how's business, Charles?" the hairdresser asked when he
got his customer settled into the plush barber's chair in front of a
wall that was all black marble and mirrors. The Back Bay business
world was a small one—and increasingly a nervous one, with rents
at historic high levels and receipts beginning to totter. Bill knew that
Chuck was general manager at Kakas, one of the oldest businesses
on the street.

"The fur industry," Chuck replied, shaking his head morosely
as Bill began to work with his scissors. He let it drop. "How are
you guys doing with all this stuff that's happening in retail?"

"I'm hanging in there. Everybody's pulling back a little, but
fortunately this is one of the last areas to really get hit. People still
have to get their hair cut, you know?"

Chuck grunted. Carol had been on his back lately about spending so much money with the baby coming. Why, she had asked,
sweetly but with that edge she had begun to show, did he need to
buy thousand-dollar suits at Louis Boston?

"So I don't look like a fucking slob," he told her, not bothering
to add the other compelling reason, which was the thrill he felt
whenever he entered the French Academic–style old museum building that housed the exclusive men's store, where the soft-spoken
salesmen knew him by name. It was the same reason he got his hair
cut at the health spa. The Spa at The Heritage was part of a new
one-hundred-million-dollar commercial venture called The Heritage
on The Garden. The portentous name and rigorously enforced capitalization of the T's caused chuckles among the proprietors of its various
salons and shops, but served to convey that all-important cachet.
While some people thought that kind of affectation ridiculous, other
people, like Chuck, were impressed.

Being a hairdresser, and as such a practiced observer of social
nuance, Bill was intrigued with Chuck precisely because he saw just

how earnestly the man went after projecting the right image. And he was awfully good at it, Bill decided; he had obviously come up from someplace; there was just enough of that flat tone of the North End or someplace left. Bill liked the man for a number of reasons, not the least of which was his audacity.

Like any good salesman, Chuck also instinctively recalled little details about the people he came into contact with. The last time he was there, Bill had mentioned that his wife was pregnant. Chuck remembered to ask how she was.

"Not to complain, but it's been rough," Bill told him. "I'm afraid my wife had a miscarriage and we lost the baby. It was really rough. You know how it is."

"I'm sorry to hear that," Chuck said. "Is she all right?"

She was now, Bill said, noticing that his customer was looking at him intently in the mirror. Chuck said, "My wife and I are expecting our first baby."

The comment caught the hairstylist off guard. He had been cutting Chuck's hair for the past six months, chatting amiably all the while, and the man had never once mentioned being married. In fact, the first day Chuck came in, complaining about how hard it was to find someone who knew how to style his hair exactly as he liked it, Bill had guessed that he was single and given to exaggeration, considering that Chuck's hairstyle was barber-school basic: Easy to cut, a stylist would have to be blind drunk to screw it up. Furthermore, Chuck never wore a wedding ring when he visited, and he exhibited an elaborate charm when dealing with female employees at the salon. Without giving it much thought one way or the other, Bill had merely assumed the man was gay.

"Your first," he repeated, concealing his surprise, nodding. Through the mirror, he met Chuck's steady gaze as he snipped at the hair above the collar of his tailored blue Turnbull & Asser shirt. "That's really nice, Charles." Bill set his scissors on the shelf and surveyed his customer's hair from either side to see if it was even. "So when's she due?"

"December."

"Oh, a Christmas baby!"

Chuck, watching carefully in the mirror, didn't reply. This silence prompted Bill to blurt, "So soon! Great! There's nothing like your first kid. Wait till the baby is born! You're going to love it."

Uninterested, Chuck tilted his head slightly to check the haircut.

"You know," Bill said, wondering why he seemed more willing to talk about the baby than Chuck was, "I didn't even know you were married."

With the focus back on himself, Chuck perked up. "Yeah," he said laconically. "I've been married for a couple of years."

"Oh. And your wife, she works?"

"Supposedly."

Bill had no idea what that was supposed to mean.

"What's she do?"

"She's a tax lawyer."

"In the city?"

"Newton," Chuck said.

"A lawyer, wow. Is she going to work after the baby?"

In the mirror, Chuck critically surveyed his three-quarter profile and asked, "You don't see any gray, do you?"

Bill blinked. "You? You have terrific hair, Charles. No gray."

"Really? You don't think it's getting thin?" In fact, Chuck's hairline was receding in front, but a decent haircut would manage to hide that pretty well for at least another five years or so. Otherwise, it was thick and healthy.

"No, it's fine," Bill said, slipping the silk drape from his shoulders and taking a wisk to brush off Chuck's shirt. He noticed a monogram, "CMS," stitched at the top of the pocket.

Paying the bill, Chuck tipped generously but not excessively, and flirted with the receptionist out front, where he bought a bottle of hair-styling mousse before he left.

He wasn't expected back at Kakas for a half hour, so he took his time as he strolled along the park, where couples sprawled on the grass in the sun. Shouts from a spirited lunch-hour softball game—all white men from nearby state offices, ties askew and shirt sleeves rolled up—drifted down from the Common. Above, kites floated lazily in the warm updrafts of a cloudless sky. Chuck loved downtown Boston on days like this; it was so unlike New York and other big cities he visited on business or, just as often, on trips to attend hockey or football games with his friends. Compared to Manhattan, but even to places like Philadelphia, the center of Boston had always been utterly lacking in menace and disorder. Chuck knew the reason for that: "The niggers stay out of the Back Bay," he would tell friends. Even downtown, "niggers" was a word still in casual use in Boston, though usually uttered now in a low voice.

Walking along the Arlington Street side of the park, he could see the white swan-shaped form of a paddleboat carrying passengers on the pond. In New York, he had read, they had literally to chain newly planted trees in place on sidewalks to keep them from being stolen. In Boston, at least in the central part of Boston that he frequented, flowers bloomed unmolested in neatly tended beds, and children ran freely on the grassy slopes.

This was a Boston that should be enjoyed while it could, he knew, because it was not to last. In fact, Boston's rapid deterioration was a subject of constant conversation in peaceful enclaves like the Back Bay and Beacon Hill. It could be seen in little things, like the fact that a bicycle was no longer safe on its kickstand outside a store while its owner ran in to buy a loaf of bread or a newspaper. And while Boston's parks and affluent downtown areas were still more effectively segregated than those of any other big city in the country, the invisible wall that had long held back undesirable elements seemed to be breached more with each day that passed. Earlier, for example, Chuck had walked past the two drunks who now spent each afternoon outside the Theological Book Store on Newbury, where they loitered on the stoop and entertained each other by making comments about passersby.

And now, on his way back, he saw another newly familiar intruder, a black man in the uniform of the urban homeless— sweater, trouser cuffs sagging over unfastened boots, plastic shopping bags brimming with junk at his sides—trudging toward him on the sidewalk, ranting at the people who hurried past, knowing to avoid eye contact.

Chuck edged casually closer to hear what he was carrying on about today. As usual, it made no sense whatsoever. "My father wasn't shit in the Navy. Wasn't shit to me," the man wailed in a sing-song cant as he progressed up the block. "My father was a chief bosun's mate in the United States Navy, and they didn't like him. Wasn't shit in the Navy, wasn't shit to me." A cluster of four well-dressed women, just out of Bailey Banks & Biddle, began giggling when they thought the intruder was beyond earshot. But the man turned on his heel and lunged toward them, aiming a bony finger: "Don't you go looking at me, bitch! White bitch! Come back here! I'm talking to you!" Frightened, the women hurried around the corner at Berkeley Street.

The derelict stood with his mouth agape for a moment, squinting unsteadily at an inexplicably empty sidewalk. Then with determination he reversed direction, taking as wide a berth as a motorboat, and continued on his lunge toward the park, muttering and ignoring the look of utter contempt that blazed from the face of the tall young man he brushed by.

On at least three other occasions during the summer, Chuck had seen the same person, always dressed the same, always trudging up or down the same stretch of Newbury, as if walking an assigned beat. Even though the man was clearly a visual threat more than a physical one, his presence anywhere in sight enraged Chuck, who saw it as still another unmistakable sign that the city was finished.

Before going back to Kakas, he stopped at a florist and bought a twelve-dollar bouquet to take home to his wife, and then he stopped a few doors down at the French deli for a sandwich to eat at his desk. Watching the young woman prepare his smoked turkey on white, Chuck was still furious. Boston was finished. Chuck knew that his own future was in the better-class suburbs, where everybody over the age of thirty with any sense and enough money to do so had already fled. There a man with talent and ambition could have his own business, could flourish through his thirties and beyond. In fact, he had already chosen the area and the business. A restaurant in Framingham, affluent and thriving, twenty-five miles west.

That summer, once his decision was made, there were only two major roadblocks remaining to impede his way.

One was money. Starting the kind of restaurant Chuck wanted required an amount of capital that neither he nor Carol had managed to accumulate despite their impressive combined income. They always spent what they made—on the house, on restaurants and clothes and travel, not to mention the money Chuck always seemed to have riding on a football game or a horse.

The other roadblock, of course, was Carol herself.

From the time he uttered his first words as his older sisters squealed in delight, Chuck Stuart knew how to talk his way to the things he wanted, and, on occasion, out of trouble. His father was a talker. A well-liked Revere insurance salesman who always had the latest joke on the tip of his tongue, the elder Charlie Stuart was known as Revere's "toastmaster general." Put a microphone in front of Charlie's face, it was said, and you had an instant testimonial.

It was a trait that ran in a straight line through successive generations of male Stuarts, and had its roots in the loquaciousness of Ireland.

In a small Irish village by the misty Boggeragh hills and not far from the Cork-Killarney Road, there is a fifteenth-century castle that towers over the nearby bracken fields and woods, and on a windy parapet high above the gray limestone south wall of that castle is a spot where a person, if he or she is so ridiculously inclined, may lie on the hard surface and stretch precariously back under the battlement to place a kiss on a great flat rock known as the Blarney Stone.

An inscription near this spot reads:

> *A stone that whoever kisses*
> *O, he never misses to grow eloquent.*

Like so much in Ireland, the castle and its stone owe their celebrity mostly to sentimental claptrap, but their place in history is owed to a land dispute with the English—in this case a claim the reviled Elizabeth I made in 1602 on certain property of the lord of Blarney, the scion of the ancient MacCarthy clan and a man famed even in that land of talkers for his smooth and persuasive tongue. Responding to persistent royal petitions with a series of increasingly elaborate blandishments, the recalcitrant Irish nobleman finally exasperated the queen, exploding that all he seemed to be able to get out of her subject was "the usual Blarney." Elizabeth went to her grave a year later, but the phrase stuck as a description of what a local nineteenth-century writer referred to as "a cajoling tongue and the art of flattery or of telling lies with unblushing effrontery," but what has become simplified over the years as merely the "gift of gab."

It was a gift that was possessed by the paternal great-grandfather of Chuck Stuart, Michael J. Stuart, the Stuart who came over in the boat, as his American descendants would later think of him, when they did so at all. The fifth son of a family that had barely survived

the successive famines that killed two million people and laid waste
to all of Irish society a decade before his birth in the west of Ireland
in 1858, Michael had been fortunate enough to reach his maturity
in a village, Kilrush, where the wretchedness of the recent past at
least had yielded some opportunity for gainful employment as the
devastated country began to dig out from the calamity. In a grim
irony, Kilrush, where the stench of death was still a vivid memory
when Michael was a boy, had actually benefited in one small way
from the famines. Due to its location on an estuary at the mouth of
the River Shannon, the merchants of Kilrush were able to profit from
the emigration that would empty Ireland of more than a third of its
population in the second half of the nineteenth century. Like the
other ports of Ireland during the era, small and large, Kilrush's chief
export was people. There and elsewhere, a thriving small industry
of shipping agents and clerks, innkeepers and dry goods merchants,
pawnbrokers, peddlers, and other purveyors of necessities to the
desperate had sprung up.

Talking himself, as a young man, into a position as a booking
agent for a shipping passage firm, the industrious Michael Stuart
canvased villages and the rock-hard countryside that was still staggered by the disaster a whole generation later, extolling the laggards
on the benefits of emigration and the safety, comfort, and low cost
of setting out on that inevitable adventure on a ship whose owners
he happened to represent. It was cutthroat and not especially lucrative work, selling steamship tickets to poor folks, but a man with
the ability to charm, to persuade, and to close the deal had an
advantage. Thus Mike Stuart remained gainfully employed in his
native village, and was able to marry, have eleven children, and
only then, two years after his fortieth birthday, arrange for his own
passage to the United States.

Well-off enough by now to be able to avoid subjecting his family
to the awful perils of traveling to America in steerage, Michael, his
wife Mary J. Cunningham, who was called May, and their lively
brood sold their belongings, bade farewell to their loved ones and
neighbors in a tearful "live wake" that had become the standard sad
bon voyage party in a country hemorrhaging its people, and set off
by carriage on the road to Cork, stopping en route for a visit to
Blarney Castle, which even then enjoyed fame as a roadside
attraction for pilgrims who wished to say they had kissed the Blarney

Stone. This brief excursion, bragged about often in years to come, would become the basis of a family joke in America that Mike Stuart, loquacious in middle age and garrulous as an old man, had not only kissed the Blarney Stone but had bitten off a piece.

In October of 1899, the big Stuart family set sail, sharing two second-class cabins, from Queenstown at Cork Harbour on the steamship SS *Belgenland* to the port in Philadelphia, where they stayed for only a short time before making their way north and settling into a rented house near the West Broadway center of the burgeoning Irish immigrant neighborhood of South Boston. There, Mike handily transferred the work skills he had acquired in Ireland and supported his large family as a freight clerk at a cargo facility a few hundred feet from the site of the Boston Tea Party on the Inner Harbor's Fort Point Channel.

Mike Stuart's industrious nature stayed his growing family well. By 1910, five of the children had married and moved off on their own. Living at home in South Boston with Mike, then fifty-two and employed as a railroad clerk, and May, then fifty, were their children Eva F., twenty-three, and her new husband John McDowell, a twenty-two-year-old dyer; Lillian S., twenty-two, a bookkeeper; Mary C., twenty, a clerk in a dry goods store; Michael C., eighteen, a porter for a furniture store; and two children still in school, Gertrude, sixteen, and Vincent, thirteen.

Underscoring the example of hard work that Mike imparted to his children was the fact that at age seventy-one, and now living in the Roslindale neighborhood of Boston, he was still employed as a railroad clerk when he buried his beloved May, who had died of heart failure, at St. Joseph's Cemetery in West Roxbury in the summer of 1929.

By this time, Mike's son and namesake Michael Cunningham (after his mother's maiden name), was himself terminally ill with tuberculosis at the age of thirty-six. A Navy veteran of World War I who had made his living first as a foundry coremaker and later as a dental lab worker, the younger Michael was known as the maverick in the family. In 1919, while in the Navy, the twenty-five-year-old shocked his parents and siblings by marrying a girl from Revere, north of the city, named Ida L. Stone. The marriage was performed in Revere, by a justice of the peace, and on a Monday, no less. What's more, the girl was Jewish, though her new husband's staunchly Catholic family relaxed considerably when she vowed her intention to convert, a promise she kept within months.

Within ten years, however, Ida's husband was dead at the age of thirty-seven, having spent the final three years of his life in the Veterans' Hospital in Rutland, Massachusetts. There were two children, Charles M., Chuck's father, born in 1922, and Mary, born a year later. Finding herself widowed with two young children at the age of thirty-four, right at the onset of the Great Depression, Ida Stuart persevered. With the children, she continued to live in the rented cottage she had shared with her husband on Revere Beach, then a popular working-class seashore town whose dance halls, restaurants, and amusement rides provided entertainment for summertime crowds that had been known to jam one hundred thousand strong along the crescent of Massachusetts Bay just above the city of Boston.

Even in the Depression, there was at least seasonal opportunity in Revere Beach, and Ida Stuart made the best of her lot, working as a waitress year-round and supplementing that with a second job as a shoestore clerk in the busy season. A strong, opinionated woman who insisted that her children stay in Catholic schools and who took no guff from anyone, Ida eventually managed to put enough money together to buy a bungalow near downtown Revere, a working-class municipality whose population of forty thousand consisted almost entirely of Italians, Irishmen, and Jews, though the latter were beginning to abandon gritty Revere for communities farther north along the shore such as Marblehead, Swampscott, and Salem. Like most Revere residents of the time, Ida spent her whole adult life there. So, as was expected, would her son.

Ida didn't have much to do with the Stuarts, except for the old man. Others in the family had long since grown weary of his stories of an Ireland that few of them knew, or recalled, or even cared about. Pointless stories, they seemed, of the look of the skies in the West and the smell of the peat, the horses snorting steam in the morning, the girls and how pretty they looked at the dances, the stirring swirl of the music, the tin whistles and harps, fiddles, and tiompáns all going like the devil himself. As Mike's eyes would mist over, his long-suffering listeners' would glaze—except for Ida, who would still be listening to the old man in the kitchen long after the others had drifted into the living room. When he finally died at the age of eighty-six in the summer of 1944, with young Charlie away in the Army, she knew sadly that the only real link she had felt with her own past in the Stuart family was gone. In his will, he left no property or valuables. But in a last testament to his industry, he did leave a savings account that had survived the Depression with a balance of $1333.68. It was divided among his six living children and Ida's two—the only of his grandchildren he cared to remember in his will.

After the war, Ida's only son, Charlie, on whom she had doted, married a local girl, Neysa Robertson. Like his parents, Charlie and his wife did not have a big church wedding. Instead, the wedding took place after mass on a Sunday in the spring of 1948 at the rectory of St. Theresa's Roman Catholic Church in Revere. Charlie and Neysa moved into a sprawling new housing project off Cooledge Street that was among hundreds of such facilities hastily constructed and subsidized by the government after the war to alleviate the severe housing shortage that confronted millions of American ex-servicemen and their brides. Charlie found work selling insurance; his wife kept her job as a telephone operator for a while, but then quit to concentrate on having children.

After several miscarriages, Neysa gave birth to their first child, a girl named Shelley, in 1953. On the day after New Year's in 1955, another daughter was born to the Stuarts at Chelsea Memorial Hospital, but there were major complications during the birth, and Neysa died at the age of thirty-three. Her husband named the baby Neysa in her memory. The funeral was held at Ida's house on Payson Street.

Ida and her son, always close, now shared a tragic link, since each had lost their spouse while in their thirties and as the parent of two young children. But while Ida had been forced to fend for herself, she could at least offer her son the succor of her home. At her insistence, Charlie and the babies moved in with her months after the funeral.

Charlie, who had dearly loved his wife and wanted nothing in life more than to be a man, like his grandfather, who would enter old age surrounded by a brood of a family, dug himself out of his grief with work. "In Revere, he was everybody's insurance man," said one old friend. Said another: "Most of his work was servicing those life insurance policies where he'd have to stop by the house every month to collect the premiums, ten or twelve dollars, or whatever it was. A lot of places, he'd just walk in without knocking—that's how much a part of the routine he was. People liked the man a lot—he always knew your kids' names, who was getting ready for their Holy Communion, who had a kid getting married. He was just a part of your family life."

In one of those homes he visited regularly, that of a big, noisy, first-generation Irish family that had moved a notch up on the social scale from Chelsea to Revere, Charlie Stuart met the woman who would become his second wife, Dorothy Frances Kingston, still living at home in her late twenties and working in town as a clerk. They were married on April 12, 1959. Again, it was not a big church wedding, but was held on a Sunday, after mass, at Immaculate Conception in Revere.

A week shy of eight months later, on December 18, 1959, their first child was born at Beth Israel Hospital in Boston, a seven-pound, four-ounce boy they named Charles Michael Stuart, Jr., after his father. During his boyhood, he would also be known as Charlie, and later as Chuck.

Charlie, an extraordinarily handsome baby with deep blue eyes and a winsome little grin, arrived in a household that was well-primed to introduce him to a world that gave all indications, from day one, of revolving around himself—as his mother's first child and living embodiment of the bond between her and her husband; as his father's first son and bridge to a new life from a grief-ridden past; as his half-sisters' precious doll. So cooed after and pampered, so appreciated upon his arrival and *adored* was wee Charlie Stuart, that one elderly Irish relative soon was referring to the infant, when its parents were out of earshot, as "little infant Jesus."

By the time the boy entered the first grade at Immaculate Conception Elementary School, the family had burst the seams of its place in the project: Two more sons, Michael and Mark, had already arrived, and another, Matthew, would be along soon, making six children in all. The Stuarts put together the down payment and purchased a little three-bedroom Cape Cod home on a dead-end street in Revere, a few blocks from Immaculate Conception, where attendance at Sunday mass was a family affair, and where Charlie, a quiet, obedient boy who struck his elders as being eager to please but hard to motivate, became an altar boy at his mother's urging.

Getting him up at five thirty on the mornings when it was Charlie's week to serve at early mass, and watching him trudge angelically off to church with his starched white surplice on a hanger over his shoulder, became one of his mother's fondest memories.

Others would recall a different boy, an avid, almost driven sports lover who, despite his strapping build, failed to excel at any sport other than spectating. "All bat, no glove," is how a former Little League coach referred to him. A Pop Warner league football coach said, "No guts," but added quickly, "But he always showed up, and you never had any trouble with him."

As an adult, long after he had moved from Revere, Chuck still came back every Saturday during the season to help coach a Little League team. Besides the fact that he always showed up, people recall that he always was impeccably dressed, and little else.

As a boy, Chuck Stuart began covering some tracks early. Only his closest friends knew that he had once lived in a sprawling housing project. He would never allow the fact to come up in conversation. It was a basic condition of the friendship. He grew up among a large group of boys, including his three younger brothers, all of whom were urged by their mother to follow Chuck's example of obedience, courtesy, and conformity. But throughout his childhood and adolescence, he also was part of a loose group of boys from Revere who grew up together, through grade school and junior high, playing Little League baseball and schoolyard basketball, hanging out on the corners as they got older, "scoping" the girls. Yet very few of them ever saw the inside of his house on the dead end at Lowe Street, a block from Immaculate Conception.

The reason, Chuck told one longtime associate, was simple: He was embarrassed by his family. "Too many kids, too much yelling and fighting. The place is always a shithouse."

"So what?"

"I just don't like anybody coming there."

Others in their group would later recall Chuck as a snob, someone who, as one contemporary put it, "always let you know he thought he was better than you." But closer inspection would find another side to the boy. Because he was the oldest boy, and his mother's first child, and a bond to a new life for his father, Chuck was lavished with attention before it was gradually withdrawn as the Stuart house became crowded with children. Perhaps as a result, he grew up unique among his siblings and friends. Thinking himself special, he became aware that there were finer things to be had beyond the grind of Revere, where he was regarded as just another good-looking ordinary kid of whom nothing more was expected than to stay out of major trouble, find a steady job somewhere, buy a used car, scope out the girls downtown or on the beach, drink some beer, go to some ballgames, and eventually find a place of his own to live and a nice local girl to raise a family with—hopefully having first obtained his high school diploma.

The Revere that Chuck grew up in as the oldest of four boys with two older half-sisters was an extraordinarily inward-looking city of 42,000 on the broad curve of Massachusetts Bay just north of Boston. First settled in 1626 after Captain John Smith's explorations, it was quickly annexed to Chelsea, the settlement that reached up from Boston. In 1871, after its southern tip had seceded to become Winthrop, and Chelsea became a city of its own, North Chelsea was left to incorporate itself as Revere, a collection of farms amid the salt marshes with a population of 1,197.

Prosperity and recognition came to Revere only with the completion of the narrow-gauge Boston, Revere Beach & Lynn railroad, which brought the summer throngs that only began fading away in the 1960s, after which the city's famous amusement resorts began crumbling under the bulldozers that left the beachfront bordered with a wall of bleak concrete high-rises, many of them dark with vacancies.

The 1980 Census found that fewer than half of the adults living in the city had even completed high school, and only 7.7 percent had completed college. Now, instead of being known for its dance casinos and such thrill rides as the Cyclone, a roller coaster with a 100-foot drop, Revere was better known throughout the Boston area for municipal corruption, to the point where a North Shore Mafia kingpin once bemoaned a regional organized crime crackdown by saying, "I'll tell you how bad business is these days—we had to lay off six cops in Revere."

By the time Chuck was old enough to enjoy it, Revere's beach was so badly polluted that sunbathers who ventured onto it stayed back by the seawall, as far from the fetid surf as possible. In a paean to her hometown that was published in the weekly *Revere Journal*, Kathleen Flynn, a Revere native who had moved to Florida twenty years earlier, wrote of coming back to Revere for a visit: "It was low tide in the nearby Chelsea Creek and the stench from the mud flats permeated the car. Some things never change . . . Revere Beach, a once beautiful, pristine, crescent-shaped beach with powdery white sand, no undertows or whirlpools . . . smelled worse than Chelsea Creek. The brown debris floating in the water also littered the shoreline." Luckily, wrote the author, the joys of seeing old friends and family compensated for "all the disappointments of going home."

This was the Revere, in which Chuck Stuart grew up, a crowded, close-knit little city sensitive to the slights of outsiders but quietly proud of what it did have: loyalty to family and friends and a sense of roots that was nurtured by the tendency of its young people to stay close to home after high school.

Chuck was the exception. While he would always return to Revere, sometimes as often as two or three nights a week after work, he would also impress people from childhood on with his desire to put distance between himself and his home town. By the time he was ready for high school, along with the rest of his mid-baby-boom generation classmates, Revere High was so overcrowded that students without college aspirations were encouraged to attend the regional vocational-technical high school in Wakefield. Chuck leapt at the opportunity. He majored in culinary arts, a curriculum designed for students who wanted to become cooks and restaurant workers.

At the vo-tech, as it was known, Chuck cemented a boyhood friendship with Brian Parsons, who shared his interest in bodybuilding and sports. Neither boy had a steady girlfriend in high school, though both were good-looking and much in demand. By the time he got out of vo-tech school, where he had a couple of part-time jobs in pizza shops, Chuck had developed a curious relationship with his home town. On the one hand, as he began to think about how he would make his living, he noticed that aside from politicians, doctors, dentists, and undertakers, the most respected men in Revere owned restaurants. Their cars, Cadillacs and Lincolns in one era, Porsches and Jaguars in the next, could be seen gleaming on the main drag outside busy restaurants with words like *ristorante* and *villa* in their names. Gold jewelry flashing from wrists and well-muscled necks, they lived in what appeared to be a gilded, late-night world of good-guy camaraderie; they knew their customers by name; they had respect and savoir faire; they knew that a flaming Sambuca bought on-the-house, with a couple of roasted coffee beans in the glass, was the right touch, the gracious way to keep a customer coming back.

But on the other hand, the impressionable teenager also saw that when the sun came up, the flashy cars were gone. And beyond the littered lots where the amusement park rides had been torn down, all that stood was a wall of decrepit cement condos, ten-story monuments to folly, corruption, and foolish lending. At noon, with the sun high over the blue-green crescent of sewage-swollen sea, as seagulls pecked through the trash on the wet sand, paunchy businessmen slouched against the pock-marked gull-splattered seawall in their long-sleeved shirts and ties munching roast beef sandwiches from a fast-food stand as the local girls strutted by in their two-piece bathing suits and heels, hair stacked up like sandcastles.

By the time he had his diploma, Chuck again didn't lose any time putting more distance between himself and his home environment. That summer, he got a job as a kitchen helper at a hotel as a short-order cook in the suburban town of Danvers, off Interstate 95 north of Revere, and as soon as he had saved enough money for the down payment and a month's security deposit, he moved into a tiny apartment in a two-story house in Malden, the next town toward Medford from Revere.

But he always returned, always drawn back to Revere, and before long, he had found a new job, as an assistant cook at a restaurant on Revere Beach that was called the Driftwood.

THREE

Carol

Carol Ann DiMaiti Stuart was one of those few people over the age of six who could spend the entire day at Disney World crying.

The tears were not from sadness. In fact, she would describe the time she spent with her husband at Disney World in the winter of 1989 as one of the happiest of her adult life. Strolling in the sun, eyes as wide as a child's as she took in the sweep of color and playful architecture, she was moved to tears merely by the anticipation of parenthood, of one day being herself a part of this transfixed swarm of parents with clinging children. At the world's most self-conscious amusement park, Carol Stuart discovered what the movies used to find in Paris. Wide-eyed, she used the word "romantic" to describe it. But the experience had also made her realize that she and Chuck, poised now at the biological edge of their thirties, were not yet whole as a couple. At Disney World, Carol's dream blazed anew. Through tears of happiness, Carol pressed close to her husband. As they strolled along, her head was filled with daydreams of them and their child, of amusement parks in the summer and apple orchards in fall; *The Nutcracker* at Symphony Hall at Christmastime, bellyflopping on a snow-sled, Fenway Park on Opening Day. In the sunny optimism of Florida, Carol decided it was time.

In just a few years, everything had come together, as she knew it would. Both of them had fabulous jobs. Together, they were making big money—spending it as quickly as they earned it, of course, but that could change with the firmer hand on the budget that parenthood would demand. Gradually, as her own income rose impressively, if less dramatically than her husband's, Carol had been insinuating herself more into the household finances, an area in which Chuck had long claimed the powers of a benign dictator. While she still turned over her paycheck to him without question, she had begun to "butt in" more often, as she put it. They didn't need to eat out so often, she had suggested, and when they did, it did not have to be at the kind of expensive places Chuckie insisted on. Each month for the past several years, as his father's health deteriorated with the effects of Parkinson's disease, Chuck had been sending money to his parents in Revere. Carol was shocked to discover recently that he was writing monthly checks for two hundred dollars. Gingerly, she had inquired about the sum, but he flew into a door-slamming rage and she let it drop. But the point had been made. The time was coming when her husband's financial dictatorship would need to accede to certain parliamentary controls.

The baby they had long spoken of would force that issue neatly, she believed. And while Chuck had lately shown little enthusiasm for talk of a family, she attributed that to the headstrong effects of making so much money. Still, someone had to plan for the future. Chuck's philosophy, Carol frequently said, was "live for today." Quietly, listening to her own biological clock, watching her friends with their new babies, Carol's confident planning for tomorrow had begun to accelerate as her confidence in her own abilities rose.

When they bought their new house in Reading the year before, one of the things Carol liked best about it was the nursery already in place in one of the bedrooms. The wallpaper in the room, which Carol had begun to refer to, with little comment from Chuck, as the "baby's room," had a design that featured Mickey Mouse, Donald Duck, Dumbo, and other Disney cartoon characters. It was perfect.

She knew that in another year or so, especially if she turned up the heat a little in the spring, she would be finished with her master's program night courses in advanced tax law. By the start of 1989, the year in which both she and her husband would turn thirty, Carol unilaterally decided to become pregnant.

Each year, the Stuarts tried to take two vacations, one in the summer and the other in the winter. Chuck, as usual, had made all of the arrangements for the most recent summer vacation, which they spent in Italy. The Disney World trip was the first one that Carol had arranged on her own. She had been adamant about going there; Chuck was set on a cruise. So Carol had been pleased with herself when she found a package deal that included a two-day cruise off Grand Bahama, followed by four days in Orlando.

By Carol's account, at least, it was a wonderful trip. While Chuck had been more content on the cruise, where he could evaluate the shipboard cuisine and work on his winter tan, Carol had been captivated by the Disney World mystique, which appealed to something basic in her but also made her feel that she and Chuck, alone without a baby stroller to push or a toddler to impress, seemed like interlopers. With a child, with children, this would all be so much richer, she thought. Children were always a part of their plan for the future. Chuck, who had grown up in a big family, claimed to love children. She knew he wanted to wait a while yet, what with his future being uncertain at the fur store. But she thought for the first time that he was too worried about his career to know what was best in his life. Sometimes, a wife has to simply make a decision, she decided.

She figured she could smooth out the rough places. On the Wednesday after they got back, Chuck's usual late night at work, Carol met three old friends for dinner. Ross Allen, Bill Jaaskela, and Barbara Williamson all had worked with her at her previous job at the Arthur Young accounting firm in Boston; they got together regularly for dinner to stay in touch, as they had this night at a Thai restaurant in Newton where, unabashedly, Carol shared her feelings about having a baby.

"We got back from Disney World feeling incredibly guilty," she told them. "Like, isn't this wonderful, and wouldn't it be better to share it with somebody? You know, we've had all this time by ourselves. It's time to have kids."

Carol certainly implied that it was a mutual decision. But she was also clearly upset at the same time. With Carol, it didn't take long for anything on her mind to come out.

"Chuckie and I had a terrible fight," she said.

"What about?" Ross Allen asked.

As usual, Carol didn't need much prompting. "Well, usually something like this wouldn't aggravate me, but this one just set me off. I got so mad." She explained that the day before, when she told Chuck she was going to have dinner with her friends, he informed her that she had better make sure she was through in time to do an errand for him. Chuck and a friend from work had plans to go for a couple of beers on Wednesday night, and his friend's wife, who worked at the same place, would be without her ride home.

"So he just said 'Oh, Carol can come on down and pick her up and take her home,' " she told her dinner companions. "What he said to me was, 'Oh, by the way, Carol, you're going to pick up Kimberly after work,' " she said, mimicking Chuck's voice. "But it was totally out of the way for me. And I was so aggravated that he just assumed I hadn't made any plans myself; he just volunteered me. He's always doing things like that. But I put my foot down. When he told me that last night, I got so mad. I didn't want to throw him out of the bedroom, but I wouldn't talk to him. I just rolled over on the other side of the bed and wouldn't talk to him."

There was a defiant look on her face. She said she demanded that he apologize for taking her for granted, but he refused, angrily. And he made matters worse by laughing in her face. It was clear to her friends that the standoff hadn't ended: Carol obviously was not planning to rush from the restaurant that night to pick up anybody.

"Usually, after we have a fight, Chuckie always sends flowers the next day," she pouted. "Today, he didn't. He didn't even call me." Carol began crying, but tried to make a joke out of it. "I guess we're not newlyweds anymore," she said, tugging a handkerchief from her purse. "We've been married a long time, I guess."

Everyone knew that Carol could cry at the drop of a hat. An announcement that the vernal equinox had occurred was enough to cause Carol's eyes to mist in appreciation. But it was unusual to see her shed a tear for herself.

The next time Ross Allen saw Carol, in May, she seemed like her old self again. In fact, she was burbling with joy. "I'm pregnant!"

she told him happily. "I don't know what happened; it was all of a sudden!"

Carol never gave her friends any reason to believe that her husband was not as overjoyed as she was about the prospect of becoming a parent. Just the opposite, in fact. When she saw them, she always made it a point to report how excited Chuck was at becoming a parent. "He's going to be a wonderful father," she would say, and everyone near her would feel the happiness and optimism radiating from her.

And she believed he would in fact be a wonderful father. It was just that he needed a little push, and for the first time in their relationship, she had acted unilaterally to provide it.

Only Chuck knew that the pregnancy was an "accident." After they returned from vacation, Carol told him, she went to her doctor worried about her weight—lately, Chuck had been pointedly mentioning it whenever she had anything to eat that wasn't lettuce, she thought—and took his advice to try going off birth control pills and using an alternate method of contraception.

Except that she forgot just once, she told her husband sheepishly. And now she was pregnant. But they had been planning to have a baby anyway, so why not now? Why not?

Chuck didn't offer a reason. She was stunned at the force of his reaction. Furious, Chuck demanded that she have an abortion immediately. Her husband had a way of clouding up and going into a fury without much notice, but she had never seen him that angry before. But this time she didn't beat her usual retreat. For once, Carol dug in, flatly refusing to even consider an abortion. It was time to have a child, she said. She had turned thirty; the clock was ticking. She was pregnant, and he had better just get used to it. Sometimes, she figured, a wife just has to assert herself.

Chuck didn't see it that way at all, however. To Chuck's way of thinking, a wife did not make the decisions, even one with a law degree. She especially did not make the decisions on her own. Not that it was any business of Carol's, but he, in fact, had begun to take out extra insurance policies as fatherhood bore down on him. Nor did he tell her that he, too, had decided to start improving his education in that winter of 1989 when he learned he was going to be a father. After work one night a few days after the surprise of learning that she was pregnant, Chuck had walked two blocks to the

Center for Adult Education in a big brownstone on Commonwealth Avenue. There, he paid his fee and signed up for a Saturday morning course. "Buying and Operating a Restaurant Successfully."

Meanwhile, to Carol's great relief, Chuck finally backed down after making a lot of noise. In fact, within a day or two he seemed like his old self again, solicitous and attentive. Keeping his seething resentment to himself, he even began telling people about the baby—she was delighted to see how much he appeared to enjoy the attention that prospective fatherhood conferred on him.

Ever his father's son, Chuck spent hours one night carefully reviewing their portfolio of insurance policies, she told her friends. Carol had never interfered in any of those details. "Chuckie is the financial whiz," she would say. Chuck did the banking, the bills, the taxes, and the planning, and Carol was happy to give him her paycheck and forget about the rest, most of the time. Only on occasions, such as when the automatic-teller machine spat out a receipt with the words "ZERO BALANCE" on it, would she worry a little about the way they seemed to be spending everything they made. Insurance was supposedly an investment, or at least a prudent hedge against the unforeseen. And finally, it seemed to her that Chuck was going overboard on insurance. "We're becoming insurance-poor," she told friends with a laugh that nevertheless underscored how pleased she was that Chuck had become so enthusiastic about planning to become a parent.

Any smart, sensitive kid who grew up in the Balkanized suburbs of Boston was familiar with the ethnic jokes. They seemed to change with the borders. An Irish kid like Chuck would have heard that a seven-course Irish meal was a six-pack and a potato, and might even have repeated it himself. A kid with an obvious Italian name like Carol's would have heard the one about the first thing a family of pink flamingos did when they moved into town: They planted a pair of plastic Italians out on the front lawn. The Boston area had been exclusionary since the day in 1630 when the Pilgrims, led by John Winthrop, landed and proclaimed both the homogeneity and the haughtiness of his "city upon a hill," which was to exist as a special place where "the eyes of all people are upon us." To a degree more striking than any city in the United States, an atmosphere of "us" as distinct from "them" would endure in metropolitan Boston, where an outsider can still be defined as someone whose parents had come from another state.

To all eyes in this self-conscious milieu—including her own—Carol DiMaiti grew up blatantly Italian, within the security of a vast, exuberant, extended clan of relatives and friends who saw nothing at all odd in the fact that her family house, a rambling wood-frame two-family brown bungalow in a neat, well-tended neighborhood, had in its front yard a statue of the Virgin Mary set off in a sky-blue grotto among the azalea bushes. As a child, this pretty, dark-haired little girl who was always known as the apple of her father's eye never had the slightest reason to apologize for her background. But that changed, almost imperceptibly, as the child grew up and wandered past the defenses of the other ethnic turfs. Inevitably, Carol DiMaiti ("rhymes with Haiti," she persisted in telling tongue-tied friends in high school and college) came to understand that no matter what else her careful upbringing and hard work in school might lead her to become, outside that cozy little neighborhood where she grew up and attended Catholic school down the block, "Italian" is how they were going to define her first.

And though she would have fiercely denied such a thing, as her ambitions led her more surely outside that neighborhood, she developed, as victims of subtle bigotry will, a self-effacing manner about her ethnic background.

"Oh," she would say with a laugh and a disarming shrug to explain certain things about herself, whenever she sensed a disapproving judgment in such arbitrary matters as perceived lapses of decorative taste. "We're Italian, you know. From the North End."

In Boston, at least until easy redevelopment money from the banks brought yuppies in to claim the edges of the old neighborhood during the 1980s, "North End" has carried a single connotation since the 1930s: Italian. In the years before World War I, immigrant Italians literally just off the boats planted deep and ultimately sturdy roots in the neighborhood, which in its earliest days had been linked to the city limits on the Shawmut Peninsula only by a sliver of land that, filled in, would become Hanover Street. In Colonial Boston, before many of its well-heeled Loyalist burghers fled with the British at the onset of the Revolution, the North End was a fashionable neighborhood. Paul Revere lived there. Later, as it became a haven for successive waves of immigrants, John ("Honey Fitz") F. Fitzgerald, the legendary Boston politician and maternal grandfather of John F. Kennedy, rose to prominence from its wards. During the early nineteenth century, as Boston claimed more space from its surrounding wetlands, wealthy North End merchants built wharves from their houses across the salt marshes to the shoreline of the harbor; and while the wharves brought commercial prosperity, they also brought the refugee-crammed steamships from Europe and airless tenements thrown up quickly to house them. Many of the early immigrants moved on to better neighborhoods away from the bustle of the wharves. But by the Civil War, as Boston's Irish-born population was bloated with tens of thousands of refugees from the famine-cursed west and south of Ireland, there was no longer any easy access out, and the North End took on an insular character. "The dear old North End," the Irish called it. While the "Dearos" eventually ceded certain sections of the neighborhood to a later influx of eastern European Jews, it was Irish eyes that looked down contemptuously on the foreign-tongued refugees from southern Italy and Sicily, lumbering in from the wharves off Commercial Street and Atlantic Avenue in the years of the great Italian immigration after World War I. Within a generation, the Irish were in full flight and the North End was Italian.

Today, despite the new brick townhouses that gild the gentrified areas with the best views of the water, the North End retains the character of southern Italy. It is a place where an old woman walking its narrow streets on her way to the store in the morning raises her hand in benediction to a potbellied cook in a fresh white apron smoking and rocking on his heels on the sidewalk in front of his restaurant. Except for the late-model cars at the curbs, the North End on a warm August morning might be mistaken for a bustling village in Calabria.

Among the multitude of Italian immigrants who embraced the North End just after the First World War were Enrico and Michelina DiMaiti, who arrived with some belongings and not much money in the early 1920s. By 1925, when their son Giusto was born, the couple were sufficiently well established to have opened a grocery store at the foot of Hanover Street, just across Commercial Street from the drydock where the USS *Constitution* was built. For the rest of their long lives together, the DiMaitis lived in the apartment building next door to the grocery, working twelve hours a day and, when they could, expanding modestly. By the time Giusto was a young man, his parents' grocery included a fish shop, and they also ran a small luncheonette nearby on Commercial Street, which their son managed.

Today, probably because of its prime location near the gentrified sections at the edge of the neighborhood, the family's grocery store is gone. A 7-Eleven convenience store now stands incongruously on the site. But nearby on Hanover Street, there still are many small shops on the ground floors of the neat five-story tenements, and many Italian restaurants. There are also two Roman Catholic churches within a few minutes' stroll of the house where Carol's father grew up at 460 Hanover Street. In a small way, the peculiar setting of these two churches so close to each other helps to explain why, in years to come, Giusto DiMaiti would strongly, if largely silently, resist the relationship that developed between his only daughter and her boyfriend from an Irish family in Revere.

One of the churches, St. Stephen's, is actually closer to 460 Hanover Street than the other, which is called St. Leonard's. But when Carol's father was growing up, St. Stephen's was the church for the Irish who still remained in the North End. Originally built by Boston's Unitarians, who hired Charles Bulfinch to design it in 1804, it was originally known as the New North Church, to distinguish it from the famous Old North Church across the square. In 1862, after most well-heeled Unitarians had abandoned the North End for more genteel neighborhoods, the church was sold to the Catholic diocese. The bishop, whose name was Fitzpatrick, renamed it St. Stephen's.

Sixty years later, when they arrived to begin new lives in the North End, the Italians found scant welcome at St. Stephen's, whose parishioners now included not only working-class second-generation immigrants but also some so-called lace-curtain Irish "Greenbloods" as they were also known, who had long since moved their families to Beacon Hill. Instead, the Italian immigrants found comfort within the more traditional confines of St. Leonard's, a little farther up Hanover Street. A sign that still faces the sidewalk from a shady grotto of religious statues and flowers outside St. Leonard's was erected to announce both their pride, and something of their tacit defiance, to their Irish neighbors gazing disapprovingly, with the special contempt the poor have always reserved for the poorer, from under the tall white cupola of their converted Protestant church across the street. "First Roman Catholic Church in New England," the sign outside St. Leonard's notes pointedly. "Built by Italian Immigrants."

By the end of World War II, the Italians were on their way to predominance in the North End, and had stamped the neighborhood with a cultural identity, which the Irish never had. In July and August, clamorous *festas* spilled into the streets in honor of various patron saints. Even in bad times, people ate, and as good times arrived, people ate with a vengeance. Everywhere, there was food: fat roped cheeses and pasta dusted with flour; salami, pepperoni, and ropes of garlic hung over counters abundant with produce, with black shiny eggplant and sun-red tomatoes and bouquets of basil, all piled high. At the foot of Hanover, across Commercial Street, was a vast terminal where freight trains and trucks lumbered in all day long, laden with fresh fruits and vegetables and chilled meats to provide not only for the shops and restaurants of the North End and the city markets beyond, but for the ships, commercial and military, that sailed from the wharves. An enterprising young man such as Giusto DiMaiti, whose parents had already given him a toehold in the food business, could not help but find opportunity in this, nor could he help noticing that a bigger world loomed beyond those wharves.

Such a young man gazing across the harbor as he contemplated his life at the time would have watched the outline of a great bridge taking shape beyond the wharves and above the masts and super-structures of the vessels docked at the Charlestown navy yard. The Mystic River Bridge, later to be known as the Tobin Bridge, opened in 1950, and threw open the suburban North Shore. A year later, leaving the North End behind, Giusto DiMaiti crossed it. At twenty-five, with a trade as a salesman in Italian groceries and pasta that enabled him to present himself as suitable husband, he married Evelyn Florence Mantia, a twenty-year-old first-generation Italian woman from Medford, a town just north of Boston. The wedding, a festive affair, was held at St. James Roman Catholic Church; soon afterward the couple purchased a two-family house on Fourth Street, a block down from the church and two doors down from the house where Evelyn had grown up and where her parents still lived. The

DiMaitis occupied the upper level of the home; and Evelyn's sister, Rosemary Leone, and her family moved in on the ground floor.

Like their respective parents, the DiMaitis sank solid roots. They never moved from the wood-frame bungalow on Fourth Street, where they raised their two children, Carl, born in 1955, and Carol Ann, born on March 26, 1959, at Lawrence Memorial Hospital in Medford.

Carol, a dark-eyed, pretty child with a ready laugh, grew up in the warmth of a big, extended Italian family. She was imbued with values that couple the age-old Italian insistence on importance of family and the supremacy of the father in that unit, with the hard-won awareness of the crucial need for education.

For the two DiMaiti children, as for many of their neighbors in a section of Medford that had become heavily middle-class Italian-American by the 1960s, there was no question about it: You went to grade school at St. James, you paid attention to the nuns, and you did well. And then you went to high school at Medford High, which the people of Medford had made into one of the better high schools in the suburbs. And after that, you were headed for college. Your parents would help out, of course. In towns like Medford, in determined families such as the DiMaitis, the emphasis on college had reached the point where a man with a couple of kids in school who didn't have both a day job and a night job tended to think of himself as a part-time worker. You probably wouldn't be bound for Harvard or Wellesley—and there was no question that you were going to have to work and pay a good part of your own way. But in Carol's family, unlike Chuck's, you were going to college. Period.

Carol's older brother had been the first to graduate from college, and when he became a high school social studies teacher, his parents had never been prouder—until Carol came along and wowed every teacher who ever met her. Yet, though she would far outpace him academically, Carol always looked up to her older brother.

At Medford High School, Carol DiMaiti would be fondly remembered for many things, among them scholastic excellence coupled with an extraordinary inclination to make herself useful. But if any of her classmates were to have been asked to predict where Carol would be ten years later, each one of them would have answered about the same: married to a good husband, living in the suburbs with a couple of terrific kids, happily ever after. Nothing, not the law degree, not the financial freedom that would come during the boom years of the 1980s, when she and her husband would have a combined salary that approached that of many corporate chief executive officers, would ever shake that basic assessment of Carol's aspirations in life.

And you could do worse in Carol's practical mind than raise your family in Medford. Often lumped with Revere and other blue-collar towns in the Boston suburbs, where the schools were often indifferent at best, Medford in fact took great pride in its school system. With its careful landscaping and eight interconnected buildings on twenty-six acres of land, Medford High looks more like a small college campus, and its students tend to respond in kind. Its facilities include an Olympic-size pool, an extensive library, and an audiovisual classroom and laboratory center that is also the headquarters for the local cable television company's public-access channel.

Although the enrollment in 1990 had sunk to 1,700, underscoring a trend that had been clear enough twelve years earlier to make Carol abandon her plans to become a teacher, during the 1970s it was more than twice that. Despite that overcrowding, and despite the years that had passed, despite the fact that kids, even smart kids with good attitudes, come and go, teachers at Medford High remembered Carol vividly.

"Academically, Carol was in the top percentage of her class. She was an A student in the honors program," said Sal Todaro, headmaster at the school. "She took advanced placement and honors accelerated programs."

"As a class leader, she would initiate group concepts and ideas for the entire student body to get involved. She was a problem solver and a critical thinker; she had that rare combination of both."

Typically, Carol volunteered to work in the administration office before classes each day. "She'd come into the office in the morning and it was like a ray of light coming in. She was always upbeat—she always saw the bright side of things. She'd take the negatives and turn them around. This kid was an optimist with both feet on the ground," said Todaro, who had met few students like her before or since.

"She wasn't bashful, but she wasn't overbearing. In class, she would phrase her presentations in a way to almost draw responses. You have individuals who ask questions—she'd ask that second, third, and fourth question. She was very in-depth, a deep thinker."

Off the top of his head, Todaro rattled off some of the things he recalled about Carol's high-school years: "National Honor Society. Tutoring in math and in English—she took the time to assist kids that needed help, strictly voluntary. She was there all the time— after school, before school. Elected treasurer in a senior class that numbered—" only here did the headmaster have to check a record— "873." Not to mention a pom-pom girl.

"She wanted to be a teacher," Todaro said. But always with Carol, the bottom line, he recalled, was this: "And after that, get married and raise her family."

The recollections never varied on that point. "Overall, her purpose in life was to raise a good family," said Robert Bonsignore, a Medford native who went to high school and later to law school with her. "She got along with jocks, burnouts, wimps, geeks, headmasters— everyone. She was a very pleasant person, painless to speak to"— and already exhibiting a trait that would always characterize her social life: "able to bridge the gap and circle in all different groups."

"In high school, people can be petty, looking to take a jab at others. But through four years in that school, I never heard anyone say a bad word about her."

To those who knew her, Carol was always either working or studying, and sometimes she managed to do both, bringing her school books to work and cracking them open in a corner when others were taking a cigarette break outside.

When she was fifteen, her father got her a job as a busgirl at the Driftwood, a restaurant on the main drag in Revere Beach a few miles from their home in Medford. As usual, Giusto DiMaiti had a second night job at the time, tending bar at the Driftwood, a decent steak-and-seafood restaurant on the beach, popular with business people who liked the food and quiet ambiance beside the ocean. Unlike many of the restaurants and bars that crowded Revere Beach Boulevard, the Driftwood didn't attract a rowdy crowd, even late on weekend nights when the cruising was in full swing outside. Once a week, the local bookies would stop by on their rounds, and occasionally it would become known that someone had radios or stereos for sale cheap, but otherwise the place was as respectable as an ice cream parlor, and about as alluring to the leather-jacket crowd that frequented many of the nearby rock joints and pickup bars. Just to make sure no one got the wrong impression upon walking in the door, the owners usually had Sinatra music playing.

Under her father's protective eye, Carol worked there a couple of nights a week and every day during the summers while she was in high school, and liked it well enough to stay on through college. The tips were good, nobody got hassled, it was nice to be near the beach, even if it was polluted old Revere beach, and the staff was like a big family—twenty-five employees in all, the kind of people who celebrated each other's birthdays with cakes blazing with Fourth of July sparklers, and stayed in touch with each other long after they had moved on in life.

The day she turned eighteen, old enough under Massachusetts law to serve drinks, Carol was promoted to a waitress job at the Driftwood. Her replacement as busgirl was a young girl from nearby Everett named Christine Baratta, whose aunt knew the owner, which was the usual way to get a part-time job in Revere, where outsiders were no more welcomed than anywhere else in the Boston area. Aside from babysitting and delivering newspapers, it was Christine's first job, and she was apprehensive when the restaurant owner warned her that she would have big shoes to fill.

For not only was Carol DiMaiti a hit with the customers but she was popular with her co-workers. Carol, who never missed a day of work, was punctual, unfailingly pleasant, energetic, chipper, and thoughtful in a demanding, messy, low-status job of cleaning tables and lugging trays of dirty dishes to the hot kitchen. Having to follow such an act was intimidating, even for a fourteen-year-old like Christine who was quite willing to knock herself out for two dollars an hour.

But when she showed up for work on a day early in 1977, frightened and certain she was doomed to not measure up, Christine was amazed to find Carol herself coming to her rescue.

"The maitre d' had told me all about what a wonderful person she was, how it was going to be hard for me to replace this woman. I was just a kid. I didn't really know what it was like to work, and they were scaring me, telling me how I was going to have to be personable, how I was never going to be able to match up to this little dynamo. So I walked in for my first night of work, and I'm nervous, and who comes bopping out but this five-foot-three little thing, so sweet and bubbly. She showed me the works. She calmed me down and taught me how to work, and just completely defused any anxiety I had."

Christine never forgot the effort Carol put into making her feel comfortable, even though Carol herself was nervous starting her new job waiting tables. Christine, who was herself the oldest of five sisters, said, "When I met Carol I met a big sister. She taught me how to drive. She taught me how to wear makeup. She taught me about clothes and hair. She helped me pick my prom gown out. God, she helped me to pick out my college, Boston University. She helped me to pick out a career. She always treated me like such an equal. In a way, she really helped me to grow up. She took such an interest that she became a very important part of my adolescence."

From Carol, Christine learned such basic lessons in a girl's life as how to use makeup, and how to drive a car. "I was going to my prom and I had never worn makeup. I was fifteen or sixteen, but being fifteen or sixteen ten years ago is different from being that now. Now, I think they wear makeup right out of the cradle. But I was just a kid, and I was going to my prom, and I was nervous about wearing makeup. I didn't know how to do it."

Carol, on the other hand, did, and it wasn't something she had learned from a magazine. "She was into naturalness, even before its time," Christine said. "She felt you didn't have to round your eyes out in deep black mascara or eyeliner. She had a wonderful face. She used light, light blush. No blue eyeshadow, just a nice brown. But she could wear red lipstick like no one."

Later, anxious to get her driver's license, Christine turned to Carol. Scared and impatient, Christine had already exhausted the patience of her father, who sent her to a driving school. That lasted one lesson, which ended in frustrated tears. "I had never even started a car, and they expected me to drive out on a highway," she said. Dismayed, she told Carol at work one night that she knew she would never, ever learn to drive.

Carol laughed, and dug into her purse for the keys to her own Datsun 210, a little white car with blue racing stripes that Christine had admired. "Come on, let's go," Carol said, dropping her keys into the younger girl's palm. "Here you go! Let's do it." The two went out to the Datsun and Carol ushered Christine behind the wheel.

Laughing hysterically, they lurched off to an empty parking lot nearby, where Carol patiently began teaching her young friend how to turn, park, and back up. Within a month, Christine came bursting into the restaurant proudly displaying her license.

By 1978, Carol's bank book showed nearly $10,000 on the bottom line, most of it diligently saved from waiting tables at the Driftwood over the years. Proudly, she enrolled at Boston College, a school that was just Catholic enough to assuage the concerns of her wary parents, who could nod solemnly to share the information that the college was run by Jesuits, and just far enough away from Medford to allow her to stake out a small measure of independence. While she loved her father deeply, and obeyed him without question, Carol had come to realize that Giusto did not fully appreciate the fact that his little girl had grown up.

Initially, she had even toyed with the idea of living fifteen miles away from home, on the Boston College campus. But even with a nineteen-year-old's ransom in the bank and a tiny mutiny stirring in her timid soul, Carol characteristically managed to look a few years ahead and make the prudent choice, both financially and emotionally. Until her senior year in college, she would live at home.

At college, her teachers would remember Carol as bright, very hard-working, self-effacing, and determined. But a few of them would also puzzle over her, as teachers sometimes do with their brightest students. Seemingly submissive, invariably prepared to recite the required academic tract, the young woman from Medford could also be deadly in argument. Blithely leading the amiable Carol DiMaiti down a well-trod theoretical path, an overconfident teacher of undergraduate political science or theology could find himself hurtling off a rhetorical cliff at the end as Carol skipped aside with a demure smile and a single pointed conclusion. In a classroom, Carol DiMaiti, despite her little-girl's voice and her engaging curiosity, was to be underestimated at one's own peril.

As Carol's confidence grew at college, where she enjoyed the social life almost as much as the academic one, the tiny rebellion that had begun to mount at high-school graduation broke through on occasion. By her sophomore year, for example, it was clear to her pragmatic mind that being a teacher was no longer a good idea. As the end of the phenomenal post-war baby boom eased its way out of the schools in the 1970s, teachers began to find layoff notices in the mail. Characteristically, Carol weighed her options silently for some time before announcing what was already a *fait accompli* in her own mind: She would become a lawyer, not a teacher. Abruptly, she switched her major to political science and plunged in with a vigor that surprised even those who had long remarked on her academic energy. Released from planning for the school-board constraints that would accompany a high-school teacher's life, Carol now felt free to have opinions, and to express them. As usual, she thought things through carefully and quietly. But before long, minute tremors of political insubordination could be felt rumbling through the benevolent patriarchate of the DiMaiti house on Fourth Street.

"Carol announced that she was a liberal, and she might have well told her father that she was thinking about becoming a Communist," a friend recalled. For the first time in their lives, father and daughter did not see eye-to-eye on an important subject: politics. Like most Italian-Americans in the suburbs where they had enthusiastically plugged into the postwar American dream, Carol's father was a committed conservative, which by the beginning of the 1980s translated into what would be known proudly as a Reagan Republican. In such a relationship, a daughter with a Carter for President bumper sticker on her car might as well be waving a red flag at a startled bull.

Suddenly, Daddy's little girl had opinions. "They had the kinds of arguments that really clear the kitchen in that kind of house, where everybody was usually so nicey-nicey," the friend said with a chuckle. "You know, people would start sort of drifting away, deciding it was time to do the dishes or watch television. It wasn't the kind of house where you were used to arguments of any sort. But sometimes, not often, but sometimes, they would keep at it for hours, just the two of them. He would never back down politically, but she wouldn't either, and it drove her father nuts and kind of scared her mother, I think. But they never got personal, never, and she never got mad. And after a while you could see that her father loved it. Even when she'd like to piss him off with some statement, you could tell he was actually pleased at the way little Carol dug in her heels and stood her ground. I don't think anyone in the family really realized just how much fun these two were secretly having arguing with each other."

Though she was attending college during the day, Carol contin-

ued to spend a lot of time in her father's presence, even at work at
the Driftwood, where both of them were on duty one night in 1978
when Chuck Stuart sauntered into their lives.

Chuck, a proficient short-order cook thanks to his vocational-
school training, had gotten the job through his boyhood friend Brian,
who already worked as a cook in the Driftwood's bustling kitchen.
Tall and good-looking, with a shy smile and a polite demeanor,
Chuck got noticed right away by the Driftwood's waitresses and bus-
girls, including Carol, who was still dating her high-school boyfriend
at the time.

One of the first things people learned about the new cook was
that he apparently had been at Brown University the previous year,
but was said to have left when a knee injury caused him to lose his
football scholarship. No one could ever remember Chuck actually
telling them that, but everyone seemed to know it. It was just one
of those basic points of information people knew about Chuck, like
his coming from a big Irish family in Revere and his love of sports.
Years later, when people learned that Chuck had never attended
Brown, they would wonder why Chuck had so casually deceived
friends, on such a trivial matter, and one on which it would have
been so easy to get caught. After all, anyone with reason to give it
any thought would realize something generally well known, that Ivy
League schools, Brown among them, didn't even have football
scholarships.

To Chuck, determined to achieve social status and painfully
aware that his own education consisted of spending his high-school
years at a vocational school, followed by flunking out of Salem State
in less than a month, it mattered greatly that people thought he had
been in an Ivy League school. The only time he really worried about
being caught in his lie was after he became interested in Carol
DiMaiti and realized that the guy she had been dating since high
school now played football at Brown. But Carol never asked.

As he settled in at the Driftwood, Chuck began paying rapt
attention to Carol. Though he was shy and, despite his good looks,
had never dated a girl more than casually, Chuck Stuart was obviously taken with the dark-haired waitress who always seemed to have
her nose buried in a book when she wasn't busy with a table. And
once they sensed the possibilities, co-workers began encouraging the
two of them to get together. Chuck and Carol, several waitresses

agreed, just seemed to belong together, although (or perhaps because) they were opposites in appearance as well as personality.

Chuck, a big, broad-shouldered young man, stood nearly a foot taller than Carol. Visually, his strength lay in a first impression that largely came from his sparkling deep-blue eyes, wavy brown hair, and a strong, firm jaw that projected what was seen as quiet confidence. It was Chuck's good fortune, or design, that the first impression tended to linger, because a good second look would discover a certain thickness of the brow that presented a disquieting appearance on those infrequent occasions when Chuck might be seen deep in thought or, more likely, sunk in a sulk. There also was a puffiness to the cheeks, an overall hint of flabbiness that was being held in check only by strict vigilance, until the inevitable time when an image sharp and handsome enough to be on the television screen would metamorphose into one more likely to be found seated in front of it.

Carol, on the other hand, fared much better on subsequent impressions than on the first. She was one of those people who, it was said, did not "take a good picture." And it was true, a snapshot highlighted her worst features, primarily a mouth that was slightly too wide to be pretty, and obscured her best, which were the finely formed contours of her face and wide, big brown eyes that burned with curiosity. Like Chuck, Carol had to work to stay happy with her weight; unlike him, at six foot three inches, she had little leeway at five foot three. But when she hovered at what she thought was her best weight, the 100- to 110-pound range she struggled to stay at during her college years, she had a figure that could and on occasion did stop the ever-observant traffic on Revere Beach Boulevard when she left her car to go to work. Yet in their later years together, Chuck would become at least as concerned about her weight as his own.

Shortly after he started work at the Driftwood, it was obvious to everyone in the restaurant that he was determined in his own quiet way to get Carol's attention. "He wanted her, and that was it. He went after her," said Christine.

Carol had a boyfriend, Jeff Cataldo, but their relationship had cooled after high school. Besides, Jeff was at Brown, and Chuck was at the Driftwood. He worked at it, and eventually, he prevailed. "She really was torn after Chuck came on the scene. Jeff was heartbroken when she broke up with him. I remember her saying he was going to take it hard," Christine said.

From his close vantage point behind the bar, Carol's father took it even harder. Intensely proud of his only daughter, Giusto carried in his wallet, and would show to anyone with little provocation, Carol's sixth-grade report card, on which she had gotten nothing but A's. He also carried her First Communion picture and a little Valentine's drawing she had made for him when she was four years old, with the D in Daddy drawn backward. For Carol, Giusto expected nothing but the best.

And this new kid from Revere wasn't good enough. It wasn't only that a union of an Italian and an Irishman was considered a mixed marriage in Medford—not to mention the North End, where it was considered a tragedy. Always keeping a discrete eye on his daughter at work, Giusto had noticed the way the new cook watched her as she moved across the room, the way he always seemed to be hanging around her when she had free time. Carol's father liked Jeff Cataldo, an Italian boy going to a good school, just fine. This new guy, who Carol seemed to be paying a disturbing amount of attention to, had two strikes against him when he walked in the door Irish and not in college. Strike three came across the plate as soon as he began making a move on his daughter.

Aware of Giusto's disdain, Chuck alienated Carol's father even further by making an elaborate attempt to win the man over with his charm, which failed notably for once. But it was a different story with Carol's friends at work. Almost from the beginning, Chuck realized that the best way to approach Carol was through the people who liked her best. The new girl, Christine, was surprised by the amount of attention she started getting from the handsome new cook.

"As a busgirl I'd come in during the early shift and I'd have to go downstairs to bring up the supplies—heavy bottles of dressing, gallons and gallons of ice, and linens. I was a young girl, and strong, too, but it took me a long time to bring the things up—many trips up and down this long, narrow flight of stairs. In the summertime it was brutal. Chuck would be down there sometimes getting some stuff for the kitchen in the freezers, or whatever, and I'd be piling all my stuff up, and he'd come by and say, 'Let me grab that for you.' Whenever he saw me down there he always helped me, which is not the case with many people, who felt, basically 'You do your work and I do mine.' A cook's job was hard enough. And he was nice about it."

To Christine, and to Carol as well, Chuck didn't display a lot of the usual rough edges of Revere. "He didn't swear—maybe he swore with his friends, but he didn't swear at work. He also wasn't rude. A lot of times the cooks were rude. He was nice. He gave you what you needed, and if you made a mistake or something, he didn't throw a pan at you like a lot of them would. Cooks are notoriously temperamental, and it was an outrageous group. But it wasn't like they were chefs in a four-star restaurant. I mean, it was simple, like baked scrod, seafood linguini. You'd think some of them were creating four-star cuisine. Chuck was different. He was always nice to work with."

Given his training, Chuck talked openly about having his own restaurant one day, but so did many others in the Driftwood kitchen who, it was clear, didn't yet have as much as their own car. But Chuck struck people as being different, with a determination that was impressive, especially as shown in his pursuit of Carol once his intentions were clear. Suddenly, he was cornering co-workers to question them about any sign of interest Carol might have shown in him. It was the talk of the Driftwood when Carol finally began sending the same signals back through the grapevine.

"She was wondering when Chuck was going to ask her out and that kind of stuff," Christine said. "They were sort of feeling each other out, 'Does she like me?' and 'Does he like me?' That kind of thing. There was a lot of joint effort among the staff to get these two together. We really tried to foster that relationship."

It worked. Before long, they were dating. And then they were going steady.

As this relationship with Chuck became more serious during college, Carol's father became increasingly alarmed. He had always placed his daughter on a pedestal, and he made no bones about his attitude that Chuck Stuart had no business being near her. Yet when Carol asked him to explain his objections, he couldn't come up with good, logical reasons other than the opinion that Chuck seemed sneaky. It soon got around at the Driftwood that Carol's father had thrown Chuck out of his house when he came calling one night early in their relationship.

"He just didn't think that Chuck was good enough for her,"

Christine said. "Even though Chuck bragged about the culinary arts training he had received at his vo-tech school, where he made it a point to tell people he had belonged to the gourmet club, in Carol's father's eyes, the best he was doing was flipping burgers at the Driftwood, and he wasn't in school or anything," Christine said. "Her father worked at the Driftwood himself, so he knew what this guy's future looked like, and he didn't think it was much. He was very patriarchal, but really, anybody who had a daughter who was the apple of his eye like Carol could have said, 'You can do better than this.' "

Carol's friends at work felt otherwise. "This guy was gaga over her," said Christine. "And we all felt he was nice. He was cute; they made a wonderful-looking couple. We were caught up in that. And she thought he was so special that we cut him a lot of slack— he wasn't vivacious like she was. He was sort of quiet—not dumb or anything like that. Just quiet. But she could be the life of the party—she was always giggling, always personable. He wasn't as personable."

During college, as her relationship with Chuck became more serious, Carol was increasingly torn between the feelings for her father and her growing passion for Chuck. Carol, who seldom could hide her feelings about anything, sometimes began crying over the dilemma, saying once: "I just wish the two men I love most in my life could get along, that it would be okay with my father because I really love Chuckie."

The more Giusto showed his opposition, the more Chuck pressed. "He was so attentive to her," said Christine. "I mean, this guy loved her. I think when he met this woman, he realized he had hit the jackpot. He just couldn't have found anyone who was going to be a more wonderful companion, friend, wife, mother. It was all there in front of him. She was smart; she had a career ahead of her; she had a real personality. It was there for him to see."

Carol "liked that he was different from, you know, guys," her friend recalled. "He called all the time. He'd send her little gifts, little tokens. He was very good on expressing love. Most men, you get flowers on your anniversary. With Chuck, it was always flowers here, flowers there. Little bunches when they went out on a date. He made it special. He was extremely attentive to her. To use an old-fashioned term, he wooed her. He sent her cards for no reason—

sometimes he'd even leave flowers for her to find on the front seat of her car when she was working. She was always so impressed by his attention."

In the early stages of the relationship, when Carol's old boy-friend tried to win her back, Chuck deftly headed him off. "Chuck, he was right there with the flowers," said Christine. "He was tough to beat."

That was the first time people noticed how he could focus on something he wanted. "When she walked into the kitchen, he'd never take his eyes off her. He was piercing, he really was. He followed her, his eyes everywhere she went, everything she did." Christine remembered helping Carol to make salads on a counter in front of the stove where Chuck worked in the kitchen. "I would turn around and he'd be right there doing what he was doing but looking at her with those eyes."

Whatever, it worked. But even after he had won Carol over, Chuck made it a point to remain attentive toward her younger friend. "A lot of times, being a busgirl, you were the last one out because you had to clean up. If Carol's shift ended, if her customers all had left, she always used to bring her books to work, and she'd go get herself something to eat in the kitchen, a piece of fish or a bowl of chowder, and she'd go sit in one of the back rooms and study for a half hour, an hour, whatever, waiting for me instead of just leaving when she could.

"Even when she and Chuck were going out after work, it was always, 'We'll take Christine home first.' They always made sure I got home." In the car, Carol often sang along with the radio on full blast. Chuck was quiet. Christine never saw her happier, and on those evenings, she also came to see a more personal side of Chuck. For such a good-looking, apparently together guy, she decided, he seemed to be almost vulnerable.

"He never talked about his family," Christine said, but he made it clear that something was missing. Carol told her friend that Chuck needed her "for things that he had never received at home—affection and attention." With her genuinely nurturing nature, Carol felt more in love with him than ever.

Since Chuck never talked about his family, people were sur-prised when, a year or so later, a kid identified as his brother showed up for work as a dishwasher. Chuck had been at the Driftwood long

enough to get his kid brother a job, but he wasn't eager to be associated with Matthew. A sullen kid with long black hair, Matthew
seemed to be something of an embarrassment to Chuck, who treated
him with a condescension that surprised the others. "Why don't you
get yourself together, get a haircut?" Chuck demanded publicly of
Matthew, who was obviously intimidated by his older brother, and
stayed out of his way in the kitchen. After his shift was over, Matthew liked nothing better than to head down the strip to a rock club,
where he and his friends drank as many beers as possible while
listening to heavy metal bands booming from the thousand-watt
speakers.

Carol clearly shared Chuck's low opinion of Matthew. One
night, looking at the leather-jacketed Matthew talking with Chuck,
who did not smoke, seldom drank more than a single beer, and
dressed like a preppy, Carol decided with a laugh that her boyfriend
was a foundling. "No way," she told a friend, "are those two guys
blood relatives."

"What's his brother like?" someone once asked her, seeing the
two together on the sidewalk out front, where Matthew was dragging
on a cigarette and shrugging his shoulders at something Chuck was
saying.

"Silent," she said, adding with a bluntness that surprised her
friend, "Almost like he had a lobotomy."

By the time Carol was nearing college graduation, she and
Chuck were deeply in love and making plans to marry. But they did
not agree on when that would be. Chuck wanted the wedding to be
right after Carol graduated from college in June of 1981. Carol
insisted that they wait until after she was through with law school.

In the interim, Chuck decided to do something about his future.
Carol was sailing through undergraduate school with honors, and
undoubtedly would do the same in law school. Which would mean
that his wife would be a lawyer, and he would be a short-order cook
with dreams of opening his own restaurant one day. That, of course,
would not do. Chuck stopped talking about the restaurant and started
looking around for a better job. In the classified section, he found
one that looked promising under "Management Trainee."

Edward F. Kakas & Sons, the prominent furrier on Newbury
Street in the Back Bay of Boston, turned out to be the best thing

Chuck ever talked his way into. Chuck moved quickly through the company's training program, and within months was making a strong impression on his new employers, who found to their delight that not only did the young man from Revere have management ability—an office manager was one thing, but no one was going to pay an office manager the kind of money Chuck envisioned—but he could also charm the clientele and move the merchandise. Within a year, Chuck was the top salesman at Kakas after the owners themselves.

Driven, he threw himself into his new career with spectacular success. By the time he had been there a year he was making more than $40,000, an accomplishment that both pleased and bothered Carol, who was happy to see her future husband doing so well but, she confided to a close friend, a little frustrated at knowing that with her law degree and years of study, she would be lucky to start at anything near the same salary herself.

It was the first time anyone had ever heard Carol disparage Chuck's education. And she was ashamed of herself as soon as she said it. Meanwhile, her future as Chuck's wife, with her father ultimately if reluctantly on board, began taking discernible shape. The degrees would just be well-planned stops along the way. "It was important for Carol to do well professionally" and become a successful lawyer, said Christine, "but she always looked forward to having kids and being a mom. I think if someone said to her, 'You can either be a lawyer or a mother,' I'm pretty sure she would have said, 'I'd rather be a mother.' "

After Carol graduated from Boston College, with honors, she worked full time for another year to earn enough money to start law school. In the fall of 1982, she enrolled at Suffolk University Law School, a school that turned out legions of Boston attorneys who ended up in criminal work and, many times, on the bench. But despite a growing interest in politics, it was the dry, mundane area of tax law that eventually drew her attention, especially after Chuck began encouraging her.

"Criminal lawyers are a dime a dozen," Chuck scoffed once when they went out to dinner with another couple who were in their second year of law school. "Who wants to be one of fifty assistant DAs copping plea-bargain deals with some fat, crooked Boston judge?" Carol nodded vigorously. Chuck had insisted on choosing the restaurant that night, something the other couple remembered

well because he had so blithely overridden their objections that it
was beyond their law-school budget. "Don't worry, I'll pick up the
tab," Chuck said expansively. Embarrassed, the couple went along,
but it was the last time they went out for dinner with Carol and her
big-spending fiancé.

By then, Carol's second year at law school, he was up to
$50,000 at Kakas, salary, commission, and bonus. He had a habit
of working his salary into the conversation.

To her fellow students, overwhelmed with the academic demands of law school and only dreaming of making that kind of
money, Carol's boyfriend was a curiosity, especially since she never
stopped talking about him. "It was 'Chuckie, my boyfriend' this and
'Chuckie, my boyfriend' that," said one classmate. When they ultimately met him, people were expecting a lot. No one could recall
having a bad impression of Chuck, but then again, no one was getting
much of an impression at all of him, despite the prior buildup.

"It was like he was there," said Carol's high-school friend from
Medford, Robert Bonsignore, who was in the same law-school class
as her and was as curious as anyone to meet the man who came to
be known disparagingly as "the fabulous Chuckie." He discovered,
however, "There wasn't anything. He could have been a painting
on the wall. My first impression was that he was not interested in
anybody."

Still, though Carol seemed oblivious to anything except his
vaunted charms, there were misgivings that stuck in the mind without
much definition. "There was something not quite right about Chuck,"
Bonsignore said. "It wasn't natural. It's hard to put your finger on
it. He seemed smooth enough, a little much with the blown-back
hair, but nicely tied together anyway. But not natural, you know?
Almost like 'Oh, I know what I'm supposed to do here. Shake a few
hands, a few niceties and move along.' Not that you gave it much
thought, but there didn't seem to be a real interest in anything that
was going on."

Some of that came from Chuck's growing awareness that his
girlfriend was starting to move in social circles that his own background had taught him to distrust as well as dislike. The only topic
he commanded with real enthusiasm and in any depth was sports—
and few of her law-school friends were able to hold forth on that
topic for more than a few minutes before they ran out of opinions,

knowledge, or interest. In fact, some law-school friends of Carol's were simply intimidated by her boyfriend. Given his good looks and ability to project apparently unflappable self-confidence, given the general knowledge about how much money the guy was pulling down, given the fact that the incredible Carol was madly in love with him, the last thing that would have occurred to them was that Chuck felt inadequate in their presence and compensated for it with a coolness that seemed aloof. Instead, they thought he was a snob.

The truth was apparent at unguarded moments when Chuck was exposed and Carol wasn't able to cover his vulnerability, as was her habit. Such as the ski weekend.

During the winter of Carol's second year of law school, she and Chuck joined a group of about fifteen people from her class for skiing and socializing at a big rented cottage in Waterville Valley, New Hampshire. After dinner, in front of a roaring fire in the living room, a half dozen or so of the young men and women sipped mulled wine and played Trivial Pursuit. Chuck and Carol were on the same team—and it quickly became clear that Chuck wasn't chiming in with the answers that were enthusiastically shouted by everyone else.

No one would have thought much about this—some people just don't have a ready command of trivia, just as some people can't play chess. But in a competitive situation some of the better players began chiding the losing team, and it suddenly became quite clear that Chuck was the reason they were losing. Instead of laughing it off, however, Chuck lost his cool. Angrily, he got up and stalked out in the middle of play.

There was an embarrassed silence. Carol sat on the floor not looking at anyone and the game ended soon afterward. As the others drifted upstairs, Chuck was still sitting in another room noisily thumbing through old copies of *National Geographic*, refusing to acknowledge even their "good nights." When he was still sulking the next day, Carol announced she didn't feel well and needed to catch up on some studying. She and Chuck drove home in silence a day early.

Still, as they had at the Driftwood, Carol's friends tended to cut her boyfriend a lot of slack just because she was so well liked. Carol was the only one in their group who could play the combined roles of friend, confidante, and surrogate mother. At one time or another, amidst the social and academic pressures of law school and growing up in the process, most of them came to know one of what they all began to call her "Carol talks."

"She wasn't abrasive, which is probably the key," said Bonsignore. "She got her two cents in when someone started acting like an idiot, or being unreasonable, or being one-sided. She would take you aside and talk to you, but she would do it in a way that you'd end up being grateful. You'd be like 'Gee, Carol, thanks for telling me what an idiot I am.' "

Except for Chuck, that is. With Chuck, Carol was as meek as a child.

In 1983, he proposed in typically grand style, taking her to a fancy restaurant on Christmas Eve and presenting her with a $4,500 engagement ring she found tucked inside a Gucci wallet. In her joy, she cried so effusively the waiter asked if she wanted him to get help. After dinner, laughing, they hurried to Carol's house in Medford, where her aunt and uncle came up from the downstairs apartment to toast the happy young couple. Carol's father was cordial but subdued as he stood by the gaily decorated DiMaiti Christmas tree and raised his glass with the others. The engagement had been long anticipated; Carol was a grown woman who had always proven herself to be responsible, even when her father thought she was being headstrong, even when she threatened never to speak to him again if he voted for Ronald Reagan. She touched him deeply. Carol was the kind of daughter who called her parents every day from school, where she had moved into a dorm. Because he loved her, Giusto had backed off his vocal opposition to Chuck, unwilling to alienate a daughter who could otherwise do no wrong in his eyes. At least the guy seemed to have career prospects, and if Giusto DiMaiti still thought he seemed like a sneak, he now kept it to himself.

In June of 1985, Carol graduated summa cum laude from Suffolk University Law School. Chuck, running to stay in place, was promoted to assistant general manager, and then general manager at Kakas. The future was bright for the happy couple. They set the date for that October.

There was only one small cloud in their blue skies that summer, and it quickly blew past. At Kakas Furs, several expensive coats that should have been delivered to the warehouse in July were not. It was not quite clear where the problem might have occurred, or even when. In a big operation, these things happen. A security firm was brought in. Each of Kakas's fifty employees was questioned individually, all the way up to the general manager, Chuck, who was furious for weeks at what he regarded as a huge insult of being interrogated. The problem was traced to a delivery service and the matter was forgotten, once the insurance company was satisfied, by everyone but Chuck.

Later in the summer, Carol managed to cheer him up with some wonderful news. She had landed a great job. Arthur Young, the well-known accounting firm, wanted her to start in its downtown Boston office in September, in a program that would use her law background as a basis for a career in tax law, just as they had planned.

"I'll have to pass the CPA exam pretty quickly," she told Chuck. "That means night courses, summer school."

That was nothing new. Carol was always studying anyway. What Chuck was really interested in was more basic than that.

"How much?" he said.

She teased him. "Minimum wage?"

"Come on, how much?"

She paused for effect. "How about thirty thousand dollars?"

"My God," he said, doing a quick calculation. "We're yuppies."

Within weeks, they began house-hunting, and found just the right place, a duplex in Medford, two blocks from Carol's parents. Like the DiMaitis, they would live in half of it and rent out the other half. It was so perfect that Carol was a little embarrassed to tell her friends at the Driftwood. Always sensitive to other people's feelings, Carol was afraid of sounding like she was bragging, a characteristic posture of self-deprecation that made some of her friends, who wanted nothing more than to exalt in her hard-won good fortune, a little uneasy.

Carol had a habit of making fun of her own taste, though many of the young women who knew her consciously followed her example in such matters as dress. Chuck, Carol insisted, was the one with good taste. It struck some of Carol's friends as odd that Chuck was the one who picked out such things as the china pattern and the towels for the wedding. They hated to sound sexist, but these were really things the bride usually handled, not the groom. However, Carol's friend Christine said, "Chuck was really into that sort of thing."

Carol shrugged it off with the usual laugh at her own expense. "You know me, Chrissie. I'm Italian. If they sent me into the store, I'd probably pick out a pattern with a big flower on it or something. Chuck has wonderful taste."

However, one Boston College girlfriend who attended Carol's bridal shower thought Carol's self-deprecation was starting to wear a little thin. While it was true that her decorative taste ran toward the neo-baroque, it was also true, this woman thought, that Carol had a well-developed sense of style that her fiancé from that fashion capital of the North Shore, Revere, seemed to denigrate subtly. She did not like the little-girl way Carol batted her eyelashes and walked in Chuck's protective shadow.

"Carol was a sweet, well-liked person who did extremely well in school," this woman said with some edge to her voice. "She was not an independent woman with a healthy self-image. Carol's life was only complete when she was a daughter or a wife, and I would guess after that a mother."

Chuck and Carol were married on October 13, 1985, at St. James, the church where Carol's parents had been married. The wedding reception was a big festive affair at Lombardo's, a banquet hall in East Boston that was popular with Italian families because of its sumptuous food and its location near the Tobin Bridge, convenient to both the city and the North Shore. The reception marked the first time the DiMaiti family and the Stuarts had ever had a real chance to assess each other over a long period of time. As such, it was a typical Boston festivity. One ethnic group, the reigning Italians, looked down their noses at the other, the Irish, who sulked in return, while the Wasps surveyed them both from a slightly superior distance.

"The DiMaitis were having a ball, dancing and drinking, eating and singing, like a big Italian family," said one guest. "But a lot of Chuck's people were just drinking. By the end of the night, they seemed hidden behind a forest of beer bottles."

A member of the Wasp contingent, Carol's law-school friend Mark Bradley, had this to say: "The wedding stuck out in my mind because it was . . . such an Italian wedding. It was this big, old, long room with a couple of levels. There was this level for the head table, the dance floor, the place where the people were seated. It was nice, but very Italian. You know, a lot of red carpet? The 'Dance with Daddy' number? This dollar-dance thing where everybody pays a buck to dance with the bride? You know, a lot of drinking, everybody's ripped drunk and having fun. People were hollering.

"At the end of the wedding, they had all these little cookies and cakes, and all the old ladies—this blew my mind—were going around just opening their purses and stuffing them in. I was sitting there with my one other Protestant friend, going 'What the hell are these people *doing*?' No one was batting an eyelash. 'It's a tradition,' someone told me. Not that it wasn't a terrific party. It wasn't my taste," Bradley said, adding, "but it was nice and I did have a good time."

Only Chuck, as usual, managed to move easily in all the worlds. But it was still clear that he had his friends and Carol had hers.

Carol didn't want to leave, even though they had to be up early the next morning for a honeymoon flight to Paradise Island. Carol loved to dance, and they practically had to drag her away that night. At the end of the evening, she was still out there, radiant in the pulsing strobe lights, dancing with her husband to a 1980s suburban anthem that both of them considered their favorite, Bruce Springsteen's "Dancing in the Dark," to words they both knew by heart. Dancing in the dark, they lip-synched the peculiar *Angst* of their era to an offbeat that pulsed under the wail of a tenor sax.

F O U R

Willie

W illie Bennett, who always wanted to be famous, first got his wish one night in the spring of 1981 when he dropped to a crouch, pointed a revolver at a bunch of angry cops, and bellowed: "You're not going to take me alive!"

Luckily for Willie, this was one of a number of incorrect statements he had made over an adult lifetime spent either in custody or in flight to avoid arrest for crimes that began with stealing nickels from Boston parking meters. On this balmy evening in 1981, he was in imminent danger of going to his death in a hail of justifiable gunfire over a problem that, bane of the life of a criminal whose weaknesses included fast cars and a hatred of cops, began as a simple traffic violation three months earlier, on the night of February 8.

Willie was only out to go to the store near the place where he was living in Mattapan. In fact, two of his kids were in the back seat. The last thing he was looking for that night was trouble. But the fact that his car had expired license plates brought him to the attention of a cop on routine patrol, who happened to come up behind him at a light.

When the cop pulled him over, Willie couldn't produce his license.

"I left my wallet at home," he told Officer Francis X. O'Brien. The cop was wary, but there were two nice-looking little kids in the back seat. O'Brien offered to follow Willie back to his place a couple of blocks away to get the license.

Willie pulled up slowly to the curb on Westmore Road, where he had told the cop he lived. The children climbed out and scampered into the brick apartment building. Willie was still behind the wheel, but as the officer got out and slowly walked toward him, Willie moved fast and grabbed something from under the seat. Before the cop knew what was happening, he had a sawed-off shotgun stuck in his belly and a triumphant Willie Bennett grinning in his face.

"Get your hands up," Willie told the cop, echoing an order that he himself had complied with on numerous occasions. Officer O'Brien complied. With the barrel of the shotgun pressed hard in the cop's gut, Willie casually reached around and removed his service revolver. By now, Willie was having himself a good time. Laughing heartily, he stepped back with a gun in each hand and aimed the policeman's revolver down toward the street, pulling off a couple of shots that flattened the front left tire of the patrol car.

Then he called the cop a name and hopped into his own car and sped away down the street, still cackling with glee.

Needless to say, this incident made a lasting impression on the police at district headquarters in the Roxbury section of Boston. It did not take them more than a few hours to ascertain the identity of the perpetrator, or to murmur with appreciation at the truly impressive range of outstanding arrest warrants that turned up with Willie Bennett's name on the top. Forget the parking tickets and moving violations—here was an ex-con police were looking for to ask about such previous crimes as assault with intent to kill two police officers, armed robbery and shooting of a legless cabbie two years earlier, as well as the armed assault and kidnapping of a parole officer, not to mention the taking of Officer O'Brien's gun and shooting his tire, and, of course, various parole violations associated with all of the above.

For a while, Willie, who always knew how to keep his head down until he forgot, managed to avoid detection by not going anywhere near his regular address. But when the police got a tip in May from an informant who gained some points by giving them Willie's current address, 42 Lawrence Avenue in the Dorchester neighborhood, they responded with a measure of enthusiasm tempered with a degree of caution that came from the knowledge that their man had already clearly shown himself to be a "shooter."

On the afternoon of May 7, 1981, with their guns drawn, and with four other officers surrounding the building, two detectives and two uniformed cops pounded their way through the door of the apartment on Lawrence Avenue. Sure enough, there was Willie Bennett, crouching and aiming his gun right in their faces.

This is the point at which the thirty-one-year-old Willie made his memorable declaration about not being taken alive, just before one of the cops, diving to the floor, managed to get off a very good shot that knocked the long-barreled Smith & Wesson .357 Magnum out of Willie's left hand.

Later, after he got out of Boston City Hospital, Willie was booked on a variety of charges and headed back to prison with this assessment of the prosecutor ringing in his ears: "Willie Bennett is a threat to all law enforcement."

Suffolk County District Attorney Thomas Horgan had meant that as an indictment of Willie's lifelong attitude of increasingly violent belligerence toward the police in particular and the public order in general. But in the Mission Hill projects where Willie held sway, it was taken as a compliment by some people who regarded Willie as a hero for his hatred of the cops. One of them, Willie's young nephew Joey, even cut out the newspaper article about his uncle's showdown with the police and put it on his bureau in an eight-by-ten picture frame.

In time, during long and angry days and nights of a frantic search for a suspect in the Stuart shootings, that framed newspaper clipping with Willie's picture would take on the aura of a protest sign waved tauntingly in the face of the police. Bennett's criminal reputation as the "baddest wiseguy" in Roxbury would mark him as clear a candidate for the role of chief suspect as if he had raised his hand and volunteered for the part. But much more than a post-puberty lifetime of bad behavior and tough luck would bring Willie

Bennett to that sorry point in his life. In the African-American experience, especially as it relates to the urban despair that is absolutely guaranteed to produce citizens like Willie Bennett, it had begun with slavery.

Willie Bennett's ancestors included a number of hardworking men and women who went through life with the kind of fierce determination to succeed that, in other ethnic backgrounds, tends eventually to produce children who become doctors and teachers, senators and even presidents, who are pointed to as shining examples of the possibilities inherent in America. Unfortunately, families like the Bennetts were destined, or sentenced, to butt their heads against a brick wall that rose around urban ghettos blocking off the traditional routes of escape to betterment.

There had been flashes of promise in the distant past, however.

Willie's first ancestor to show up on a public record was John F. Franklin, the son of a Virginia slave who had escaped from the South and made the arduous journey to Nova Scotia, where the British government had earlier taken advantage of a growing abolitionist movement to recruit escaping slaves for duty against America in the War of 1812.

Born in 1827, John never learned to read or write; he worked for most of a marginally prosperous life as a shoemaker who married and helped raise a large family and died destitute after a severe economic depression rocked rural Canada in the early 1870s.

John's eldest son and namesake, born in 1852, left home and moved across the river at age nineteen to Halifax, where he soon found steady, if dirty, work sweeping chimneys. The youngest son, Joseph, born in 1857, soon followed his older brother's lead, journeying across the harbor to Halifax, where he lived with John, who found his brother a job as a chimney sweep. In time, Joseph found his own place and married a woman with whom he raised eight children.

With the economy of Nova Scotia staggered by depression, and as the Industrial Revolution beckoned with jobs from the shores of New England down across the Bay of Fundy, many enterprising blacks fled Canada to settle in what they referred to as the "Boston states." Among them was John Franklin, who put down new roots in Portland, Maine, where the port, the U.S. facility closest to Europe, was bustling with the steamship trade. Close on John's heels, as usual, was his eager brother Joseph, who arrived with his family in tow in 1891.

Again, Joseph enjoyed his brother's hospitality for a while, with all the Franklins living in a district of the working-class Carlton Court section where each of the 271 blacks among Portland's 58,000 residents lived. But Joseph's family soon exceeded the bounds of John's household; he took a place for his family a few doors down, and also got a job with Portland Railroad, the city's main public transportation company, which was then beginning to make the transition from horse-drawn cars to motor-driven trolley cars. Still, by 1895, the company's lines operated on twelve miles of tracks, with more than 225 horses to care for. Joseph, who had been fond of horses on the hardscrabble farms of Nova Scotia, worked taking care of the horses kept at the Beckett Street car barn on Munjoy Hill.

But the horses were gone by the end of the decade, and Joseph found another job, as a janitor at Portland's famed Jefferson Theater on Free Street. In those rowdy, prenickelodeon days of American vaudeville, a self-conscious preoccupation with imported "great European artists" had given way to a growing appreciation of homegrown talent, not the least of which was the famous "sepia dance" craze that brought the first legitimate black performers to the American stage. In his days of sweeping up at the "Jeff," as the theater was known, Joseph Franklin would have been able to stand in the shadows and see the likes of Bill "Bojangles" Robinson begin to define a new entertainment that would soon lead to a revolution in popular dance and music. For the first time, he would have been exposed to the nascent rhythms of jazz and blues, even as pumped out by a vaudeville pit orchestra.

It was obvious that this exposure touched Joseph Franklin deeply. From then on, after he left his janitor's job when Portland Railroad invited him to come back to work, this time as a "car washer," there would always be a piano in the parlor of Joseph's house on Lafayette Street. And one of his sons, William Joseph, grew up playing it.

Born in 1893, William Joseph Franklin was always called Willie. A talented, fun-loving young man who had accompanied his father to the theater on many nights as a boy, Willie enlisted in the Army during World War I and was sent with the Maine 103rd Regiment to Massachusetts for training prior to being shipped to action in France. Willie apparently liked what he saw during training, because after the war he settled in Boston, which had a thriving black community that had already carved out territory for itself in a strip of Roxbury that was hemmed in by overwhelmingly larger Irish and Jewish immigrant neighborhoods. For a time, he worked as a chauffeur, and then as a porter, living on Tremont Street.

Two things at the time stand out as a measure of the painfully slow but steady upward mobility of the Franklins in America. In 1923, Joseph Franklin's death was marked with obituaries printed in two Portland daily newspapers, an unusual tribute for a black laborer. Both articles noted the elder Franklin's long years of service in his jobs. And by 1925, Willie, the son he had taken to the theater on so many nights, was employed as a professional musician.

It was not an easy life. But it marked a watershed: For the first time, a Franklin was able to go beyond menial labor and be paid for doing something he loved, which was to play the piano. By 1930, Willie was married to the former Alice Hogue, a pretty daughter of Virginia slaves, and living in a comfortable apartment on Cabot Street. So close was Alice Franklin to the slavery experience that she remembered her elderly parents telling her about "jumping over the broom," the slave ritual marriage.

During what seemed to have been a happy marriage, Willie and Alice had six children, but Alice's life was cut short by cancer at the age of thirty-six. Her death left Willie with six children to raise. By night, he was a chain-smoking jazz pianist who was a well-known fixture at such famous spots as the Hi-Hat on Columbus Avenue and Wally's on Massachusetts Avenue, nightclubs where whites and blacks would mingle in the smoky haze, in a part of town that was known as Crosstown, where cocaine and booze were king and vice was easy for anyone with a few dollars. But by day, Willie Franklin was apparently a diligent single parent who rode herd on his brood at 68 Ruggles Street and kept the kids out of trouble.

Willie's oldest daughter, Pauline, had her mother's looks and her father's style, and he increasingly came to depend on her for help in raising the younger children, which she did enthusiastically. Then, at the age of twenty, with her brothers and sisters old enough to fend for themselves, Pauline used the one marketable skill she had developed at home, cooking, and got a restaurant job that enabled her to move into her own apartment on Columbia Road. Almost immediately, a young man named William Bennett, two years her senior, came into her life. On January 5, 1950, at the age of twenty-one and nine months pregnant, she married Bennett, a twenty-three-year-old dishwasher who had come to Boston a few years earlier from Philadelphia, in a storefront church in Roxbury. Nine years later, Pauline's now aged and ill father would move in with them for the last few years of his life. When he died in 1962, Pauline and her husband thought enough of the old man that they paid to have a classified death notice printed in the *Boston Globe* to honor him.

Pauline and William's eldest son was named Willie after his father. And for the first decade of his life at least, with the combined influences of a strong, loving mother, a steadily employed father, even if he was washing dishes or hauling boxes, and a grandfather who was an abiding presence in his boyhood and a reminder that life did hold at least some small potential, it almost looked as if the young Willie Bennett might have had a chance to make it.

Twenty-six days after his parents' marriage, Willie was born in Boston on January 31, 1950. The newlyweds, with their healthy new baby boy, had rented a small apartment on Massachusetts Avenue, and two years later were able to move to a nicer place above a store on Cabot Street in Roxbury.

For a black man who had come to Boston from Philadelphia in search of better opportunities, the future still loomed with a certain amount of promise in 1952 for Willie's father. Soon after his marriage and the birth of his first son, the senior Bennett, who was only slightly over five feet tall, had left the drudgery of dishwashing at the Massachusetts General Hospital kitchen for a better job as a rubber worker. It paid enough to allow his wife to quit her restaurant job and concentrate on raising a big family. A second son, Ronald Bruce, was born to the couple in 1953. Over the next seven years, the Bennetts would have five more children, all girls: Linda in 1956, Paula in 1958, Diane in 1959, Veda in 1960, Tarita in 1963.

But as the family grew, the laborer's once-sufficient paycheck seemed to shrink. "Goin' down hill," friends began saying sympathetically of the man, who was once genial and almost courtly, but whose temper, the boy told friends, often flared. Until the boy got to be bigger than his father and able to defend himself, his wisecracking oldest son was a particular target of his wrath. From those rages in his formative years, the young man would tell friends later that he learned three things: contempt for an increasingly irrelevant father, respect for the travails of his mother, and an ability to move fast to save his own skin.

As for the senior Willie, what little joy he managed to scratch out in those years came from fishing. For eight hours at a stretch, saying nothing, staring at nothing more distracting than the sparkle of the sun on the water, he would stand on a rotting old wood pier at Dorchester Bay and quietly fish. Nothing made him happier than to lug home a pail heavy with flounder or fluke, too many for one family to eat, and to proudly pass out the extra ones for the neighbors to cook.

But those occasions were the exception as the family grew larger, the money got tighter, and the living space got more cramped. His wife and children were glad for those increasingly frequent occasions when he did not come home at all to the crowded two-bedroom apartment near Dudley Square.

As young Willie reached his adolescent years in the 1960s, the civil rights struggle occupied the attention of the nation in the papers and on television, but a different struggle was underway in the old urban neighborhoods of Boston, where manufacturing and other steady blue-collar jobs were in swift decline just as a new immigrant group of poor blacks, many of them postwar transplants from the Deep South, swarmed in. Between 1960 and 1970, Boston's black population nearly doubled, to about 100,000—and fully 92 percent of them were confined in a wide corridor that plunged down toward Mattapan from the South End and now included most of Roxbury and the western flanks of Dorchester. The middle-class Irish and Jewish residents who fled outward from this thrust left behind abandoned tenements, boarded-up stores, churches and synagogues, and once-thriving neighborhood schools that were suddenly reeling from the shock.

Almost without notice, schools that had few black students when John F. Kennedy was elected president in 1960 were predominantly—in many sudden cases overwhelmingly—black by the time Martin Luther King, Jr., was assassinated eight years later. At the same time, there was no concurrent adjustment in employment or political power, as there had been for the white ethnic immigrants who had occupied the neighborhoods in earlier years. Only 4 percent of Boston's city payroll in the 1960s was made up of black employees.

The Timilty School was just such a place by the time Willie Bennett showed up with his schoolbag and pencils to start the seventh grade in 1963. One of the model junior high schools in the system until recently, the Timilty had begun a dizzying deterioration in the 1960s, when teachers long accustomed to preparing students for high school and college found themselves unexpectedly confronted with students who couldn't even read. Within a few years, the "racial imbalance" of such schools would become a national issue, and Boston's school crisis would finally erupt in a tumult that would define race relations in the city for decades afterward. But Willie Bennett wouldn't be among the students affected by any of that commotion, because his junior high school tenure only lasted through Christmas vacation of the seventh grade, when he had already been officially classified as a "mental defective" by school authorities.

Which was no problem for Willie, who liked the freewheeling life on the streets of Roxbury a lot more than he liked any classroom. In January of 1964, after failing to return to school for the winter semester, he had his first serious run-in with the law when he was caught rifling parking meters for coins and charged with larceny. Five months later, Willie was charged with purse-snatching. He made the first of what would become an utterly predictable progression of trips to juvenile court, until a breaking and entering charge finally put him away. It had been an amazingly fast descent. On February 16, 1966, when he should have been worrying about tenth-grade geometry, seventeen-year-old Willie was sentenced to the Youth Service Board's juvenile facility at Shirley, Massachusetts.

In 1968, a year after he got out of jail for the first time, several things happened. Willie, already street-hardened and cynical, barely noticed one of them: Dr. King was murdered in Memphis. The others were closer to home: Willie's father lost his factory job and was unemployed for the first time since the end of the war. By the end of the year, Willie's father had left his wife and children, who had then moved into the public housing project in Mission Hill that would become their permanent home.

A year later, Willie was back in jail, this time as an adult, after being convicted again of larceny. When she could, his mother found someone to watch the children and took the bus to the state correctional facility at Concord to visit him. At the time, she and her older children began a habit of writing to Willie in prison that would continue, off and on, for many years.

While prison was in some ways considered a "rite of passage" for the young men Willie knew on the streets, it was also an experience none of them consciously planned on repeating once they got out. Paroled in 1970, Willie met and fell in love with a young office receptionist, Kimberly Jones, who prevailed upon him to straighten out, get a job, and start making plans. And for the first time, he began to respond to the idea that he might have legitimate adult options. After he started work in a decent job as a stock man at a downtown department store, Kimberly agreed to marry him. They were married on November 6, 1971, in a big church wedding at her parish, St. Francis deSales, in Roxbury.

A year later, when their first child, Nicole, was born, Willie was doing as well as he ever had. He got a better job, as a painter. Two years later, Willie found a nicer apartment and a better job yet. It looked then as if he might be following the pattern of steady progress that had brought his grandfather to Boston.

Unfortunately, however, Willie continued his association with his friends at the projects, where he became known for expensive tastes and apparently decided to begin supplementing his income in the best way he knew how, illegally. He developed a reputation for auto theft, and a flair for it, too. Not only would he steal a car but he would often make a point of publicly thumbing his nose at the cops in the process. In a ghetto version of an escapade that the Irish kids had made a tradition in Charlestown, Willie would steal a car in Roxbury and head directly for the Mission Hill project, where he would impress his friends by careening down the narrow, litter-strewn streets and driveways at breakneck speed, screeching around dumpsters and hurtling down deserted alleys, often with a patrol car in furious pursuit.

"He was a legend," one friend from the projects recalled with admiration undimmed by the years. "He was known for his daring."

He was more of a legend than he bargained for, however. From those years forward, police officers assigned to the increasingly thankless job of patrolling the Mission Hill projects would know and hate the name of Willie Bennett, who had so often laughed in their faces.

And, inevitably, their patience would pay off; occasions would arise when they would have the opportunity to deliver a comeuppance to their smart-assed torturer. In 1973, for example, Willie pressed his luck one night on a daredevil joyride with a companion. This time, with Officers Michael McQueeny and Keith Carlson in dogged pursuit, the cops won, flushing the car Willie was driving out of the projects and eventually cornering the vehicle in Jackson Square.

Willie wasn't laughing at that point. He and his friend jumped out of the car and ran, but the cops were determined. One of the officers, Carlson, followed on foot while the other, McQueeny, raced around the block and trapped the two men on Columbus Avenue. McQueeny stepped carefully out of the cruiser, but he didn't find cover quickly enough after the shooting started. The cop wasn't killed, but he was hit twice.

At the age of twenty-three, leaving behind a young wife who loved him and two children who needed him, Willie was convicted and given a nine- to twelve-year sentence at Walpole State Prison.

This was hard time. But Willie's sense of humor apparently served him well at Walpole, where he became known as an entertaining fellow in a place where amusement was scarce. Willie's clever tongue often left guards shaking their heads with confusion—had he just made a fool of them or not?—and left his fellow inmates in stitches of laughter. A bitter rage that he managed to keep simmering just below the surface allowed him to wield a verbal stiletto with precision.

One of the other sources of amusement at Walpole was drugs. While prison tensions were exploding at institutions like Attica, a tense standoff was maintained at Walpole, where ex-inmates say that relatively easy access to booze, pot, heroin, and other substances tended to keep the lid on loosely. With his father's medium build and short stature, Willie was not a formidable physical presence at Walpole, so he honed his natural street charm and got by on pure good-natured jive. "He was one funny dude," said a former fellow convict. Often, a guard would have no idea just how ridiculous Willie was making him look to other prisoners.

After eating, getting high was the main preoccupation of any day, and the drug of choice at Walpole then was a prescription painkiller, Talwin, that was considerably cheaper than heroin. "People would shoot them, like an aspirin," said a former inmate. "It was cheap. A good buy."

Ever the raconteur, Willie loved to get stoned and talk about his exploits on "the streets" where he had been since the seventh grade. He always seemed to have a good story or two. One friend from the projects, whose prison nickname was "Broadway," remembered Willie spending hours regaling other Walpole inmates with reminiscences about dodging the cops, fast cars, good money, pretty women, and lucrative scams like "working the till," which was the art of opening an old cash register while using one hand to muffle the sound of the bell.

In the complex meritocracy of prison, Willie was known as a good man to have around—cool enough, and surrounded by enough tough friends, not a patsy. Street smart. "If Willie could con you out of something, that was your loss," a friend from prison remembered. "For him, it was a game. But he wasn't into playing dirty."

Said another, "People kind of liked him because he wasn't disrespectful." He was also an easy touch. In a pinch, Willie could be depended on for a cigarette or a Talwin, a fellow convict said. "He'd give you his last one."

In 1979, Willie was paroled for good behavior, but as usual it didn't last long. Soon after he got back to Mission Hill, Willie was in big trouble again, and this time for an incident that would fatefully mark Willie for the first time in the minds of policemen as something other than a troublesome wiseguy thief. Now they began to think of him as a mean, violent criminal with that worst of combinations, a bad drinking habit and a trigger finger.

On July 3, 1979, just after three o'clock in the morning, a thirty-one-year-old handicapped cab driver named José Moreno stopped on the street near Horadan Way in the Mission Hill projects to drop off a fare, a black man who was about the same age as Moreno. The passenger, who appeared drunk, refused to pay. What's more, he took out a gun and ordered the driver to turn over his cash box. Moreno, who had lost both legs in an accident in the Virgin Islands before emigrating to the United States, had a wife who was seven months pregnant at the time; he was working overtime to earn money for the baby and for a better pair of artificial legs. Unhappily, he turned the precious cash box over to the assailant, who then ordered him to get out of the cab.

Hampered by his prosthetic legs, the cabbie apparently did not move fast enough. Neighbors heard two gunshots, and ran to the scene to find Moreno alive but unconscious in a pool of blood beside his taxicab. The incident was outrageous enough to make the papers, and in the stories about the "legless cabbie" gunned down in Mission Hill, police said they were looking for a black man from the projects, a punk well known to them, as the suspect. While he was never charged with that crime, he was a highly publicized suspect. It was the first time, but by no means the last, that Willie Bennett would see his name in the paper.

F I V E

Ambitions

Chuck had already set up housekeeping in the duplex near the DiMaiti's house in Medford, so when the newlyweds got back from their honeymoon on Paradise Island in the Bahamas the bride moved in. From the beginning of their married life together, Chuck handled the money and made most of the decisions. Carol did what she knew best: She worked, studied, and dreamed of her own family.

They had agreed that the family was a least a few years off, when they were more settled and more financially secure. For the time being, Medford, the town where Carol had grown up, appealed to both of them. Unlike other working-class towns clustered in a loop that spread outward from the city limits, sections of Medford have an almost country atmosphere, especially where the historic old town backs up against the hilly green expanse of the 4,000-acre Middlesex Falls reservation in the north, and also near the southwest border, where the Mystic River starts its plunge from the Mystic lake system to the inner harbor of Boston. The town is also the home of Tufts University, sprawled on a 150-acre campus across the river—with about 7,000 students, just big and selective enough to have a beneficial cosmopolitan effect on its surrounding community, but not so large or full of itself as to overwhelm it, as Harvard does a few miles south in Cambridge.

Carol dedicated herself to her job. The hours at Arthur Young turned out to be brutal—by the end of her first year, 65-hour weeks were routine. But since her husband was also immersed in his work at Kakas, it all seemed normal. The pace was enough to divert Carol's attention from the one thing she wanted most in life: to raise a family.

As they had first at the Driftwood, then in college, her new friends came to know Chuck through Carol's eyes. At Arthur Young, co-workers would hear her on the phone to him, at least once and usually several times a day. "I love you" was the way she closed every conversation. At work, in a cramped office she shared with two other junior tax attorneys where the only expanse was the sprawl of Boston visible before them through their twenty-eighth-floor window, she chattered constantly about her husband, and her deskmates got an impression of a marriage that resembled episodes of "I Love Lucy," with her as the scatterbrained wife and Chuck as the long-suffering husband-knows-best.

Carol recounted the time, on a long autumn weekend holiday in Maine, when they rented a condo that had a hot tub out back. While she was busy unpacking, Chuck announced he was going to try out the hot tub, and disappeared onto the deck.

"I'll be with you in a minute," she called after him. When she was ready, she slipped on a bathrobe and went out to a wooden deck where Chuck was submerged up to his neck in the big steaming tub. "Hi Chuckie!" Carol said, dropping her robe and posing on the platform stark naked, which was how she thought one dressed for a hot tub. What she didn't realize was that it wasn't their own private hot tub—it was a communal facility, shared by the adjacent units. With her husband screaming at her and pointing over her shoulder, she turned and was mortified to see another couple in their bathing suits, gaping at her from deck chairs where they were sipping drinks.

"Chuckie almost had a fit. He practically didn't talk to me the rest of the weekend," she said, describing how she had to scramble back into her robe and run inside, where she stayed for the rest of the weekend.

"He was so mad at me last night," she told her co-workers in another anecdote showing how hapless she was. Her Labrador retriever, Midnight—a dog Chuck quietly loathed—decided to take a bite of the electric blanket on their bed in the middle of the night, and chewed right into the live wire. The commotion woke her up, but not him. Growling in frustration, the dog was getting a mild shock biting into a wire, but he wouldn't let go. Carol was beside herself.

"Midnight's getting electrocuted!" she cried, trying to rouse her husband, a heavy sleeper. "He's dying!"

"What are you talking about?" he mumbled finally when she shook him awake.

"Midnight! Midnight!"

Finally, Chuck groggily rolled half over and saw the dog with its teeth sunk into the electric blanket,

"Pull the damn cord out of the wall!"

"What?"

"Pull the damn plug out of the wall!"

"Oh!" she said, leaping at the socket. Released from its charge, the dog shook its head, wimpered, and padded off.

"Now why didn't I think of that?" Carol said sheepishly.

Only occasionally did she come out prevailing in these anecdotes. Before Christmas she announced, "Well, Chuck has such good taste in things that I usually let him make the decisions, but I have to say I make an exception when it comes to decorations for the Christmas tree."

"What did he do?"

"Well, he ordered a set of Christmas tree ornaments that UPS delivered Saturday. He said I shouldn't look at them until Christmas, but I made him show me, and a good thing too."

"Why?"

"Can you imagine spending over a hundred dollars for twenty-eight glass tree ornaments, each one with the insignia of an NFL football team? Can you imagine? I made him send them back. I told him, 'Chuckie, there's no way we're going to decorate our first Christmas tree with ornaments advertising football teams. Do you realize how idiotic that would look in our new home? On our Christmas tree? Honestly, Chuckie, do you know how *Revere* that is?' "

"So what did he do?"

"Well, it was the Revere part that did it. He looked real embarrassed and said he'd send them back. Which he did. Pronto."

Not long afterward, when she invited a half-dozen friends from work to a Christmas party at their home, they arrived expecting to meet Ricky Ricardo. Surprisingly, he was nothing like what they had imagined—instead, they found a quiet, apparently humorless young man who didn't seem to be interested in much of anything except sports. It was an unusual social affair for the Stuarts, in that both Carol's and Chuck's friends were invited. But after the introductions, Chuck and his Revere friends drifted into one room while Carol and hers stayed in another, with Carol occasionally going back and forth.

"What I remember is that Chuck's friends all looked like football players, and the women all had big hair—incredibly huge hair—and they never left the sides of their husbands. They just kept to themselves," said Ross Allen, a friend who had started work at Arthur Young on the same day as Carol.

As they got to know Carol's husband, her friends also noticed other little things that struck some as vaguely disquieting. The way she doted on him, for one thing. For another, he appeared to be absolutely vigilant about her whereabouts. Not overtly jealous—Chuck never appeared to mind Carol's going out with groups of male and female friends, as long as he could keep his own hours with his buddies in Revere. But he always wanted to know exactly where his wife was.

"I'm such a baby," she told one girlfriend after she returned from a business trip to Chicago. "The minute I get to the hotel, I have to call my husband."

As he advanced in his job at Kakas, his employers gave Chuck full-time use of a company van, which he used to commute to and from work. Carol drove the family car, but Chuck made sure she was in touch with him even when she was on the road.

"She always had this damn car phone," said Mark Bradley, one of a group of friends Carol first associated with in law school. She sometimes gave him and others a ride home, usually stopping to pick up Chuck after work, in the Toyota her husband had bought for her. "We'd leave school, and she'd pick it up and report in. We'd get in the car, and that was what the deal was. They always spoke. It was, 'Chuckie, we're leaving now. We'll be there in a little bit.' I could never believe that any couple would talk that much together."

At Chuck's behest, Carol found another job during the summer of 1987—at Cahners Publishing in Newton, as a tax lawyer. "Chuck wanted her to be home more," said Bill Jaaskela, a friend from Arthur Young who was sorry to see her go.

Even though her hours improved, Carol couldn't seem to stay out of school. Cahners had her and several co-workers enroll in a masters program in tax law, taking night classes at Boston University in the Back Bay, not far from where Chuck worked on Newbury Street. She threw herself into the new regimen with her customary energy and skill. One of her teachers, a Boston tax lawyer named Martin S. Allen, recalled her as a "very pretty woman who seemed very much alive—very bright and very eager, unassuming and unpretentious. She seemed like she had people around her all the time. She just stood out as being joyous and unique and excited about what she was doing with her life." In class, he noticed that Carol was always willing to challenge, and to take a chance on being wrong. "She was a strong student in a very strong class—the strongest class I've ever had," he said. "She got an A. There weren't a lot of A's."

All the while, almost without her realizing it, Carol began to develop more self-esteem. Her friends began hearing more often of times when she was actually putting her foot down, such as throwing her brother-in-law, Matt, out of the house. They were still living in the condo in Medford, in the spring of 1987, when Chuck, Matt, and a friend of Matt's came in late one night from a Bruins game at the Garden. Matt and his friend had gone through an impressive number of beers at the game and afterward, and were in no shape to drive back to Revere; Chuck, sober but too tired to drive them himself, told them they could stay the night.

Carol, who had been asleep when they came in, got up around dawn to go to the bathroom and was shocked to find two males in their underwear collapsed in a heap across the bed in a dimly lit room that adjoined the master bedroom on the way to the bath. She ran back to her bedroom and shook Chuck awake, demanding: "Who is that out there?"

"Matt. Matt and his friend."

"What are they doing here!"

Chuck tried to focus on her agitation. "I told them to stay," he said groggily.

"Get them out."

"It's six o'clock, Carol."

She was standing on the bed, stamping on the comforter with her bare feet. "I don't care! Get them out."

"Later, dammit."

"Now! I am serious, Chuckie. I want them out of my house this minute!"

Afterward, she would confess to her friends at work that she was being unreasonable, and wouldn't have blamed Chuck if he had just turned over and gone back to sleep. But amazingly he didn't. Cursing under his breath, he got up and pulled on a pair of pants. She heard him in the next room rousing the others. After some grumbling and thumping around, he was back. She heard Matt's car starting in the drive.

"Are you satisfied?" Chuck said with disgust.

She pretended to be asleep. But later, gingerly, she would decide that it was good she had stood up for once. Maybe she would do it again.

She thought Chuck quickly forgot about it, but he didn't. Actually, it marked the first time he began wondering if she was getting the upper hand in their marriage.

Neither of them ever had a hard time spending money, and even though they had a lot of it, there never seemed to be quite enough at the end of the month to cover all of their expenses. Inevitably, money became a problem. While Carol was always willing to go along with dinner at a restaurant—she hated to cook, and disliked cleaning up after Chuck when he did—she was the more temperate of the two, buying her conservative suits and good-quality blouses at places like Filene's Basement.

Chuck, on the other hand, spent money like a man with inherited wealth. His suits and shirts had to be from Louis or Brooks

Brothers. He seemed unaware that you could buy a pair of shoes for less than $200. A pair of Patriots or Celtics tickets for a hot game was never a problem, even at scalpers' markups. There were frequent out-of-town trips with the guys from Revere, to go to hockey or football games, even the Olympics. Beyond that, there was the money he sent each month to his parents. And to Carol's further dismay, the more money he made, the more cavalier Chuck became about tossing down $50 or $100—maybe more, for all she knew—on a sports bet at a bar.

Carol's friends always noticed how well Chuck dressed. Sometimes, without meaning to sound exasperated, Carol made a point of saying how ridiculously much he had paid for something.

"I mean, I have never even *seen* a twelve-hundred-dollar sweater before," one of her law-school pals, Mark Bradley, said once with an appreciative laugh.

Occasionally, she defended his extravagant tastes with an embarrassed and good-natured shrug. It wasn't as if he didn't buy *quality*, she would say. Time and again, Chuck extolled to his wife the virtues of what he called "the Best," to the point where she had become fairly knowledgeable in such arcane matters as the intrinsic differences between a four-hundred-dollar good wool suit and a thousand-dollar one—the *hand-sewing*, he would stress; the fact that it is shaped with a *hot iron* and not a steam press. Its *memory* of the way it fits the torso. And so on, until she would roll her eyes and nod assent.

Not that Carol was a shirker herself when it came to spending money on clothes. Friends often remarked on the range of expensive suits, sweaters, and shoes that filled the walk-in closet that housed her wardrobe. But oddly, as her own salary increased, Carol became more deliberate in her spending habits than her husband, more content to wait for the markdown of an expensive item at Filene's. It didn't matter much, since Chuck made all of the major money decisions anyway. But she finally began to wonder why.

"The moment he sees something he wants, Chuckie has to have it," Carol confided to another close friend, who was surprised to hear her complain about her husband in any way. "We spend every penny we're making. He has this philosophy of living for the present. He says you should enjoy life while you can."

One side effect of this that Carol didn't know about, since she simply turned over her paycheck to her husband and got an allowance in return, was a household credit rating that, while not totally negative, showed a history of delinquent payments and overdue accounts.

Just as Carol had nurtured her dream of a family, Chuck had never made a secret of his ambition to own a restaurant. Each had faithfully affirmed continued support for the other's aspiration—in what they would mutually agree to decide was due course. Until then, there were the pressing demands of career for both of them. And, not to be discounted, they were enjoying their well-financed lives, taking weekend trips and vacations without much thought to the expense, stopping to eat at the best restaurants in Boston whenever the impulse moved them.

As 1987 rolled around and the real-estate boom hit its peak, an agent appraised their Medford duplex at a selling price that would make for a killing. With their combined income already nudging up well over $100,000 a year, Chuck wondered if the time hadn't come for the restaurant. But the shockingly quick profit they could see in the real-estate they owned was very enticing. Carol, by now a whiz at tax accounting, wondered if they shouldn't consider selling the Medford place and "buy up," to a single home in a more remote suburb with an even better prospect for appreciation.

This made sense to Chuck, who supposed the restaurant could wait a bit. Things were going very well at Kakas, where he was making more money than he had ever dreamed possible. And Medford did not have the kind of cachet that Chuck was beginning to aspire to. Besides, it was uncomfortably close to her parents. "I got the impression that Chuck wanted to move out of the duplex," Carol's friend Bill Jaaskela recalled from his conversations with her.

Late that summer, right before she started her new job at Cahners, they sold the duplex and bought a house with a big swimming pool in Reading, a suburb thirty minutes north of Boston, for $239,000. They made enough on the sale of the Medford place to be able to put down $62,000 in cash.

Reading, just beyond the belt of suburbs clustered around the city, was more suited to Chuck's evolving style. With a village green dominated by a white clapboard church, the town looked the way Chuck thought New England towns were supposed to. The house they bought, a slate-blue bi-level on Harvest Road, had three bedrooms and a bath-and-a-half, but it was the landscaping that sold them on it, with richly mulched beds of flowers, lots of trees, and a wood-board fence out back surrounding the free-form pool, which was edged with quality tile and had a heated whirlpool tub adjacent to it. There was a built-in gas barbeque and a walk-in shed to keep the tools and lawn implements Chuck quickly began acquiring. On the upper level, a big sunroom looked out through glass right above the pool. The kitchen, to Chuck's satisfaction, was also big and sunny, with good white tile and blond wood cabinets. The dining room was small, but Chuck decided to make that into a parlor. The real living room, a spacious expanse at the front of the house, would become the dining room. People coming to visit were immediately struck by the fact that you seemed to be in a restaurant as soon as you came up the short stairway just inside the front door.

Actually, it was a fairly standard frame house of a style and workmanship that characterized the Northeast suburbs in the early 1970s, when it would have sold originally for not much more than $50,000. Mostly because of the landscaping and the expensive pool, it appeared to be one of the nicer houses on a street of similar dwellings built close to each other, with plots of lawn between, on a street pocked with potholes. On one side, the property bordered a drainage ditch that siphoned water off a lake a little distance away. Chuck referred to the ditch as a creek. On the other side, the houses were not in good shape; some of them, in fact, were old mobile homes that had been cemented into place and added to by do-it-yourselfers. Broken-down cars stood in many of the driveways. Even if it meant going out of his way, Chuck seldom drove home that way, and he never took visitors along that route.

And there were a lot of visitors, now that Chuck had a proper forum for entertaining. To the neighbors, they seemed to come in vastly disparate shifts, especially in the summer—one Sunday, his noisy family and friends from Revere with their countless kids screaming "Marco! Polo!" from the pool and all the adults with beer bottles and cigarettes; the next, her family, quieter, more likely to be eating than drinking, less likely to stay out back listening to music half the night. Other times, her friends, a much quieter, yuppie-like crowd.

Entertaining on Harvest Road, Chuck polished his reputation both as a chef and host.

"They didn't have a lot of dinner parties, but when they did, he knew how to make you feel comfortable at the table," said one friend of Carol's who had not seen this side of Chuck before. "I swear, you felt like you were in a four-star restaurant."

Chuck, of course, did the cooking. Carol couldn't be bothered with cooking; not only was she busy but she was totally disinterested. To her, the refrigerator was a place to keep cold snacks, celery sticks, and diet cola, its door a convenient bulletin board for displaying photographs, such as those of the growing number of her girlfriends who seemed to be having children. So inept at the basics of suburban cuisine was Carol that when she brought home friends from tax class one night and they decided to cook hot dogs for dinner, she didn't know how to turn on the backyard grill until Chuck came in. Once, making dinner for his parents, she roasted the chicken upside-down.

As a cook, Chuck favored the big gesture. His favorite recipes involved hours of work, such as a red snapper bouillabaisse with Grand Marnier. The liqueur was a culinary staple at the Driftwood, and Chuck had concocted an impressive dish that brought raves: The sauce was creatively seasoned with tomatoes, fennel, orange rind, garlic, and butter, ladled sumptuously over fresh snapper fillets with mussels and clams arranged around the side.

He encouraged his guests to eat. Except for Carol, that is. Carol, who was chronically worried about her weight and seemed to subsist most days on what her friends chided was "rabbit food," nevertheless enjoyed food and would have loved to feast on her husband's cooking along with their guests. But she told a friend once that Chuck had a way of making her feel guilty on those rare occasions when she allowed herself to really savor good, rich food. The fact that since their marriage he himself had put on weight and was beginning to accumulate a pot belly did not exclude him from indulging. Each day before work, he stopped at a gym in Revere to try to work it off.

During his high-school years at the vo-tech, Chuck believed, as did most of his classmates, that along with enough money to sign the lease for your own place, the culinary arts courses formed the basic requirement for being a successful restaurateur. Later, with several years of experience, especially running the daily operations of the fur store, where he also came into frequent contact with other

Back Bay business people, he learned the truth: Most restaurateurs went broke in the first year after opening their doors.

Characteristically, Chuck had investigated the restaurant industry carefully over the years he toyed with the idea. Among the magazines he subscribed to, besides *Sports Illustrated, Playboy,* and various bodybuilding monthlies, were several restaurant-industry publications—not cooking and dining magazines but trade publications aimed at the working industry itself.

So in the spring of 1989, by the time Carol told him she was pregnant and he decided to finally put his long-gestating business plan into motion, he had a fairly good idea of what to expect. He signed up for the course on buying and operating a restaurant mostly as a final item on his preliminary checklist.

The course met for four hours on a Saturday morning at the Center for Adult Education on Commonwealth Avenue in the Back Bay. The teacher, Charlie Perkins, a Newburyport restaurateur and Back Bay restaurant broker, kept his focus on the business realities—leases, lawyers, financing, and other such matters—rather than the perceived glamour. Though he described his students as "people who have a dream and want to be entrepreneurs," he also was well aware that a good majority of the twenty or twenty-five people in the class wouldn't get beyond the dreaming. He wanted those who did to know that owning a restaurant was not the same as dishing up a spectacular meal at a home dinner party a couple of times a year.

The soft-spoken Perkins told his students, "If you want to practice medicine, you go to medical school. If you want to be a lawyer, you go to law school. And if you want to own a successful restaurant, you need an education."

Being in the minority who had already done years of homework, Chuck nevertheless made careful notes as he listened to Perkins, who told his students:

"It's not that restaurants are more prone to failure than any other form of business—it's just that they tend to attract high-risk takers. So many people get into the restaurant business with a little bit of education and a little bit of money, but then don't have the foggiest idea of what to do. Then they call us to sell when the business is in the latter stages of terminal cancer and it really doesn't have any value left. I just hate to see people get started and really lose their shirt.

"If you're a good business person, your chances of being successful are much greater than if you're a good cook, because basically, the product isn't that important. It's handling people and making business decisions."

Chuck took note of the three main reasons Perkins gave for failure in the restaurant business: "one, undercapitalization; two, partnership problems; three, a lack of discipline."

The way Chuck had figured it, reasons two and three on Charlie Perkins's list were no problem. The problem was item one, capitalization. Chuck's calculations squared roughly with Perkins's ballpark figures: A modest-size restaurant like the one he wanted to own, a place with fifty or sixty seats where you could get to know the customers and welcome them back again and again, would require from 1,500 to 2,000 square feet. In the Boston area, where healthy, established restaurants typically changed hands for 40 percent of the previous twelve-months' sales, the ballpark figure for opening a new one ran between $100 and $200 a square foot; therefore, a reasonable figure for what Chuck had in mind was $150,000, with another $50,000 in working capital—in all, $200,000. Charlie Perkins also had some good tidings for those who might actually follow his advice carefully: Assuming it's done right, with the right business acumen, with hard work and of course with enough capital, Charlie confirmed, "There's no reason you can't be profitable in a month or two."

That sounded fine to Chuck Stuart, always hoping for the fast result, who now only had to work out the details for item number one, capitalization. The way he had it figured, by the time the flowers came into bloom and the warm weather brought the strollers back to the paths and lawns of the Public Garden that summer, $200,000 wasn't going to be any problem.

SIX

Drumbeat

Nationally, most people who are murdered die at the hands of someone they personally know; in Boston, it is almost a certainty. According to police studies in recent years, nearly nine out of ten Boston homicide victims knew their killer. The figures simply translate into the demographic fact that chances are exceedingly high in Boston that a murder victim is black and poor, and that the murderer is too. Focused against the backdrop of the city's severe *de facto* racial segregation, indications are that a white person in Boston, statistically speaking, can expect a relatively high degree of security from violent crime. In the late 1980s, in fact, Boston was one of the safest metropolitan areas in America, especially for its citizens who were not black and who did not live in the ghetto. In 1988, when Boston had ninety-three reported homicides, it was ranked twentieth among U.S. cities—after Indianapolis—in per capita murders. Indeed, it had long been a matter of civic pride to Bostonians, who tend to

worry over their city's national image with a fervor unmatched elsewhere in the cynical Northeast. Unlike New York, Bostonians would
say with little prompting, their city was *safe*.

And so it came as a matter of shock, and no small civic dismay,
that the news media began telling Bostonians a different story in the
latter half of 1989, when there began a steady drumbeat of crime
news that seemed to indicate, in its frequency and its breathless
presentation, that all hell had broken loose in the Hub.

This impression came about mostly because hell *had* begun to
break loose by the end of the 1980s with the relatively late arrival
to Boston of the crack cocaine culture and its attendant public gun-
play and gang activity. In a community where, since Colonial times,
each segment of the loosely federated population had traditionally
monitored the behavior of every other segment, the sudden rise of
strutting sixteen-year-olds armed to the teeth on crack dollars caused
a degree of alarm that hadn't been felt by Boston's white residents
toward their black fellow citizens since the terrible days of the
school-busing crisis had made the city a convenient national symbol
for bigotry in the mid-1970s.

But there was another factor at work in Boston, which some
news professionals consider to be the most media-conscious city in
America: a good, old-fashioned newspaper circulation war, the likes
of which had not been seen in Boston for generations, and a fierce
battle for what journalists shudder to be told is "market share."

It had begun quietly enough in the early years of the decade.
Then, long after newspapers with names such as the *Post, Advertiser,
Record-American, Transcript, Herald Traveler,* and *Journal* had been
consigned to dusty clipping files, the city of Boston had two daily
newspapers, the prosperous *Globe*, which bestrode the region like a
great advertising-fattened colossus, and the anemic *Herald-American*,
a tabloid that was the direct answer to what used to be known
unkindly in the newspaper industry as the Publisher's Prayer: "Dear
God, if I must have competition, please let it be Hearst." The reference was to the once fearsome Hearst newspaper chain, whose daily
newspapers, mired in working-class demographics in old urban cen-
ters, had ultimately become a laughing stock among modern
competitors.

Hearst was losing a million dollars a month on the skinny *Herald-*

American, and the company was overjoyed when another tabloid press baron, the Australian Rupert Murdoch, offered to buy the paper in 1982. Again, there were jokes: The Boston *Herald-American,* it was said, was so bad that it was the only newspaper published in America that could conceivably get better under Murdoch ownership.

But the sneers stopped when the paper, beefed up, toned down, and renamed as simply the *Herald,* did just that, against all odds in a time when fewer than five United States cities had competing newspapers published within their borders. Patrick Purcell, a young tabloid veteran installed as publisher at the *Herald* shortly after Murdoch purchased the paper, saw the competitor across town as "arrogant." Flabby from a lack of serious competition in recent years, it was also, he said, "a ponderous read," a newspaper that was heavy on global think-pieces and light on news about Boston. With a young and hard-working staff, Purcell's *Herald* went to work making the *Globe*'s life harder, emphasizing aggressive local-news and police coverage and, for good measure, also going after the *Globe* in an area where it never expected tabloid competition: political and foreign news. By the late 1980s, it was clear to amazed observers in the industry that Murdoch had succeeded to a degree no one would have anticipated at the start of the decade. While the *Globe* continued to dominate in circulation, advertising, and reputation, the *Herald* had at least become viable competition, at least for a while. By 1988, the newspaper had cut its losses to the point where Purcell believed it was about to begin showing an honest profit. In such a situation, this is little short of a triumph.

In the *Herald* newsroom, reporters accustomed to writing two and three stories a day had once held a contest to see which of the colleagues on the well-staffed other paper had the fewest bylines in a month. Suddenly, it was obvious by the quickening of pace that the competition was taking its toll at the slumbering *Globe.* As 1989 dawned, the two newspapers were slugging it out for every break in local news, especially the crime beat. The print reporting likewise energized the city's television news operations. By the end of the eighties, as the crack epidemic broke in a wave over Boston, crime in Boston was suddenly being covered with a vengeance. As the summer of 1989 waned, the drumbeat became louder.

*   *   *

On September 1, under the front-page headline "A Merciless
Final Verdict on the Streets," accompanied by the photograph of a
black man who was the subject of the story, a *Globe* account began:

> Jimmy Cade laughed at adversity. He was bad. He was down.
> He was an O.G.—original gangster—with the Corbet Street
> Crew in Mattapan.
>
> When they hooked Jimmy on a murder rap a few years
> ago, he laughed. "Ain't got no case, man," Jimmy said. He
> was right.
>
> Yesterday, Jimmy wasn't laughing. He was lying dead
> on a metal slab at Southern Mortuary, across the street from
> Boston City Hospital. . . .
>
> "Jimmy beat the justice system," a Boston police detec-
> tive was saying. "But he couldn't beat street justice. It got
> him."

Two days later the same newspaper acknowledged that gang
violence in the city had occurred at an unexpectedly low rate during
the summer. "We just be chillin' out," the article quoted a black
gang member as saying. It added: "There are ominous signs for the
future. In a six-day period last week, three gang-related murders
shattered the relative calm. . . . School opens next week, and feuds
that have been on hold since June will be renewed."

The *Globe* attributed part of the decline in gang activity to the
success of a controversial policy underway in the highest-crime
police district, Area B, where police had been given the authority
to stop and search suspected gang members on sight, a practice that
had accounted for a 25 percent increase in arrests over the year-
earlier summer.

"Give the devil his due," the article quoted John Codwell, a
lawyer who had successfully argued in court against the policy. "One
thing about unconstitutional police tactics—they often work." But he
added, in an ominous note that would find an echo months later,
"What they're doing is alienating a whole generation of young black
kids. And it doesn't have to be done this way. You know why they're
calling this a war? So the good guys can cheat. . . . Now every black
kid they arrest is in a gang. If you live on one of the streets that is
known to have a gang, you're in that gang. If you don't, and they
arrest you, they say you're the leader of a newly emerging gang."

Not long after, an almost eerie foreshadowing found its way into the news. On September 8, under a headline, "A Life Taken at the Peak of Its Promise," the *Globe* had the story of a thirty-five-year-old white woman, Frances Cunningham—"a bright, straight-arrow, sensible person, in no way involved with shady people or with drugs"—murdered in her car in mostly black Mattapan. Said a relative: "It's hard to comprehend that she is dead. She was so unlike a murder victim."

But her story soon faded. A *Globe* headline on September 9 alluded to the police commissioner's support of the search policy: "Roache Backs Crackdown on Hub Gangs" and quoted him, "police continue to walk a tightrope when they try to balance the rights guaranteed by the Constitution against the public safety needs of the community." Later, the commissioner says that police in Area B were responding to an "unusual time in terms of violence in this country."

In the September 10 *Globe*, a correspondent sent to compare Boston with the crime in New York City began: "For an indicator of what will happen to Boston's drug scene next, look to New York."

The same paper a week later:

Two men and one woman who were shot on a Mattapan side street Saturday night appear to be victims of a random shooting spree in the drug- and gang-infested area, according to neighbors.

On September 21, in the *Herald*: "4 Shootings Leave 5 Injured."
The next week, in a *Globe* column by Mike Barnicle:

Six cruisers sit like blue-and-white blocking backs at the corner of Castlegate Road. Cops with shotguns and rifles are going door to door, hallway to hallway, looking for a kid who has just taken a shot at two guys in a car. . . .
"Shots fired" the dispatcher is saying on nearly every call that comes across the police scanner.

October 2, in the *Herald*: "Mom Says Teen Shot over Drugs."
Two days later in the *Herald*: "Youth Slain on Bike in Possible Gang Hit."
October 8, in the *Globe*: "Another Life Is Lost to the Violence."
The next day's *Herald*: "Hub Gang Violence on Rise."

Two days later: "Cops Shoot Dorchester Man; Bounty Reported on Police."

The next day, on October 12, the *Globe* reported:

In the heart of the Franklin Hill housing project in Dorchester yesterday, police were doing what they and residents say they always do: frisking a group of teenagers.

The almost constant searching and questioning of young blacks by police has set off a series of eruptions and controversies that has been felt from the police stations to courthouses by a community torn by violence.

Tensions reached a new peak Tuesday night when a policeman, investigating reports that a Franklin Hill gang, the Giants, had put a bounty on the head of officers, shot a bystander after mistaking a set of keys for a weapon.

A story accompanying spoke of "rumors" that "one gang had offered a $1,000 bounty on the life of any Boston police officer" and quoted a police captain who bemoaned a recent court ruling curtailing the police stop-and-search policy, saying that the court injunction against searches of teenagers not suspected of committing a crime had "made them more bold and brazen. Officers say that the kids are saying, 'You can't touch me' or 'The judge says you can't touch me.' I think what's happened is the kids have read the newspapers and become more brazen."

A headline from the *Herald* the same day: "Bullets Fired at Apartment Door of Black Family in South Boston."

The *Herald*, October 16: "5 Injured as Boston Streets Erupt in Gunfire."

The same day, under a front-page headline bellowing "As Shootings Spread, Police Vow Searches," the *Globe* said:

Boston police reacted to a rash of shootings among young people over the weekend by pledging to continue their disputed searches of suspected gang members.

Police say that gangs are believed to have been involved in at least some of the six shootings reported in a twelve-hour period Saturday night and early Sunday morning in Dorchester and Mattapan. . . .

"It was a very violent weekend," said Deputy Police

Superintendent William Celester, commander of the 320 officers who patrol Roxbury, Mattapan and part of Dorchester.

After a relatively quiet summer, the number of shootings
has increased sharply in the past two weeks, Celester said.

On October 18, a *Herald* headline said: "Turf War Tied to
Shootings—Retaliation Likely Motive in New Spree of Violence."

On October 21, the *Globe* had this headline across the top of
its front page: "Police Cite Reign of Violence in Neighborhoods."
One of two stories on the subject reported "a widening split within
the black community over the police department's role in ending
an accelerating cycle of drug and gang-related violence." And an
accompanying article spoke of "an unprecedented reign of violence
. . . more than 100 people were shot in the inner-city neighborhoods
of Boston during a 40-day period that began in early September. . . .
At the current rate, 10 persons are being shot every four days in
Area B, an area of about 1.5 square miles.

In quiet, tree-shaded Reading, in the far reaches of the Boston
suburbs where he kept careful track of the alarms being rung now
with loud insistence in the news, Chuck Stuart, ever alert, sensed
an opportunity.

SEVEN

Debby

While Chuck's interest in women had always been somewhat indirect, in that he saw any glimmer of interest from the other sex mostly as a ratification of his own assessment of his attractiveness, he did find himself paying close attention in June of 1989 to a pretty college student who came to Kakas to work in a summer job as an office assistant. Tall, slender, with delicate features, dazzling white teeth, and a frosty yet provocative élan that reminded some people of the young Grace Kelly, Debby Allen carried herself with a poise that belied the fact that she was barely past her twenty-first birthday. The quiet confidence she exuded was undoubtedly a product of years of training since girlhood as a figure skater.

Her mother had been a nationally ranked amateur skater, and Debby followed naturally and inexorably. Often, a lifetime of such relentless training and competitive pressure within a discipline that was as much performing art as athletics produces little more than

preening narcissists who never recover from the devastation of finding
themselves miserably washed up by the time they are old enough to
vote. But Debby Allen hadn't turned out like that. Instead of encouraging pipe dreams of an Olympic figure-skating gold medal, her
parents helped her channel ambition into an academic career—first
at Noble and Greenough, the prestigious prep school in suburban
Dedham, and then at Brown University, where she had just completed her junior year and was informally engaged to the senior
captain of the football team.

Chuck noticed her the minute she walked in the door.

"Jesus," he said to an associate, with whom he had been
reviewing repair orders at Pete's desk outside Chuck's office. "I think
I'm in love."

This joke mildly surprised the colleague, who had never known
Chuck to express much vocal interest in women other than the occasional contribution to locker-room badinage when the guys got
together. But she was stunning, he saw, as Jay Kakas led Debby
over for an introduction to the two men she would be working for
during the summer.

Debby was majoring in organizational behavior, an innovative
business management program at Brown, and she welcomed the first
real opportunity to practice some of the things she had learned. She
dressed simply but nicely, in a manner that could only be called
understated. At work, her demeanor was crisp but friendly, and
steadily placid. She laughed easily, being careful never to giggle.
She wore her blond hair pulled back neatly. She did her work well,
quietly pitching in whenever someone else seemed swamped. She
impressed her co-workers with what they soon realized was a genuine
sensitivity to other people's feelings. And at five-thirty, she went
home, often on the arm of her equally good-looking boyfriend, Brian
Heffernan, when he came by to pick her up after work.

"Barbie and Ken," is what one wisecracking secretary called
them. "The two whitest people in Massachusetts."

But to Chuck, watching as they strolled arm-in-arm out of Kakas
Furs onto the bustle of Newbury Street, there was something terribly
alluring about them. He left work himself about a half hour later
than Debby, and some nights he would see them sitting happily
together at a sidewalk cafe a few doors down from Kakas while he
waited outside for a ride home from Carol. She looked so different

then, so *feminine*. The football hero and his beautiful blond girlfriend, aglow in the sun, perfect accoutrements for the best block of
Newbury Street, Chuck's block. He could see himself at that table,
leaning in close to her, making her laugh. He even knew what he
would order, too. A Campari and soda was just right for this time
of the year, for sipping in the sun in a place like this with a companion like that. Not American beer, like the Ivy League football hero.
Actually, that was a chink that he had noticed very early in the
boyfriend's armor. He would sit there drinking his beer, with the
can right on the table beside her glass of house chardonnay.

Unlike his father and brothers, Chuck was never much of a
drinker, even on those football and hockey weekends holed up with
the guys in some guzzling mecca like Pittsburgh. For Chuck, who
never liked the idea of losing control, three drinks were New Year's
Eve. Sometimes, if someone had some cocaine, he'd indulge. Sometimes, he'd get his own. But not often—blow was expensive and,
worse, time consuming, both to obtain and to consume. Besides, it
was something you did in secret. With drink, at least, you could
make a statement about yourself, if you were moderate, and Chuck
considered it important to show some people that he not only knew
the right wines, aperitifs, and beers but the wrong ones as well.
Fashions changed rapidly, of course; Chuck read the drinking-men's
columns in *Esquire* and *Playboy,* and even these he considered hope-
lessly out-of-date. It was really a quite complicated field of expertise,
but he made it a point to stay current, picking up signals where he
could find them in magazines and on television.

Wines had been a formidable early obstacle, but as he became
more savvy, Chuck realized that there was so much pretentious bullshit over wines, what with sniffing corks and trying to remember
where to put the accent, that a man could be considered cultured
merely by disdaining all of that. All you needed to know was how
to pronounce a couple of the French and California standards, red
and white, and to know what time in November the new Beaujolais
came in. Hard liquor had been déclassé for years—all you had to
remember there was single-malt Scotch. Beer was complicated
because it was so aggressively marketed that class lines sometimes
blurred. Expensive beers like Heineken, for example, suddenly lost
cachet when guys like Matthew started showing up at parties with a
twelve-pack on their shoulders. A Mexican beer that was all the rage

for a while got dropped in a flash when a competitor began snidely referring to it as a favorite with yuppies. You just had to stay current. Canadian beers were always a sure bet, but only in the bottle. And Chuck had recently been reading that on the West Coast it was now the thing to swig imported beer right out of the bottle. They were doing it at all the Hollywood parties.

Wine, women, and song—it was all a guy who needed to be hip could do to keep up with new developments in any one of them. Which is why Chuck welcomed Friday nights, his night to be himself with the people he did not need to work hard to impress, the crowd in Revere. Carol never really understood why he had to spend Friday nights with the guys in Revere. She just didn't get it when he tried to explain that it was his only night off.

Revere was the only place Chuck could have a conversation without spending an hour afterward analyzing it. By the end of the week, he could barely wait for the respite.

On Fridays, a friend from Revere would usually swing by after work to pick him up. They'd have dinner, usually at Reardon's on Broadway, Revere's main drag. Nothing fancy—a burger and fries, or maybe a big bowl of clam chowder. The owner, Steve Reardon, was a Stuart cousin. Reardon's was the place the Stuarts went after family funerals for sandwiches and beer. Chuck and some of his friends had waited tables there when they were in high school—it was only a few blocks from their homes, and while the tips were lousy, the crowd was jovial. Even now, until later at night, when some of the rough characters from Chelsea would drop in as they drank their way steadily north on Broadway, Chuck and his home-town pals usually knew every other customer in the place by his or her first name.

And after dinner, sometimes a bunch of them, sometimes just two of them, would cross Broadway and walk a block down to the Speakeasy to watch a hockey or basketball game and have a few laughs before heading home happy for the night.

This was the night out with the boys. Nobody in the crowd really drank heavily; the only women hanging around usually tended to drift away as the testosterone level began edging up in the din. As such Friday nights were almost dress rehearsals for the regular out-of-town sports weekends. You could say whatever you wanted, you didn't have to watch your language, and with no women around, or at least none that mattered, nobody got their *feelings* hurt. Nobody ever had anything to apologize for the next day, even if someone did unexpectedly tie on a load.

To Chuck, Friday night with the guys meant he never lost touch with his roots. On Friday nights, when Chuck drank Coors from the can and never uttered any of the dozen or so French words he had troubled himself to learn, Chuck felt he could let his guard down.

It was really the only time one friend could recall him discussing what had already become quietly obvious to those who worked at Kakas—his fascination with Debby Allen.

The friend brought up the subject at the Speakeasy after he picked up Chuck one Friday night in the middle of the summer. Chuck wasn't out front, so he double-parked on Newbury Street and found him inside, very engrossed in a conversation with Debby over a repair order that had caused them both to stay later than usual. He could see that Chuck was working hard both to charm her and to let him know he was being effective at it.

"So hey, man, who *is* the blond chick?" the friend asked casually that night. There was a Red Sox game on the television above the back bar, but neither of them was a great baseball fan.

"I don't know who or what you're talking about," Chuck replied with a poker face as he sipped his Coors.

"The blonde, Chuckie boy. With the —." Here his friend cupped his hands in front of his chest as if weighing something, while leering at Chuck.

"Jesus, did anybody ever tell you you got a fucking sewer for a mind?" Chuck snapped, more with amusement than annoyance.

"All the time, man. So what's the story?"

"She's twenty-one years old, man. A kid —."

"She needs a babysitter you think?"

"A *nice* kid, dickhead. And smart, also. She went to a fancy prep school. Now she's at Brown, Ivy League, man. And she lives at home with Mommy and Daddy. And she's going steady with some guy on the football team. She's summer help."

For some reason, the other man started singing "See You in September." Chuck hit him with the back of his arm.

"So, you getting any of that?" he asked.

"What, are you kidding me? Come on. You seem to forget I'm a married man."

Being one of Chuck's Revere friends, this was not hard to do. Few of the guys in the Revere crowd knew Carol, and some didn't even know he was married. After work on Friday nights, Chuck had this odd habit of discretely twisting off his wedding ring, slipping it into his pocket in the car on the way to Revere, and then just as quietly slipping it back on again as he was being driven home to their house in Reading. It wasn't as if he was fooling around with other women. Even on the out-of-town trips with the guys, when some of the others occasionally did end up in bed with someone they'd met in the hotel bar, Chuckie talked a good game, he flirted and tested the water sometimes, but at the end of the night, Chuckie was true-blue.

The oddest thing about Chuck and his attitude toward his wife that some close friends had noticed was that in Revere, he referred to his wife, when he had occasion to, as "my old lady." Anywhere else, it was "Carol." But to some people, that was just Chuck's way of not seeming to put on airs in his home town.

At the bar, Chuck's friend realized he hadn't seen Carol in months, not since she got the new job in Newton. "So how is Carol?" he said. "I never see you guys together anymore."

"Okay."

"What's okay?"

"Carol. She's okay." Chuck finished his beer and ordered another round. The friend knew this beer, Chuck's second, would be his last. Chuck was the only guy he knew who made a beer last three innings.

"She wants to be a mommy," Chuck said. He had lowered his voice.

"A what? A baby?" The friend laughed incredulously.

Chuck looked at him without mirth. "I knew it was coming, just as soon as things started falling into place."

"What do you want with a kid at this point, Chuckie? I mean, you got lots of time for that."

Chuck's expression hardened. "To hell with the baby," he muttered. "I don't think I even want a wife at this point."

"Come on, Chuckie."

"Man, I'm serious. I'm going to be thirty next year and my life is starting to look just like my old man's. Another fifteen years and I'll be standing in the upstairs hall with the newspaper under my

arm, pounding on the bathroom door to chase one of the kids out so
I can take a crap in peace."

"Jesus, Chuck, lighten up."

He was surprised by the firmness with which Chuck grasped
his forearm. "Listen, nobody knows me better than you do. I hope
she gets hit by a fucking truck. I really do, man."

The companion was alarmed because he had never heard Chuck
talk like that about Carol. "Don't say that, man, even kidding. This
is your wife."

Chuck snorted. "Who's kidding? A wife you can divorce. A
wife and a baby gets a lot more complicated."

"So just put your foot down and say no. No kid! Not yet! It's
your life too, Chuckie. Tell her to cool her jets, man. It takes the
two of you to get the job done, you know."

Chuck shook his head sadly. "You don't understand. She'll
drive me fucking nuts until she gets her way."

After all of these years, growing up together in Revere, he knew
his friend well. Chuck was a little like Revere Beach—tough and
macho on the outside, all chrome and headlights till the sun came
up. Then, in the harsh light, it was just another lost cause. You
went to work, you pounded sand; you had your kids, you died; if
you were lucky, sometimes there was the Bahamas or Vegas or a
little fling in between. But it was Revere when you woke up in the
morning, and no matter how hard you worked or how much money
you made, you never really got away from it. For proof, here was
the famous Chuckie, as miserable as any of the poor bastards sitting
all around them battling nascent beer bellies in their muscle shirts,
Chuckie with his long face on a bar stool a couple of blocks from
where he had made his first Communion.

But suddenly Chuck surprised him when he looked at him
intently and said, "Let me ask you something very serious."

"What?"

"What if something happened to Carol?"

Chuck's friend shrugged. Though he had known Carol for years,
he hadn't particularly cared for Chuck's wife. Carol DiMaiti was a
little goody-two-shoes. From the beginning, he had thought that Carol
was wrong for Chuck; he'd even tried to warn him, but the guy was
gone. And though he couldn't quite admit it to himself, he had
resented the way Carol barged into their friendship, wedged her little

ass right in there. Carol was always polite and friendly to the few of her husband's friends from Revere that she knew. She knew better than to present Chuck with any kind of a choice. But some of them sensed she believed Chuck was better than his friends. And after their marriage, they inferred, correctly, that Carol had begun working on Chuck with subtle insinuations that parts of his old life, his Revere friends among them, might be better left gently behind.

Always alert for a slight, Chuck's friend had noticed the way she acted when they kissed on occasions such as Christmas and New Year's—invariably, Carol would pull back ever so slightly, and her lips would never touch his cheek. A well-tuned Revere Beach radar easily sensed that Carol DiMaiti, as she matured into a young woman from the cute Italian chick who used to wait tables at the Driftwood, had come to regard some of Chuck's old friends as lowlifes, reminders of what she believed she had helped Chuck grow out of. But like Carol, this friend knew better than to chance shifting his weight on the tetherboard he reluctantly shared with Carol between Chuck's two worlds. So he lied: "Man, you know I think the world of Carol," he told Chuck. "What do you mean, something happening to her."

"Like what if she *did* get hit by a truck?"

"That's nuts, Chuck."

"Or something like that. What I'm saying is, she's starting to make me fucking miserable." The companion was alarmed to see tears in Chuck's eyes and feel his hand gripping his forearm harder. "Just when things are looking great, the sky's the limit, she wants to screw it all up."

"Maybe you should get out, then," his friend ventured uneasily.

"What?"

"Get out, man. Leave. What's stopping you, really?"

"Are you nuts? I couldn't afford that! Do you know how fucking complicated that would be, with the house and all—and lawyers? Do you know how many fucking lawyers she knows? It isn't as if she don't know some lawyers who would be happy to do her a favor, you know."

"Well, I guess it would be easier if someone got hit by a truck," he said with a forced little laugh. He made sure to say "someone" rather than "she."

"You want to drive the truck? With all the life insurance I have on her, it might be worth it," Chuck said, laughing mirthlessly.

"No thanks, pal." The friend stopped laughing and looked straight ahead at the bourbon bottles lined up on the shelf beside the cash register. He felt Chuck's stare.

"Hey," Chuck said, demanding attention.

"What, man?"

But Chuck only shook his head and muttered, "Nothing." He drained the last of his beer and put the can down on the bar.

They sat silently for a long moment until the friend asked tentatively, "What about the restaurant?"

"What about it?"

"Is she down on the restaurant now?"

"Naw," Chuck said, drumming his fingers on the bar. "She's still on board—or she says she is. If this kid thing goes down, it won't be until next year at the earliest anyway. We're not really discussing it right now, the kid, I mean. It's all like hints, you know?"

"She going to keep working?"

He shook his head. "She says, after the kid is born and all, after it gets to be six months old, then she'll go back, maybe a year. . . . What are you laughing at?"

"They all say that, is all."

"So what am I supposed to do? I got to move along. I'm pulling down good bucks."

"I'll say good bucks," his companion allowed with admiration.

"And this restaurant is going to fly, man, when the time is right. Okay? And maybe she comes around and drops the kid stuff for a while."

"Okay," the friend said dutifully, watching the dark-haired bartender as she bent to scoop ice into a glass.

"I'm working on it, reading up, asking questions, looking around. You know that." Chuck was talking about the restaurant again. He had been talking about a restaurant on and off almost since high school.

"I know you, Chuck. You don't do nothing half-assed, I know."

"Damn straight," Chuck said. "It's going to be hard work. Running a restaurant is no picnic at the beach, you know." Chuck was satisfied. Slowly, his finger circled the ring left on the shiny bar by his now empty beer mug. "And since you mention that blonde?" he said.

"Yeah? The one at the store?"

"Debby, is her name. And she don't know it yet, but she's going to be getting to know me a lot better very soon."

The friend was relieved to hear this braggadocio. "You going to make the move?" he asked with a lascivious grin.

"You bet your ass I am," Chuck said as he pushed three dollar bills across, flashing that charming grin at the bartender as he stood to leave.

"You need a ride home?"

"I ain't walking to Reading, man," Chuck said.

The two men swaggered out the door and headed for a car down the block with the Red Sox game blaring on the television behind them.

EIGHT

A Decision

No one on Harvest Road would remember the exact date, but it was late on a Friday night, Saturday morning actually, well along in the New England summer—August, most likely, but cool enough that everybody's windows were open at night for sleeping—and there was a battle royal raging at the Stuart house. Neighbors recalled it for two reasons: Except for the occasional angry word here and there, the Stuarts were not known for having loud fights in their home. And this one, happening as it did around two o'clock in the morning, was enough to wake the neighborhood.

"You just don't care!" Carol could be heard screaming through tears. "Do you! Do you!"

In reply, a window thumped down.

"I am pregnant, and you stay out half the night with your friends? This cannot continue!"

More windows banged down shut, one after the other.

"This cannot continue after the baby is born!"

"Fuck you!"

"Don't you care?"

A crash was followed by a muffled shout, and then crying that lasted for some time as the neighbors set about closing their own windows. The next morning, some of them noticed that Carol's face was red and puffy when she came outside to tend her flowers.

Through the rest of the summer, however, Chuck kept up appearances, presiding at several pool parties with his wife, hosting her parents and friends, bragging about the son they now knew she was carrying. "I got her pregnant the first time we tried," he crowed to male acquaintances. But in Revere, the few intimates among his friends sensed that Chuck had become a very unhappy man. There, several other friends heard him use a new term to describe his wife. "That fat wop," he called her.

In Revere, that summer, Chuck swore out Carol's death warrant.

First he tried sounding out his brother Michael. At twenty-seven, Mike was closest to Chuck in age and, since he was the only other of the boys who was married, in experience. One night in late August, Chuck took Mike aside and told him that things weren't working out between him and Carol. He asked for help in getting rid of her.

Mike brushed this off. "I don't know exactly what you're talking about, but I'm not getting involved in any sort of crazy thing you're talking about," he said with an astonished laugh.

Chuck didn't miss a beat. His face broke into the crooked half-grin that people found disarming.

"Hey, I'm kidding," Chuck said in a tone that accused his brother of taking life too seriously. "Come on!"

Mike soon put the conversation out of his mind. Chuck had been under a lot of pressure lately, and he was always joking around. For a while, Mike thought nothing more of it.

Chuck, on the other hand, brooded for days about the rebuff. Had he ever been a tough guy from Revere, as he sometimes liked people to think he had been once, it would have been no problem to find someone. For days, he mentally worked through the names of people he knew, searching for a candidate.

David MacLean has no idea what made Chuck think of calling him. Shortly after the Labor Day weekend, MacLean, a casual friend from the vo-tech school who hadn't even seen Chuck in months, got a surprise phone call from Chuck wanting to know if they could have dinner and talk something over.

They met at a restaurant in the suburbs. Throughout dinner, during which they spoke mostly of sports, MacLean wondered what this was all about. It wasn't as if he and Chuck were bosom buddies—they had barely seen each other in years. They had both majored in culinary arts at the vo-tech. Chuck, as everyone knew, went on to make tons of money in the fur business. MacLean— "Frank" to his friends—drove a truck.

After dessert, Chuck finally got down to business. His manner, sitting back in his chair with a terribly earnest look on his face, made MacLean think of the way corporate board meetings were depicted on television.

Speaking in a clipped tone, Chuck explained how he had always wanted to open a restaurant. MacLean knew that, of course. Anyone who had known Chuck even in high school knew that. Describing the fur store job as a dead-end career, despite the money, Chuck told MacLean that he didn't want to spend the rest of his life "working for somebody else." He had plans, options, talent, drive, determination. The only problem was his wife, who saw things differently, who was cautious and timid. Besides, she had gotten herself pregnant, and stubbornly refused even to consider his pleas that she have an abortion. And now it was too late even for that. To a young businessman ready to roll the dice, she was a serious obstacle.

Why are you telling me this? MacLean wondered. He had no idea what this had to do with him, but his instincts told him he was about to get some sort of a business proposition. The one he got practically knocked the wind out of him. MacLean would later recount the story to David Ropiek, a reporter for WCVB TV in Boston.

"So, do you know anybody I could get to, you know, take care of my wife?"

"What?" MacLean asked, unsure of what he was getting at.

Chuck leaned forward and made himself more clear. "You know . . . kill her."

"What?"

"Kill my wife. You know?"

"You're kidding!" MacLean felt panic and did the only thing he could think of to make it go away. He turned the matter into a joke. "Yeah, right," he said, laughing tightly. "Like you couldn't find somebody in Revere to do a job like that, man!"

"I asked my brother Mike."

MacLean looked at him blankly. "Mike?"

Chuck chuckled and shook his head no. "All of a sudden, he's got morals," he said sarcastically, and added: "So?"

MacLean still wasn't sure where this was leading. All he knew was he wished he was somewhere else. "You're nuts, man." He began laughing again, a little more loudly this time.

Studying his reactions intensely, Chuck decided he had miscalculated. Naively, he had assumed that truck drivers had contacts for anything. But from the man's nervous laugh, he knew he had figured MacLean all wrong. So he instantly joined the joke, laughing himself, dismissing it all as bullshit talk.

Chuck called for the check soon after that. After they shook hands in the parking lot, MacLean never saw him again.

That left only poor Matthew, the brother who tended to ask "How high?" when Chuck said "Jump." Chuck knew that Matt would go along with just about anything he told him, but the two earlier rejections taught him to be more careful this time. To Matt, he outlined the suggestion of an insurance scam.

At first, his kid brother balked. It was worth some money, Chuck importuned him. A couple of thousand. Even though he was as afraid of Chuck as he was in awe of him, Matt had other problems of his own, and he didn't need more. His girlfriend, Janet Monteforte, pretty, self-assured, eager to find a good husband, and increasingly alarmed that it wouldn't be found in the youngest Stuart boy with whom she had been going steady since high school, had recently left him dismayed at his good-natured but stubborn inertia. She made it clear that a guy who drank nights and worked in a paint factory days wasn't the catch of the century. But these two went back a long way; she loved him despite herself, and she left an opening: *If* he quit drinking, *if* he took some classes, went to night school . . . well, maybe then. Desperately in love, Matt resolved to win her back. Declaring himself on probation with his girlfriend, he astonished the

gang on Revere Beach by actually "going on the wagon." Furthermore, he said, echoing an admonition kids in Revere had heard for
generations, he was making every effort to "keep my nose clean."

So getting involved in an illegal scam with Chuckie didn't seem
like an especially wonderful idea to a young man brimming with the
headstrong euphoria of the early stage of good intentions. But Chuck
could be very persuasive.

"All right," Chuck had said, bearing down. "How does ten
thousand dollars sound?"

Now he had Matt's attention. *Ten thousand dollars* was about
eight months' take-home pay. To a twenty-three-year-old pining to
win back the woman he loved, ten thousand dollars would solve
every problem in the world. With exhilaration, Matt recalled how
thrilled Janet had been on her last birthday when he blew a week's
pay to rent a limousine and take her out for a grand night on the
town. For a night, at least, he had felt as rich as Chuckie! Ten
thousand dollars would pay for a lot of limousine rentals. To a twenty-three-year-old, ten thousand dollars would last forever! It would
be like hitting the lottery.

Finally, at the end of October, Matt agreed to go along with the
scam. This one was a little tricky, Chuck explained, and not without
an element of risk: On Monday night, the twenty-third, he would
leave the store after work with what he implied would be the day's
cash receipts from Kakas. He would later say he hadn't had time to
deposit the money right after work, because he and Carol had to
rush down to the birthing class. Afterward, Chuck explained, he
would report that he and Carol had been robbed in the car near the
hospital. Kakas's money, as well as the jewelry he and Carol had
on them, would be reported stolen. That was where Matt came in.
It would be Matt's job to meet Chuck secretly at the supposed robbery scene and drive away with the cash and jewelry. Kakas was
insured, Chuck said reassuringly, aware that his brother had no way
of knowing that he never in fact handled the cash receipts at Kakas.
The jewelry, of course, was insured. Carol's ring alone was worth a
small fortune. So everybody made out.

Chuck laughed off any misgivings over apparent potential
glitches such as where Carol was supposed to be during this stunt.
Matt couldn't imagine the saintly Carol going along with anything

like an insurance scam. "I'll explain it all to you later," Chuck assured him with a dismissive wave. "Everything will be okay."

For his part, Chuck kept up appearances on all personal fronts, including the one that represented the future in his own mind, with Debby Allen firmly, if unwittingly, fixed in place beside him. It did not matter to Chuck that nothing overt had occurred between the two of them. He always got what he wanted, and there was no reason to believe this case would be any different. During the past summer, Debby had become a good friend, working closely with him taking dictation for letters to customers while he inspected their stored fur coats for repair-work possibilities. He had even bought her small gifts—a pair of sneakers, a sweatshirt, a cheap little joke of a two-dollar wristwatch that he presented like a medal for a job well-done.

Working as they did alongside a married couple, Pete and Kim Jaworski, Chuck and Debby became seen as a sort of in-office couple themselves. To a healthy mind, the flirting associated with such a relationship was innocent and harmless. Chuck knew Debby's boyfriend Brian; Brian and Debby knew Carol. They had all gone out together a couple of times. Recently, during a conversation about the differences between public and private schools, Debby had offered to take the Stuarts on a tour of her prep school, the Nobles. But when the date arrived in October, Carol feeling bloated and huge in her last trimester of pregnancy, suggested that Debby and Chuck go alone.

It was exactly the sort of omen Chuck had been hoping for. Strolling with such a beautiful companion in the dappled autumn sunlight of the school's 175-acre campus, Chuck knew that this must be the next step. Having graduated from Brown that spring, Debby was about to enroll in the masters program at Babson College in Wellesley. Babson, the Harvard of entrepreneurs—a school founded in tribute to the entrepreneurial spirit that fired his own soul. And on weekends, she taught ice skating, as she had since high school. She was a hockey nut! A jock! There was nothing in the world that he wanted more. And soon the way would be clear.

Around the same time in October, an old customer at Kakas who came in to upgrade her fur coat was directed to the young general manager, with whom she had not previously dealt. The first thing she noticed was how handsome and solicitous Chuck seemed. In the course of conversation, she mentioned that she lived in Framingham, an affluent town in the suburbs, about twenty-five miles west of Boston.

"You know, I really like it out that way," Chuck said with a wide friendly smile. "You're just far enough away from the city, but not so far that it's a hassle to commute. In fact, my fiancée and I are considering buying property out that way."

As she left, the woman wished him luck; she thought nothing remarkable about that conversation until a few weeks later, when she saw in the newspaper that he had a wife.

On October 13, Chuck and Carol took one last pre-baby holiday, driving to a resort hotel in Old Lyme, Connecticut, for a weekend to enjoy each other's company amid the splendor of the autumn foliage farther south, where it was then approaching its peak. They promised each other it would be their last expensive splurge of the year.

Then, on Monday night, Carol picked him up after work and they went to their first birthing class at Brigham and Women's Hospital in Boston. Among their two dozen classmates were women who noticed how attentive the tall, dark, burly young man was to his wife, who attracted attention because she was so obviously petite, but so hugely pregnant for seven months.

On Wednesday, his late night at work, three of Carol's friends were visiting her in Reading. They had never seen her more radiant. "Pregnancy appeals to you," said one. "Not at this stage it doesn't," Carol replied with a laugh. Chuck phoned to say he'd be home soon. "I love you," she told him at the end of the conversation, as her friends sat by, thinking how happy her life was. Carol didn't know it, but the three friends were in on the surprise baby shower for Carol, scheduled for a week from Sunday. Chuck had already told them that he would find a way to get Carol to her mother's house without knowing it was for a shower.

Two nights later, on his usual Friday night with the boys in Revere, Chuck became a little rowdy as he sat at the Speakeasy's bar with a beer in front of him. People remembered it because Chuck was usually the quiet one. They thought he must be drunk, the way he was sounding off. The conversation had turned to the crime wave that seemed to be engulfing Boston, and Chuck was leading the way in condemning it.

"The city's gone to hell," he howled. "Every time you turn around, there's another nigger killing somebody."

Two nights after that, on Sunday, he and Matt were riding in Matt's car in Boston. First they cruised by the hospital where Carol would have the baby, Brigham and Women's. Then they crossed over Huntington Avenue to a neighborhood Matt had never visited before, Mission Hill. Making sure the doors were locked, Chuck had Matt take a left off Tremont Street, where they drove to a deserted area near some fields, far enough away from the housing project that no one was around. Chuck, who had timed the drive with his watch, pointed to a corrugated steel fence near the corner of one dark intersection. He told Matt to meet him there the next night.

He gave Matt a hand-drawn map showing the immediate streets and the way back to Revere, and added a sharp warning: "You better be on time." At work the next morning, Chuck casually looked inside the open safe that the Kakas brothers kept near his desk. Inside, way in the back, was a gun, a snub-nosed .38 that Jay Kakas had bought years ago to fulfill an insurance-company requirement over a fashion show and had seldom thought of since. Beside it, in a cardboard box, were three bullets.

NINE

Murder

After work on Monday night, Carol took the Mass Pike into the city, making good time against the outbound flow of rush-hour traffic. As she got off the turnpike at Copley Square and edged into the slow traffic of the Back Bay, Carol used the car phone to let Chuck know that she was running ten minutes early. Chuck didn't like even minor deviations in their daily schedule, and lately, since she got pregnant, he had been supervising it with the vigilance of a Swiss station-master.

Sure enough, Chuck was outside on the sidewalk under the green awning of Kakas Furs on Newbury Street when she pulled up to the curb a few minutes later at five-fifty. He glanced at his watch, tossed the gym bag with his morning workout clothes into the back seat, and got in, slumping in the passenger seat beside his wife, who saw that he had already changed out of his business suit and into an open-collar shirt with tan slacks and sneakers.

He muttered a greeting, but he didn't lean over to kiss her, and he also didn't offer to drive, even though it was more apparent each day that being behind the wheel of a car was uncomfortable for Carol, who had already, at seven months, put on more than the forty-pound overall limit set by her doctor. But she kept her annoyance to herself, not being inclined to listen to Chuck complaining about his own difficult workday—this was the beginning of the hectic retail season in the fur business, and Chuck seemed to hate it more each season—all the way down to the hospital through the heavy traffic that slogged its way out of the city.

Besides, Carol was happy enough to have Chuck on board with the birth classes. While she was relieved that he had gotten over his initial snit over her getting pregnant, she had worried that he would balk when she first broached the subject of the birth classes a month earlier. Being part of a group of motivated young prospective parents earnestly discussing cervical dilation and afterbirth was not Chuck's idea of a great way to spend an evening. It certainly was not the way things were done in Chuck's family, where the women tended to talk about these things among themselves while the men rolled their eyes and watched the ball game.

But as she had always said, Chuckie was full of surprises. Just when you thought you had him completely figured out, he fooled you. The same man who wouldn't talk to her because she dug in and refused to have the abortion now appeared to be proud and enthusiastic at the prospect of parenthood. The week before, during a coffee break after the first session of the childbirth class, some of the other wives had even mentioned to Carol how solicitous they thought her husband was. Carol beamed. Chuck, she knew, was going to be a wonderful father. She wondered if an infant was too young to take to Disney World.

With him sitting silently beside her, she drove toward Brigham and Women's Hospital, looking forward to the class. The traffic on Newbury Street moved well, but after turning left onto Massachusetts Avenue where it crosses the Mass Pike, she hit a snarl. Chuck, looking toward the light towers of Fenway Park above the warehouses, was not happy. Oddly, for a person who had lived all of his life in one of the most heavily congested areas of the country, he always reacted as if surprised by a traffic jam. He would take the inconvenience personally, as if he had never encountered such a mess before, and as if he were the only one among the backed-up motorists who actually wished that things would move forward. By contrast, his wife, so sensitive to most things, was usually unflappable in traffic, smiling and shaking her head when drivers flung their middle fingers at each other. Carol was always alert for the opportunity to allow someone else to merge in, figuring that it was better to get there in good spirits, since she wasn't going to get there any faster anyway.

This attitude sometimes drove Chuck to a fury, and under these circumstances she was not unflappable, sometimes bursting into tears while he shouted at her abusively, as if she were responsible for his pique. These outbursts always shocked and frightened her when they occurred, which was infrequently and invariably with only a hint of warning that Chuck was tense and unhappy. Carol, for whom kindness was instinctive, could not understand why any human being would deliberately make another, especially a close loved one, feel so awful. But the fright was fleeting: Every traffic jam eases eventually; every tantrum ends. After a while, Chuck settled down and the outburst would be forgotten, as if it never had occurred.

Nevertheless, she was very glad when she could edge to the right alongside Symphony Hall, where a big billboard protruding from the building had a single word on it: "POPS!" As they waited for the light at Huntington Avenue, Chuck looked at his watch again and sat back more relaxed. Huntington is a broad avenue that slices southwest from Copley Square to suburban Brookline along the spine of the monumental nineteenth-century landfill project that gave present-day Boston its contours. Traffic was moving well on Huntington, where commuters were rushing out of town for the leafy neighborhoods beyond the city limits.

More than a commuter route, however, Huntington Avenue had become a border in recent years between two very distinct parts of Boston. On one side of Huntington—it happens to have been the side that Chuck saw as he gazed out his window while his wife drove—some of the most venerable institutions of Boston had built their monuments, as if to gild the edge of the Fenway district that had been developed a hundred years ago on drained mud flats. Not only Symphony Hall but Horticultural Hall across the way, and soon after that elegant edifices such as the Museum of Fine Arts, and out of view beyond that, the Venetian villa where the eccentric Isabella Stewart Gardner housed her world-famous art collection and sometimes was seen walking her pet lion on a leash. Lured by the ambiance of the Fenway, the Harvard Medical School had moved down from the Back Bay in 1906, and was quickly followed by other medical institutions, all of which settled into a section of the Fenway that came to be known as the Longwood Medical Area. Many residents of Boston had been born there, among them Chuck himself, at Beth Israel Hospital, not far from Brigham and Women's, where their baby would be born.

On Carol's side of Huntington Avenue, however, was an entirely different city past the Green Line transit tracks, where the gray brick sprawl of Northeastern University gave way to the drab tenements of Roxbury, an area whose population had changed, in the decade that spanned World War II, from 80 percent white to 80 percent black, just as if someone had flipped a switch. As they neared the intersection where she would turn right to head for the underground parking garage at Brigham and Women's, she could see the two tall steeples of the Mission Church against the twilight in the Mission Hill neighborhood. As she took a ticket from the machine and drove through the gate of the parking garage, looking forward to spending the next two hours with her husband in a class that would teach them to prepare for the birth of their first child, Carol also had no idea that her husband, sitting there so impassively, had recently made it a point to acquaint himself with every street in Mission Hill, a neighborhood that most suburbanites, like Carol herself, scarcely knew existed.

The same could not be said, however, of the Longwood Medical Area on what was regarded as the "good" side of Huntington. Unlike most old American cities, and because of the superior reputations of many of its urban hospitals, Boston throughout the 1980s remained a medical center to its own suburbs, many of whose residents had no other reason, besides a Celtics game at the Boston Garden or a Red Sox game at Fenway—both of them located just off major highways—and certainly no inclination, to expose themselves to the dangers they perceived growing ever worse in the city.

Nevertheless, in choosing to have their baby born at Brigham and Women's, and in deciding to attend weekly childbirth classes at Brigham during Carol's last trimester of pregnancy, the Stuarts impressed some of their less-citywise neighbors and even some close relatives as adventurous to the point of risk. After all, having a baby wasn't like being treated for bone cancer or some other complicated disease in which seeking the finest specialty care would be important, no matter where it was located. A baby could be born at any good hospital in the suburbs. But Carol's doctor was affiliated with Brigham, which appealed to both her and Chuck because of its reputation. Furthermore, Carol had gone to college in Boston; she knew very well that people in the suburbs grossly exaggerated the perils of the city. If you used your head and kept your wits about you, Carol believed, you didn't have to worry about a city like Boston. She, in fact, had never had the slightest trouble there.

"Besides," Carol had recently told a friend at Cahners who gave her a quizzical look when she mentioned taking the childbirth classes at night at Brigham, "Chuckie knows how to take care of himself."

Chuck himself, despite a lifelong uneasiness about physical danger that he was usually able to disguise by his size, had shrugged off warnings from his own family about being in that part of Boston at night.

"It's not the best kind of neighborhood," his brother Michael had recently told him. Michael, whose own son had been born at Brigham two years earlier, said he and his wife never would go back, not with what was happening in the city. Every time he picked up the paper, Michael said, there was another shooting or stabbing in Boston, and usually it would turn out to have happened somewhere in Roxbury, near that hospital. "I would never send my wife in there by herself," Mike told Chuck. Even at work, Chuck's friends warned him to be careful parking near Brigham.

That same day, in fact, Chuck and Pete Jaworski, one of his co-workers, had been complaining again about crime in Boston. Day after day there was more violence. Drugs, gangs, stabbings, drive-by shootings: Things were getting out of control, and nothing was being done about it. Chuck had on his desk a copy of the Saturday *Globe*, and he stabbed his index finger at the headline across its front page: "Police Cite Reign of Violence in Neighborhoods," it said over the article that spoke of a "widening split within the black community over the police department's role in ending an accelerating cycle of drug and gang-related violence." Next to that, another article spoke of "an unprecedented reign of violence" in which "more than 100 people were shot in the inner-city neighborhoods of Boston during a forty-day period that began in early September." At that rate, the article pointed out with jarring mathematical precision, "ten persons are being shot every four days" in Area B, the Roxbury police district. Everyone who worked at Kakas knew well that it included the neighborhood where Chuck and Carol were now spending each Monday night at a birthing class.

"You're nuts, going down there after dark with Carol," another co-worker told Chuck just before his wife picked him up that night.

"I know what I'm doing," Chuck replied.

In fact, as Chuck knew, the immediate streets around the sprawling complex of Brigham and Women's bustled with activity, none of it showing much evidence of danger. The transit authority's Green Line trolley cars stopped in front of the hospital at Brigham Circle, where Francis and Tremont streets abut at Huntington Avenue. Even at night, people are around, visitors coming to and from the hospital, nurses, doctors, and other employees on a break. On the corner, a cluster of sidewalk vendors often can be found selling flowers and other things. The intersection has a bank as well as two taverns that do a brisk business; there is also a twenty-four-hour convenience store just across the street from a busy shopping center. The area is well lighted. By all outward appearances, the only menace it posed came from drivers practicing the time-honored local option of making pedestrians run across the intersection. Any lawbreaking that police officers who cruised by were likely to observe usually would be covered under the motor vehicle code. Except for the occasional store robbery or purse snatching at the hospital, felonies were not a common occurrence on that stretch of Huntington.

Still, in Carol's mind, it was nighttime and it was a big city—no place to be stupid. The week before, Chuck, one of those suburbanites who fervently believe in a god-given right to free parking, had insisted on cruising around until they found a parking place on a little street a few blocks from the hospital. Carol had been very unhappy about that. But looking for the parking place had made them a few minutes late for the first class, and if there was one thing Chuck hated more than shelling out four dollars to park, it was being seen coming in late. So this week, there had been no problem when Carol insisted that they use the garage.

The birthing class ended a few minutes early. Chuck and Carol—a classmate noticed that they walked out hand-in-hand—left by the front doors under the tall granite columns of the hospital's Greek Revival façade, into a brisk October night that defines autumn in New England. When they got off the elevator on the lower level of the parking garage, Chuck asked to borrow his wife's car keys to drive home.

He took the ramp onto Francis Street and turned left toward Brigham Circle. He could have gone right, toward Brookline Avenue, which would have been a slightly more direct route to the Storrow Drive along the Charles River that links with Interstate 93 going north to Reading. But Chuck, who hated getting lost even more than he hated being late, always made it a point to go home the way he came, so there was nothing unusual in the fact that he went left on Francis toward Huntington Avenue and Brigham Circle a half block away. Huntington would take them easily enough back up to Massachusetts Avenue, and from there Chuck knew the way to the Storrow—left on Beacon, hard right at Charlesgate toward the river.

Nor was there anything especially extraordinary in Chuck's sailing right across Huntington, missing his turn. It was a tricky intersection, with cars merging from three directions. Carol, uncomfortably pregnant beside him, eager to get home, but always trusting Chuck's ability to make the right decision, might have been impatient, but not alarmed. Crossing over onto Tremont Street, which climbs toward the church that crowns the hill, he seemed to be heading toward Columbus Avenue, which intersects Tremont near the Orange Line's Roxbury Crossing station. Tremont was too busy to make a U-turn; going up to Columbus and turning left there would have made sense.

Downhill from the church, in a large pie-shaped wedge between Tremont, Huntington, and the Amtrak right-of-way just to the west of Columbia, the squat brick buildings of the housing project lay, out of sight from the traffic passing on the main streets. At Terrace Street, a narrow, dark thoroughfare one block before the lights of the Roxbury Crossing station at Columbus, Chuck casually flipped on his turn signal and made a left.

This turn would definitely have gotten Carol's attention. As Chuck headed slowly down Terrace, the projects loomed ahead, just past a block of open fields and dark two-story warehouses.

At a deserted intersection where Terrace meets Station Street, Chuck made a right, and then a quick left onto Mindoro Street. Now

Carol would have been alarmed. This was obviously not the kind of area one ventured into lightly. But it still made sense to explain that he was merely trying to turn around to get back onto Tremont, headed in the other direction.

Across the lots, lights shone yellow and bright in windows of the three-story blocks of apartments in the projects. Chuck stopped the car on the left side of Mindoro Street, with chain-link fences bordering the desolate parking lots on either side. He parked in a pool of darkness farthest away from the street lamps and the glow of the parking lot security lights. On the sidewalk, where weeds poked knee-high through the cracks, a soggy pile of junk—used tires, old mattresses chewed through by rats, rusted mufflers, even a discarded refrigerator—attested to the seclusion. It was a spot people found convenient for quietly discarding possessions that no longer had a place in their lives.

Chuck rolled down his window. Some city-tough crickets were still chirping in the stubby weeds despite the night's chill. From the projects across the field, a boom box thumped out a pile-driver rhythm, gangster rap, its pitch rising and then falling, and finally fading away with the stride of an unseen stroller. Chuck reached into his gym bag in the back seat, and gazed for the last time into the wide brown eyes of his wife, who now was frightened. Being that close to her face, he may have kissed her, perhaps, for reassurance, maybe as a diversionary tactic. Slowly, he reached back into the gym bag and brought the gun up behind her head. From the project, muffled voices, a woman's sharp laugh, the whump of a screen door banging shut on its creaky spring drifted through the night, as if over a dark, quiet lake.

Two quick gunshots echoed from the curbside on Mindoro Street.

The first, at point-blank range, smashed into Carol's skull, high on her jaw, on the left side of her face. She gasped as the force of the blast slammed her shoulders against the passenger door. Then, with gunpowder searing his nostrils, Chuck carefully positioned the revolver over his right shoulder and deliberately fired a second shot into the roof of the car just above the visor on the driver's side.

There was no one to see him besides his dying wife, but at last it would have been clear to a clinical observer who had the earlier clues that had begun to gather in the dark fury of Chuck Stuart's

mind: By his cold lack of sympathy alone for this dying woman whose
love he had once desired more than anything in his world, it would
have been clear that a sociopath was at work in the front seat of the
chilled car.

Beside him, Carol struggled frantically to suck air into her
lungs. She clawed at him in desperation, her brain unable to grasp
the horror her eyes had just seen. She struggled desperately, lunging
toward him. He pushed her away, furious now. She was supposed
to be dead, goddamnit! This wasn't how it was supposed to happen.
She should be dead and still.

But Carol tried to fight her way back to life, struggling to pound
against him and make him make it not be true. Chuck was sweating.
He tried to hold her back, horrified at her gasps. He wished he had
an extra bullet to solve the problem, but there had only been three
stored with the gun in Kakas's safe. And he needed the remaining
one for himself.

It had never occurred to him that three bullets would not be
enough. Besides, he would not have risked attracting attention buying ammunition in Massachusetts, even if he knew where to, which
he did not. Soon, however, the fight went out of his wife. She
slumped against her shoulder belt, breathing shallowly.

The boom box throbbed through the darkness. Chuck took a
deep, shaky breath and gazed down at his wife. She was still now.
Holding up the back of his wrist into what little light was reaching
the car from a street lamp, he checked the time. It was twenty
minutes to nine. Matthew had promised to be there without fail at
ten of. Chuck considered his kid brother a dolt—"numb nuts" was
the term he used—but he had made it clear that there would be no
excuse for showing up late, or worse, not showing up at all.

He exhaled, then breathed in deeply again, remembering that
Carol's keys were in the ignition. She was gasping faintly—she wasn't
dead, but he guessed that she wasn't able to say anything, either.
Looking around nervously, he saw that the sidewalk and street
remained empty. No one had been near enough to come and investigate the gunshots—not that anyone in this neighborhood would be
idiotic enough to head toward the familiar crack of a gun. Warily,
he removed Carol's keys from the ignition and got out of the car,
tossing them over the fence into the field, where they would be found
days later by police. Then he dug his own keys out of his pocket

and got back into the Toyota, where he reached over and took his wife's little hand. It was cold; he felt the full weight of her nearly dead arm.

He held fast, avoiding her eyes, and laboriously twisted her rings off, her fingers swollen from the pregnancy. First he removed the marquis ruby with the cluster of tiny diamonds, and then the one-and-a-quarter-carat diamond engagement ring that he had given her on Christmas Eve so many years ago. When he got them off her fingers, he dropped the rings into the blue-and-tan Gucci handbag that lay partly open near the car phone on the console between them. Then he placed the gun in and snapped it shut.

Though the day had been sunny and mild, the night was now cold, in the low forties, but Chuck didn't roll up his window. He needed the brace of the air for the next part. After glancing around again to make sure no one was loitering nearby, he steadied himself with a deep breath, then took the revolver and held it gingerly in his hands for a second, summoning the courage. Teeth clenched, his mouth tight in a grimace, barely aware now of the sound of Carol's attempts to pull air into her lungs, he pulled his right elbow back between the bucket seats and twisted his right hand back awkwardly to position the barrel of the gun at the flesh of his waist, a few inches above his right buttock. He had made it a point to learn that a bullet would make an ugly wound but, if aimed straight out through the side of the belly, it would exit without tearing through anything more vital than a layer of fat. It would be just nasty and painful enough, though. It would take balls to do it.

Chuck closed his eyes and held his hand still at its awkward angle. But just as he went to pull the trigger, something went terribly wrong. Carol seemed to lunge toward him, and the force of her body pushed his elbow forward, causing his hand to shift position just as he fired. Instead of exiting neatly from back to front, the bullet tore through his intestines, and with a sickening sensation, lodged deep in his abdomen. Only the fact that the ammunition was so old prevented it from continuing on its path and severing his spinal cord.

Chuck knew immediately that he had shot himself in the wrong place. He was overwhelmed with pain, terrified that he was about to die. He realized that the blood pooling cold against his crotch was his own. Despite his fear, he was also furious at his wife for causing him to do such a thing. For a few excruciating seconds, he lay back with his mouth open, as if to vent the pain, and waited for the cold darkness to fall over him.

But he didn't die. He opened his eyes and quickly took inventory, groping at his belly with his left hand. Though the pain was terrible, he realized that he was not losing consciousness. Taking short measured breaths, he reviewed his options. Should he just drive back to the hospital to save his own life? After all, Brigham's emergency ward was only a few minutes away. No, that was stupid. She was still alive, after all—with a story to tell if she ever pulled through. He could still see her breathing. No, he realized, there were no options. The only alternative to pressing on with the plan despite his wound was to spend the rest of his life in prison. Chuck pulled himself together and started the car. He groped for the gun on the floor, finding it near his feet. Painfully he slipped it inside Carol's Gucci purse and snapped the catch.

Slowly, stiff with pain, his eyes scanning the dark empty sidewalks, he drove down Mindoro Street and turned left where it dead-ends at Prentiss. From Prentiss, which borders an abandoned section of the housing project where a high chain-link fence protects the property, Chuck made the first left onto Halleck, a short, rubble-strewn block with a parking lot on one side and darkened warehouses on the other. At Station Street, he made a right toward the lights of the project and drove slowly toward the intersection of Parker Street, where the desolation at last gives way to life that spills out from the project. At first he didn't see Matthew's car parked on the left side about two-thirds of the way up the block, facing oncoming traffic. Silently, Chuck cursed his younger brother, whose mother often joked that he would be late for his own funeral. But then he saw Matthew's expressionless face caught in his own headlights.

Chuck slowed to a crawl. Grimacing, he managed to use his shoulder to force Carol as far down on her seat as possible. It was difficult because she was still gasping. Then he drove carefully toward Matthew's car, as they had planned, driving up beside the open rear window behind Matt. When he looked over, Matt was startled by the fear he saw frozen on his brother's face as he edged by, but too scared to do anything other than what he had been told, which was to look straight ahead and plan on getting away as fast as possible without attracting attention.

Leaning out his window, Chuck tossed something into the back

Carol and Charles Stuart on the day of their wedding, October 13, 1985. *(I. Wyman, SYGMA)*

Charles Stuart in 1987. *(Wide World Photos, Inc.)*

DiMAITI, CAROL A.

Carol's high-school yearbook photo. She was trying to conceal the braces on her teeth.

BOSTON HERALD

WEATHER: PAGE 26
Sunny Highs in the 60s
TV: PAGE 61
LOTTERIES: PAGE 75

25 Cents   35 Cents Beyond 35 mile zone   ★★★   Tuesday October 24, 1989

'A terrible night!'

Gunman invades car, shoots couple

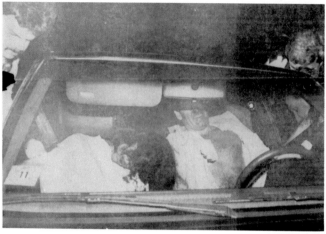

GRIM TASK: EMTs work to get into the car of Carol and Charles Stewart, who were shot by a robber in Mission Hill last night.

Herald photo by Even Richman

By DAVID WEBER

A pregnant woman and her husband were shot in Mission Hill when a man forced his way into their car and robbed them after they left Brigham and Women's Hospital last night, police said.

The woman, Carol Stewart, 33, of Reading, reportedly on her way home from a prenatal examination when she was shot in the back of her head, was in grave condition on life support early this morning in Brigham and Women's Hospital, said police.

Her husband, Charles Stewart, age unknown, was in stable condition in Boston City Hospital, with a gunshot wound to his side.

The couple's 7-month-old fetus was delivered by Caesarean section following the shooting, but its condition also was grave.

Mayor Ray Flynn visited the victims' families at the hospitals and later said, "This is a terrible, terrible night for us" in the city.

Flynn said he saw a

Turn to Page 4

Front page coverage in the *Boston Herald* of the Stuart shooting. *(Reprinted with permission of the* Boston Herald.*)*

An abandoned car marks the isolated spot in Mission Hill where Carol Stuart was murdered. *(Joe Sharkey)*

The residence of Willie Bennett's mother in the Mission Hill project. *(Joe Sharkey)*

The house on Lowe Street in Revere where Chuck Stuart grew up. *(Joe Sharkey)*

The house of Chuck and Carol Stuart in Reading, Massachusetts. *(Joe Sharkey)*

Shortly before Carol was murdered, she hung this holiday wreath on their front door, anticipating the expected Christmas birth of their child. *(Joe Sharkey)*

The Kakas fur store where Chuck Stuart worked on fashionable Newbury Street. *(Joe Sharkey)*

Debby Allen after Chuck Stuart's suicide. *(Rob Crandall)*

Carol Stuart's body is carried from St. James Roman Catholic Church in Medford. Matthew Stuart is the pallbearer at left. *(AP/Wide World Photo)*

(FOREGROUND) Carol Stuart's parents, Giusto DiMaiti and Evelyn DiMaiti, announcing a scholarship fund in their daughter's name. *(Rob Crandall)*

Matthew Stuart helps his father Charles into a car outside Woodlawn Cemetery in Everett, where Chuck was buried. *(AP/Wide World Photos)*

Willie Bennett being taken into custody. *(SYGMA)*

Chuck Stuart after identifying Willie Bennett as his wife's murderer. *(Picture Group)*

Chuck's half sister, Shelley Yandoli, and his brother, Michael, at a press conference days after Chuck's suicide. At the session, the family denied it had any prior knowledge of Chuck's plot, but Michael conceded through his attorney that Chuck had engaged him in a "vague" discussion months earlier about murdering his wife. *(AP/Wide World Photos)*

Stunned by what he had just learned, Suffolk County district attorney Newman Flanagan announces that Chuck Stuart has become the prime suspect in the murder of his wife. Minutes later, Chuck's body was pulled from Boston Harbor. *(AP/Wide World Photos)*

The Tobin Bridge on January 4, 1990. From it Chuck Stuart jumped to his death in Boston's Inner Harbor. *(Joe Sharkey)*

Chuck Stuart's body being pulled out of Boston's Inner Harbor. *(I. Wyman/ SYGMA)*

seat of Matthew's car. Reacting to the motion, Matthew glanced over and thought he saw through the darkness a form, perhaps a suitcase or a laundry sack, on the seat beside Chuck.

"Take this to Revere," Chuck gasped between clenched teeth.

Matthew tensed, aware that something had gone seriously wrong with the plan. But he did what Chuck told him. Without a word, Matthew slammed his car in gear and tore off down Station Street and, tires squealing, made a right turn onto Terrace Street. The rendezvous had taken no more than fifteen seconds. Motionless, panting, Chuck watched the red taillights of Matthew's car across the empty field as it sped toward the bright escape of Tremont Street with Carol's Gucci purse containing the jewelry and the gun lying on his back seat.

Chuck continued to the intersection and made a right before pulling over at Parker Street. A couple of hundred feet behind, a bar and an all-night grocery were crowded with customers, but the place where he stopped still had the cover of darkness and relative seclusion. He turned off the lights and the engine and collected his thoughts as Carol's breathing became weaker beside him. Then he started the car again and drove, very slowly, down the forlorn street with his car lights out.

At least one person did notice Chuck at that point. Yvonne Jenkins was on her way to the store to buy a box of Pampers and a lottery ticket when she noticed the white man at the wheel of the Toyota, driving slowly, with his lights out. Except for the pained expression she saw on his face, she didn't think much of it. Just another white man from the suburbs down to the project to score some drugs or pick up a black girl. The only thing that made her remember him at all, besides his expression, was the fact that he was fumbling with a car phone as he drove by.

In fourteen years as a civilian dispatcher with the Massachusetts State Police, it was the most harrowing call Gary McLaughlin had ever received. The thirty-five-year-old McLaughlin was into the final hours of his three-to-eleven shift at the windowless state police dispatch center on Commonwealth Avenue in Boston—its denizens referred to the facility as "the Bunker"—when the call came in on the cellular phone line.

"State Police Boston," McLaughlin said crisply into the phone.

He stiffened at what he heard after a burst of light static from the other end.

"My wife's been shot! I've been shot!"

Frowning, McLaughlin grabbed a pen and started making notes, though he could see tape was running. He motioned abruptly to a colleague, dispatcher Danny Grabowski, who picked up the phone at a nearby desk and after silently monitoring the call, stabbed at a button to hook feed the conversation into a direct line to the command turret at Boston city police headquarters, where Sergeant Brian Cunningham got on the line too.

"Where is this, sir?" McLaughlin was asking calmly, pen poised over the pad on his desk.

"I have no idea. I've been coming from Tremont . . . Brigham and Women's Hospital.

"Try to give me an indication of where you might be—a cross street or something, anything," McLaughlin said, hoping to coax usable information from the caller.

"Someone got into the car at Huntington Avenue. He drove us—he made us go to an abandoned area," the caller gasped.

"Okay, sir. Can you see out the windows? Can you tell me where you are?"

"No! . . . I don't know. An abandoned area, I don't see any signs. Oh, God . . ." The caller had a slightly high-pitched voice with just a trace of a Boston accent.

"Okay," Gary said. "How far—how long ago did you leave Brigham and Women's and in what direction did you go?"

"Oh, two minutes, three minutes. Oh, man . . ."

"Are you near Brigham and Women's Hospital?"

"No. I don't know."

"What kind of a car do you have?" McLaughlin asked.

"Toyota. Toyota Cressida," said the caller.

McLaughlin jotted that down and took a breath. At least the man was articulate, he thought hopefully. "Are you in the city of Boston?" he asked.

"Yes."

"Can you give me any buildings?"

"Oh . . . no."

"Has your wife been shot as well?"

"Yes, in the head," the caller said, and added almost as an afterthought: "I ducked down."

"Bear with me," McLaughlin pleaded.

"Should I try to drive or should I stay right here?" the caller asked.

"Stay exactly where you are," McLaughlin instructed the man, desperate to get a fix on his location. "Are the people that shot you, are they in the area right now?"

"No, they took off. Or they left . . . Should I drive up to the corner of the street?"

"If you can drive without hurting yourself, yes. If you could, just try to give me a cross street."

"I'll try to start the car. He took the keys but I have a spare set. Oh, man . . . I'm starting the car."

"What's your name, sir?"

"Stuart. Chuck Stuart." Chuck groaned in pain. "Oh, man . . ."

On the pad he was hunched over, with the phone wedged between his shoulder and his left ear, McLaughlin wrote down what he had heard, "Chuck Stewart," and drew a line under the name.

"Okay Chuck," said Gary. "Stay with me, Chuck. Help's going to be on the way. Bear with me. Is your wife breathing?"

"She's still gurgling. There's a busy street up ahead. Oh, shit. My lights are out." Chuck's voice drifted out, then came back. "Oh, man . . . I can't see where I am."

"Hang in with me, Chuck. Just try to give me any indication of where you might be. A hospital, do you see a building?"

"Oh, man, I'm pulling over. I'm going to pass out," the voice groaned.

This was the last thing McLaughlin wanted to hear. Desperately, he called into the silence on the other end of the phone, hoping his voice would rouse the wounded caller: "Chuck. Chuck! Chuck? Chuck? Are you with me, Chuck?"

Finally, after what seemed like a very long time, the voice answered, "Yeah."

During the next five minutes, McLaughlin called on everything he knew about handling terrified crime victims, and in his years with the state police, he had learned a lot. There had been a shooting, a bad one. The victims—a man, a woman—were obviously inside an automobile. They seemed to be lost somewhere in the Mission Hill neighborhood, not far from where Huntington Avenue draws the boundary between the complex of hospitals around Brigham and Women's, and Roxbury, Boston's worst neighborhood. Skillfully, McLaughlin elicited information and offered comfort to the caller. He was afraid the man might pass out before he got the vital information—*A cross street! Give me a goddamn cross street!* he thought frantically—to pinpoint the location. The car was a blue Toyota, the victim said. That at least was something to go on.

But then the caller seemed to give up.

"Oh, man, I'm going to pass out," he gasped. "It hurts, and my wife has stopped gurgling. She's stopped breathing. I'm blacking out."

"You can't black out," McLaughlin said, trying to hide his exasperation. "I need you, man. Chuck? Chuckie? Is anybody going by? There's got to be people out there."

"What?" Chuck groaned.

"Chuck, open the door. Can you open the door? . . . Try to talk to someone on the street."

The caller didn't seem to hear this suggestion. "I'm going to try to drive straight to the hospital," he said.

McLaughlin persisted, "If there is anyone in the street, stop a passerby in the street so they can tell me where you are."

"Oh God," Chuck said in reply. "I can't move."

"Can you see anyone in the street?" McLaughlin insisted.

"I'm going to try to drive," Chuck said.

McLaughlin was speaking gently. "Chuck, pull over—someone on the street."

"I'm looking," came the reply. "I don't see anybody."

"Chuck, pull over to the side of the street right now," McLaughlin told the caller.

"Yeah," Chuck said.

"Open the door and talk to anyone passing by, my friend."

"There's no one there. Ah, man."

Gingerly, McLaughlin managed to keep the man lucid for a few more minutes. The dispatcher's mouth was totally dry now, but he worked calmly, being sure to form his words distinctly and to speak clearly into the mouthpiece. The atmosphere was charged in the

Bunker, but the only sounds were soft murmurings into telephones and quick, nervous little taps on computer keyboards.

"You hang in there," McLaughlin told the wounded man. "Help is on the way. Chuck, you talk to me now, brother. You talk to me, brother." McLaughlin knew that his caller was losing blood and entering shock.

"Yeah," came the response.

"Have you pulled over?"

The reply was almost defensive, but McLaughlin didn't notice that in the crisis. "There's no one walking by," the caller insisted.

A few desks away, Grabowski, jockeying two lines, was in rapid-fire contact with Cunningham at police headquarters. Cunningham, who had ordered cars to flood the Mission Hill sector, could be heard telling the cops to turn on their sirens, one by one, and turn them off again. "Bravo Two-One, shut off your siren," Cunningham was saying on the police radio. "Bravo One-Four, sound your siren. . . ." Cunningham hoped the sound of sirens in the vicinity might indicate who was close to the couple's car. The idea worked something like the children's game. Dispatchers might be able to tell a cop in a patrol car that he was getting warmer, getting colder, getting warmer again, getting hot—home the cruiser right in there—if they could hear that siren on the phone.

Meanwhile, McLaughlin knew there wasn't much time left before Chuck lost conciousness. "We're on the way," the dispatcher assured him. "But you've got to tell me a little better where you are."

Static crowded the line. Chuck, having wound his way through the lower end of the project, had pulled the car over on St. Alphonsus Street. Carol, at least, was silent. And none too soon. Chuck knew that he could not go on much longer.

"Hello, Chuck?" McLaughlin was saying desperately. "Chuck, can you hear me? I lost him! Chuck? Chuckie? Chuck Stuart?"

Just then—the digital counter said it was past twelve minutes into the call—McLaughlin heard a thin pulsing wail through the phone, well in the background. He tensed.

On the phone, he heard Grabowski say excitedly, "Wait a minute. Can you hear a siren over there?"

"I can hear a siren!" McLaughlin confirmed. To Chuck, he said,

"Can you hear me, buddy? Chuck? Chuck Stuart? Are you with me? I can hear you breathing. Chuck? Pick up the phone. I need a better location to find you."

All he heard now was the breathing. "Damn!" McLaughlin muttered.

"Are you still hearing the sirens?" Grabowski asked nervously.

"Negative on the sirens," McLaughlin muttered.

But Cunningham had heard the wail, too, and he worked quickly, having cruisers sound their sirens on and off. At last, it paid off. The sound of a police siren came clearly over the phone line from the street.

McLaughlin tensed. "Chuck. Chuck? . . . Do you hear a siren?"

Chuck finally came back on the line and groaned, "I can hear a siren."

On the dark, glass-strewn streets of Mission Hill, police radios cracked with the information that one of them was closing in. Everyone in the Bunker was fixed on the call. Voices were getting a little louder.

"I hear the police." Chuck said, perking up. "Right here, there's Boston police."

"Put the Boston police officer on the phone, Chuck," McLaughlin said, collapsing back against his chair. There was commotion on the other end as police warily approached the Toyota, which had stopped on St. Alphonsus where Horadan Way leads into a parking area of the project, and then quickly pounded their way inside.

"We've located him!" a cop shouted into the phone.

McLaughlin heard the caller say only one more thing that night: "Get my wife out."

On St. Alphonsus Street, a half dozen police cruisers and two ambulances converged on the Toyota almost simultaneously. Three paramedics, Rich Serino, Dan Hickey, and Kevin Shea, jumped out of the first Emergency Medical Service ambulance that reached the scene. Hickey ran to the passenger side where a woman was slumped on the front seat, bleeding profusely from the head. Shea rushed to the driver's side, where Serino was already reaching in through the open window to unlock the door. To Shea, the bloody scene looked like an extreme case of those domestic violence disputes that cops and emergency workers see so much of. "Rich, make sure he's not sitting on a gun or something," Shea hissed to his colleague. But he immediately felt guilty for having even thought it.

It was clear that the couple was in very, very bad shape. The man was conscious, writhing and pressed back against the seat with his right arm raised over the passenger's seat where the woman's bloodied head was bent toward his shoulder. His teeth were bared in pain. Shea cut the front of Chuck's shirt away and helped Serino to ease him onto a stretcher while Hickey did the same with Carol on the other side. The woman was unconscious and obviously the worse off. If she wasn't already dead, it would not be long, they knew.

"Take care of my wife," Chuck pleaded as he was wheeled in the street to the ambulance. "Take care of her."

"Jesus Christ," a cop who was helping get the woman out said as he saw her distended bare belly over the waistband of her stretch pants, "she's pregnant!" It was clear that the young woman also was in cardiac arrest. Hickey cut the shoulder harness away from her body and helped to lower her onto a stretcher. The paramedics were aghast to see how pregnant, and now nearly dead, the woman was. They knew the odds were very low that either she or the baby could live. Guessing how long the woman had been without oxygen, they figured they had less than ten minutes to save the baby, if it was to have any chance at all. As they hurried the gurney toward a separate ambulance, Hickey pushed and pushed on the woman's chest to get her heart going.

"This one's going to Brigham," a cop shouted, slamming the rear door shut behind Carol as the ambulance lurched away toward the hospital where less than an hour earlier Carol and Chuck had left the childbirth class together.

At this moment, as Chuck lay inside the ambulance conscious and lucid while the paramedics labored to save his life, fate played a second trick on him, one far worse than the one that had caused his mortally wounded wife to knock the gun into his gut: It put him on national television. In the ultimate tribute the decade could pay to one of its own, Chuck Stuart promptly received his fifteen minutes of fame.

This came about ironically by the same phenomenon which had brought Chuck to believe he might be able to get away with murder. Hungry, as usual, for dramatic pictures, alerted by the drumbeat in the news media that seemed to indicate a crime wave explosion on Boston's streets, a television crew from the CBS network program "Rescue 911" happened to be in Boston that evening, riding along with an emergency crew, hoping to chance onto some kind of street excitement—"a traumatic-injury story that the audience would be sympathetic to"—the "911" cameraman, Mike Parker, would later explain. Then Chuck Stuart made his call for help. Along with news-paper photographers alerted by the police scanners in their cars, the television crew arrived on the scene and found more than it could have hoped for: a national symbol. With grim wonder, the long lens of a video camera fixed itself on the victim. On the sidewalk, a handful of project residents had been drawn by the sirens and the pulsing red lights. Murmuring in quiet appreciation, they stood in the shadows, intently fascinated by the smooth motions of the televi-sion crew whose presence ratified the moment's awful importance.

Inside Chuck's ambulance, a cop crouched by the wounded man's head. "You see who did this?" he barked, with a notebook poised in his hand. "One guy? Two guys?"

"A black male," Chuck mumbled.

"What did he have on for clothing, do you remember?" The cop was practically shouting.

Chuck replied with difficulty through the oxygen mask strapped over his nose, "Black running suit."

Shea, ready to shut the door and get the ambulance off to Boston City Hospital, which had one of the best trauma units in the city, was impressed by how alert the grievously wounded man was, and by his attention to detail.

The cop wanted to know if the running suit had "any stripes on it."

Chuck nodded shakily.

"What color?"

"Red," Chuck replied weakly.

"Did he have a mustache?" The cop was leaning directly into Chuck's face now.

"I don't remember."

With the cop still on board firing questions, the ambulance lurched off to City Hospital less than a mile away.

At Boston City Hospital, the chaos followed Chuck in. Because he was the conscious one, and because of a prior arrangement that guaranteed them access to the city hospital, the television crew, lights blazing, had chosen to focus their attention on Chuck, who was flabbergasted by the unexpected attention that would make him a media icon within twenty-four hours, when television viewers across the country would sit stunned Tuesday night as they watched scenes of the dramatic emergency rescue and heard excerpts of the taped conversation with the dispatcher. But the hospital's emergency room staff had little inkling of that as they hurried to prepare the critically wounded young man for major surgery to save his life.

"My wife," Chuck muttered as he lay naked on the table with the commotion raging all around him.

"She went to another hospital," a young intern told him briskly. "We can't keep an update because we're taking care of you, okay?"

"Okay," Chuck replied softly. He did not say it, but despite the searing pain and weakness he felt, he was desperately anxious to know if Carol was still alive. But the efficient emergency room staff had no idea, except that the guy's wife was at Brigham, and it didn't look good for her. All they knew for sure was what was in front of them. Chuck sensed now that he would live, but he was terrified of the possible consequences. *What if she regained consciousness and started talking? No! That was impossible! The woman slumped next to him in that car was as close to death as anyone could be!*

A voice startled him. It was a woman in street clothes, an admissions clerk, addressing him in a businesslike manner. She was holding a clipboard. "Charles," she said, "is there anyone you want us to call for you? Charles?"

"Yeah?" Chuck said, blinking into the bright lights above him. He hadn't anticipated being asked such a simple thing.

"Is there someone you want us to call for you?" the woman repeated.

"No."

The woman sounded surprised. "No?"

"No," Chuck repeated firmly.

The woman left with her clipboard.

Most of the hospital personnel around him were too busy readying him for X-rays and subsequent surgery to notice. But several nurses thought his response so odd that they began noticing other things about the handsome young man who had just been savagely attacked along with his wife by a robber on the streets of Boston.

For example, the way he kept licking his lips and mouthing words with his eyes closed, as if by rote. One nurse leaned in close enough to hear him repeating in a whispered monotone, "Shot me, shot my wife. Black male. Shot my wife. I ducked. Shot me."

TEN

Panic

If Matt Stuart had a motto, it would have been: "No problem, man."
Amiable, laidback, usually open to suggestions for a good time or a
quick buck, Matt nevertheless had learned early in life, growing up
as the youngest among six children who were starting to become sick
of each other in the crowded three-bedroom house on Lowe Street,
that the best way to get along was to go along. If you could prosper
in the process, all the better. But if there was a single major force
that drove Matt, it was the impetus to keep everybody happy and off
his case.

To some extent, he had succeeded at that. His friends liked
him fine. Except for the few typical minor scrapes with the local
cops, some of which involved behavior during drinking, he had managed to stay off the police blotter growing up in Revere. As was
expected of him, he had graduated from high school, in 1984. He
got a job, first in a liquor store stockroom where his brothers Michael

and Mark had worked before him, then at an outdoor lighting-fixture company where he impressed people by his fearlessness in scampering up ladders to change lamps at heights that would terrify most workers, then at the paint factory in Malden where he was making $10 an hour in 1989. His employers, in jobs that required mostly the ability to show up on time and do what you were told, would describe him in roughly the same words: Good kid, no trouble. Avoiding trouble, at least to the extent of not getting caught, was something Matt did fairly well.

And now as he drove from Mission Hill like a bat out of hell, he suddenly knew that he had plenty of trouble.

Matt was no rocket scientist; he knew that as well as anyone. But he was smart enough to figure that Chuckie wasn't paying him all that money for returning an overdue library book. He knew the deal in Mission Hill had to be big enough to be worth well over the $10,000 that was supposed to be in it for him. Chuck had described it as a lead-pipe cinch—Matt had been around the block enough times to know that nothing worth ten grand was easy—but the stricken expression he had just seen on his brother's face had told him that whatever it was that Chuckie had going, it had gone terribly wrong.

Once on Tremont Street after the fleeting rendezvous with his brother in Mission Hill, Matt knew he had to let up on the gas pedal. No sense in attracting the attention of a cop right now, before he knew what was going on himself. He watched the red lights, the speedometer, and his turn signal. When he got back to Revere, sweating and scared, he took the bag up to his room and looked inside.

The gun, of course, was the first thing he saw.

Chuck hadn't said anything about a gun. It didn't take Sherlock Holmes to know that the gun meant major trouble. And something else was wrong. The other stuff inside the purse was either Carol's or Chuck's—her wallet with her driver's license and other papers and a few bucks; her rings; Chuck's fancy gold watch. Besides the gun, the other trouble was the loot: The numbers didn't add up. Matthew knew enough about jewelry to come up with an "estimated value" to put down on the insurance claim form for this stuff, and it was a hell of a lot less than the $10,000 that was supposed to be his cut alone.

Bewildered and frightened, he stayed in his room and waited for the eleven o'clock television news, which he turned on for what he hoped would be reassurance. No such luck. Instead, he got a kick in the stomach that left him breathless. The report was sketchy, but the words reverberated with furious urgency: *shooting . . . Mission Hill . . . police . . . white couple . . . pregnant.*

The rest of the night is a blur of alcohol and household commotion, once the call came to the Stuart house from the hospital. There was one fixed point for Matt, whose first impulse was to call his best friend, Jack McMahon, whom he had known since the first grade, and with whom he had shared any number of scrapes. He pleaded for help.

There was only one thing to do, they decided sometime around midnight. Ditch the gun. Since boyhood, the two had spent practically every day and night of their lives in Revere; the town was their own back yard. Revere was the kind of place where people joked that their neighbors had sunburn in slats on their faces from peering out through the Venetian blinds—nothing much went by there without at least one busybody noticing it. They knew that the railroad bridge was the one place you could go and not have to worry about anyone watching you—or coming up on you abruptly in a police car.

The old Boston & Maine tracks run parallel to the ocean, but the Boston & Maine is long gone and now the Massachusetts segment of the right-of-way is used by MTA commuter trains rattling up and down along the cusp of Broad Sound off Revere as they traverse the North Shore. The tracks are borne across the Pines River between Revere and Saugus by a trestle bridge that reaches across the salt marshes off Oak Island, a good quarter-mile inland from where the easternmost highway, Route 1A, runs up the coast over Point of Pines into Lynn.

There are houses posted at each corner of the intersection of Bridge and Glendale streets, where the railroad crossing gate is, and so it made sense to park the car a few blocks away and walk to the tracks. North of the crossing, the tracks amble into the marshes atop a gravel roadbed that crunches underfoot. It's a long, dark walk from the crossing to the bridge over the river, but the roadbed is good and the cars rushing by on the highway across the sawgrass throw off enough light to keep the path in sight even on a moonless night.

Except for the whoosh of the traffic, it was still and windy on the marsh. Ahead, the glow of the North Shore cast an eerie pall on the low-slung iron contours of the double-track bridge, underneath which the Pines River swirled black and fast on its course through the salt flats to the sea.

Jack McMahon always had the better arm. He flung the gun sidearm off the bridge, and the two young men heard it sail across the dark expanse and fall into the river with a tiny faraway splash. Next they tossed in Carol's pocketbook, weighted down with handfuls of the clean, jagged gravel from the railroad roadbed. It splashed in, closer. Then it was silent except for the cold, whipping wind off the ocean a mile away. Silently, the two young men walked back down the tracks and found their car. They said very little on the short drive home. Matt did have one throbbing fear that made him frightened even to consider going to sleep lest the next thing he would see was the face of a cop at his bed: "I think I got set up," he told his friend.

About this time, five miles away in Brigham and Women's Hospital, Carol Stuart died.

A little after ten o'clock on that night, her parents had gotten a telephone call from the hospital. Rosemary and John Leone, Carol's aunt and uncle who were also her godparents, drove them to Brigham and Women's, where emergency room nurses took one look at the stricken expression on Giusto's face and his hobbled walk and immediately had a physician sedate him.

From the moment they arrived, as the eleven o'clock news was pumping out the first reports of the shooting on the television in the brightly lit emergency waiting room, it was clear the situation was grave. In disbelief, the relatives settled down to wait it through. Again and again, in their desperation for comfort, they recited Our Father. They said Hail Marys. And they cried when it was obvious that a brave front was futile.

A little before midnight, they were told that Carol's baby had been delivered by emergency cesarean section and were led into the neonatal intensive care unit to see the tiny three-pound, thirteen-ounce infant boy. His parents, Carol's mother told the nurses, had planned to name him Christopher, because he was to be a Christmas baby.

"He's going to need a lot of love," a nurse told the relatives who stood by the baby's incubator. A priest arrived to baptize the baby. Again and again, Carol's aunt Rosemary stroked his cheek. She noticed how delicate his features were as he struggled with the first hopeless glimmers of life.

"He's the image of his mother," she said, and she saw that it made Giusto smile for the first time.

A doctor entered in his surgical scrubs and explained that things would be touch and go with the baby. The mother's blood pressure was so low when she was brought in that there had been a severe deprivation of blood flowing to the infant through the placenta. He was not encouraging.

As the cold dawn came, and with it the new shift of people with their coffee and little crisp bags of doughnuts, it was clear that there was no hope. Carol was removed from all life-support equipment, and her family was told she had died.

Outside, beyond the family's private sepulchral despair, newsrooms in the city would soon begin stirring to life amid the scrap-paper rubble of the night before, and the hospital switchboard operators were already under strict instructions not to give out information beyond the number of a spokesperson who could confirm only that Mrs. Stuart was dead and the baby was not.

"The baby is alive," was all the hospital would say.

E L E V E N

'A Terrible Night'

The shooting in Mission Hill raised such a hellish ruckus on the police radio that Evan Richman, a photographer for the *Herald* who was routinely monitoring the emergency bands on the scanner in his car, managed to get to the crime scene before the victims were taken away in ambulances. His shocking photograph showing a blood-spattered Carol with her head resting against the shoulder of her pain-wracked husband leapt out at horrified readers on the front page of the tabloid, under a headline that screamed: " 'A Terrible Night!' Gunman Invades Car, Shoots Couple."

The *Herald* story and photo made it in time to appear in nearly 280,000 of the more than 360,000 papers sold on Tuesday morning. It was another *Herald* scoop on local breaking news over its more flat-footed rival, the 515,000-circulation *Globe*, where aghast night editors had to scramble to bang a story together late Monday night for the final edition. Because of the timing, neither of the first-day stories—and nothing that appeared on local television Monday night—managed to convey more than a basic police account of the shooting.

By morning, however, every news organization in town was at full throttle, setting a tone for the story that would not waver for months, appearing, as it did, as the long-feared crescendo to the march of peril that had been playing in the news media since the summer. For the inevitable had finally occurred: An innocent white suburban couple, a pregnant woman and her handsome husband who had heroically summoned aid despite his own life-threatening wounds, were victims of the festering urban menace of Boston, gunned down on the city streets by a black male in what the *Herald*, also minding its arithmetic, now calculated as a "53-day stretch of violence during which more than 110 people were shot in Boston's neighborhoods." The sense of alarm was conveyed breathlessly in the *Globe*, which saw "Boston's streets exploding in a cacophony of violence—a cacophony punctuated . . . by the murder of a pregnant woman and the shooting of her husband."

By Tuesday afternoon, the Stuart shooting was virtually all that people in the Boston metropolitan area were talking about. And even beyond Boston, after two of the national television networks played long excerpts from Chuck's call to the dispatcher on Tuesday night, it had become an emblem of urban menace. All across the country, the tragedy of the Stuarts was front-page news. NBC News anchorman Tom Brokaw introduced the story dramatically: "A young couple and a baby . . ."

One national report described the shooting as an American tragedy that can occur "when nice people enter the urban jungle." Across the country, few television viewers could have missed the dramatic footage; some stations showed it on their noon news and repeated it at six o'clock and, after the network shows, at eleven. Again and again, the Stuarts were identified as an "all-American couple."

The Boston mayor, Raymond Flynn, who was seriously considering making a run for governor in the next election, had not been previously forthcoming in addressing what the news media had been painting as a mounting crisis of street violence in his city. Flynn now lost no time making known his feelings, which reflected those of people in every neighborhood in Boston, but especially in his core constituency in neighborhoods such as South Boston:

"This is a terrible, terrible night for us," a grim-faced Flynn said at a hastily convened news conference hours after the Stuarts were gunned down. Flynn was accompanied, as usual, by his full-time staff photographer. "It just breaks your heart. These are good, decent family people having their lives snuffed out."

The mayor vowed that no effort would be spared to find and prosecute the perpetrator of the heinous crime. "I have asked Police Commissioner Roache to put every single available detective on this case to find out who is responsible for this cowardly, senseless tragedy. If there is someone who is not convinced that there is a drug problem in society today, they ought to be convinced tonight," said the mayor, who prided himself on having substantially beefed up the police department's budget and personnel since he took office in 1983. The police commissioner, Mickey Roache, was one of the mayor's closet friends, a trusted ally who grew up with Flynn in the white Irish bastion of South Boston—Southie, to its intimates—and who had been plucked by the fiercely loyal mayor from a rank of acting lieutenant to be named commissioner in 1985. With Roache at his side, Flynn called the Stuart shooting a "tragedy that touches us all" and a sobering example that "anyone who lives or works in Boston" can be the victim of random violence.

Even as police poured into Mission Hill to beat every bush they could for information about the assailant Chuck had described, homicide detectives had already addressed the standard question anyone involved in police work knows to ask in such a case: Did the husband do it? They decided on their answer fairly quickly: No way. One reason was obvious: When a murderer turns a gun on himself to cover up his crime, he tends to wound himself in a place that will do little damage and cause the least amount of pain. A flesh wound in the lower leg, or a bullet through the wrist, is a sure signal to a detective to exercise profound skepticism.

But Chuck Stuart, as anyone could see, had a life-threatening wound that kept him in surgery for ten straight hours, with more operations to come as his mangled intestines began to heal. A fraction of an inch in any direction, and the bullet lodged in his gut could easily have killed him before the ambulance arrived. Dr. Edwin Hirsch, the imperious chief of surgery at Boston City Hospital who had operated on Chuck, actually scoffed when a homicide detective asked him the next morning whether it looked like Chuck could have shot himself. Hirsch didn't hedge a bit: "There is absolutely no indication of a self-inflicted wound," the surgeon said. Prodded, he explained that the trajectory of the bullet and the severe nature of the wound were "not consistent" with any possible indication of self-infliction. Hirsch, who had served with a combat surgical unit in Vietnam, spoke with the kind of hard-won authority that police respected instinctively. That was that.

The other reason was more complex. From the moment he had decided to kill his wife and try to get away with it, Chuck had sensed that the time was right. From cynical street-smart cops to hard-nosed editors on assignment desks, from the townhouses of Cambridge to the triple-deckers of Chelsea and the cottages of the North Shore, white people in the metropolitan area were primed to give automatic credence not only to the plausibility of Chuck's story but also to its absolute inevitability.

As a *Globe* front-page account that ran the Wednesday after the shooting put it, "Coming after a recent wave of shootings that have involved innocent bystanders, the attack on the Stuarts, who were planning their first child after four years of marriage, sparked *particular outrage* yesterday in Boston."

As that outrage was fanned, a local radio station set up a tip line for information on the shooting, and a Boston businessman offered a $10,000 reward for the arrest of the killer, a man who, in the words of an anonymous police source quoted without question by the *Globe* on Wednesday, "lives in or routinely commits crimes around the Mission Hill housing project."

The day after the shootings, Brigham and Women's announced that it had lowered the parking fee at its underground garage to $1 for the estimated 400 couples enrolled in its childbirth and parenting classes, City Councilor Albert "Dapper" O'Neill promised to introduce legislation to give the police department a $10 million supplemental appropriation to hire more cops, and even respected black leaders such as City Councilor Bruce Bolling jumped firmly onto the reactionary bandwagon, saying that "the Stuart family has become a symbol" of the "carnage" on Boston's streets. "People thought that as long as all this violence was in the Roxbury neighborhood, it's not going to affect us. Now we see it is not confined to a single race or ethnicity." Bolling, Roxbury's representative on the city council, likened the situation to the Vietnam War: "The only question now is, what is the body count? Every day, there is another shooting, another murder. It's an emergency situation that has to be dealt with systematically."

On Beacon Hill, there were loud calls in the state legislature for the restoration of the death penalty.

And people couldn't get enough of the story. "The overnights are going through the roof," a local television executive said of the news ratings prompted by the Stuart case. Said Pat Purcell, the publisher of the *Herald:* "We couldn't print papers fast enough to keep up with the demand."

Within days, the story would take a cast that would remain in place for months. In a front-page feature story by Sally Jacobs that ran under the headline "The Shattering of a Shining Life," the *Globe* defined the tone. Jacobs had gone to Revere for the Stuart family's reaction to the tragedy, and spoke with Chuck's brother Michael, the Revere fireman, who told her: "You know, I see this kind of thing all the time in my work. But this doesn't happen to us. Not to us." At the time, of course, only a few people knew that Michael was the first brother whom Chuck approached in his plot to kill Carol.

The *Globe*'s accolade continued: "For Carol and Chuck Stuart, death came at a time rich with potential . . . the brutal end not just of the couple's dream of family, but of a relationship that by all accounts was so loving that it warmed even those at its edges." It concluded, "Out in the Stuarts' Reading neighborhood . . . several neighbors said they knew precisely what to do: Stay away from Boston. 'I wouldn't go into Boston if you gave me $100,000,' said one. 'It's just not safe.' And over in Revere, where Chuck's brothers and his friends gathered, a moment of silence hung heavy late in the afternoon. 'We're numb from it,' Mark Stuart whispered hoarsely. 'Numb.' "

Not to be outdone, the *Herald* found a "close friend" of Chuck's who likened the couple's "almost idyllic life" to *Camelot*. This story had the headline, "Dreams of *Camelot*—Christmas Birth of Baby Was to Cap an Idyllic Life." In it, Michael Stuart again was heard from. "Carol was a little angel," said the brother who a month earlier had declined to help Chuck murder her. "She didn't even swear. My brother is the same way—a perfect gentleman." In the *Herald* account, Maureen Vajdic, the neighbor in Reading with whom Carol had begun to jog on mornings before work, also spoke of her fears of random violence. "It's not safe to go any place," she said.

In its Wednesday editions the *Herald* displayed on its front page an editorial that was widely quoted all over Boston: "The Time is Now," declared the editorial, which managed to skirt the fact that violent crime in Boston had actually *declined* in the past year:

> When will it stop?
> When will public outrage reach such a level that we make it stop?
> When will we demand that the random shootings, the gratuitous violence that we all too often accept as a part of urban life, cease?
> When will we insist the people be able to walk the streets of this city—in any neighborhood of this city—in safety and comfort, without fear?
> Now. The answer is now.

On the front page next to the *Herald* editorial was a banner headline "Hub Set to Call Crime Emergency" over the lead story, which reported that the "outcry" over the Stuart murder was raised to "a feverish pitch" as Republican members of the state legislature angrily called for a restoration of the death penalty. "It is indeed a tragedy that it takes a crime of this brutality to bring to the forefront the need to do something that should have been done long ago," said Ray Shamie, chairman of the Republican State Committee.

Mayor Flynn called another press conference to say: "As a city, we're consumed with anger and outrage. We must all unite in compassion for the Stuart family to work with the police to apprehend the ruthless killer." In conjunction with a local television station, the *Herald* commissioned a poll that found growing support for a reinstatement of the death penalty in Massachusetts.

"Death in the City," was the headline over an editorial in the *Globe*:

> It was the most frightening crime and the least frequent. A stranger enters a family's life briefly, terrorizes, kills and then disappears.
> Carol and Charles Stuart were visitors to a city for one of the reasons cities exist, medical care. Boston's renowned medical complex suddenly became a brutal battleground.
> New England grieves for the Stuart family because of the poignance and innocence of their story. The Stuarts were

shot—Carol Stuart was killed—after they attended a child-birth class. She was about to deliver a child, which lends a terrible sadness to her murder. The child's fate and her husband's gallant calls for help, recorded by the police, increased public interest in the case.

Like twelve-year-old Darlene Tiffany Moore, who was killed in Roxbury last year, Carol Stuart was a visitor. . . . Perhaps drugs were to blame here, but, more ominous, the Stuarts were gunned down by a stranger—the worst fear of city dwellers. . . . The murder, which began as a robbery, is a reminder of the violence that lurks beneath the surface of this prosperous city.

Citizen cooperation with police is essential if the crime is to be solved. The gunman had the couple at his mercy. Why was he not content to steal their money but leave them their lives? That question will nag until the killer is brought to justice.

The *Globe* also ran a front-page article that was no less alarmist in its view of the urban menace that seemingly had suddenly begun to threaten the comfortable well-being of the newspaper's bedrock suburban readership.

"Violent Attack Jolts the Public," read the headline. "Randomness Is Seen Reinforcing Fear, Racism."

The story began:

"Monday night's brutal attack on a Reading couple leaving childbirth classes at Brigham and Women's Hospital brings home the worst fears of those who live in and around Boston: that violent crime can happen to anyone, anytime, anywhere."

The story went on to quote a Brandeis University "historian of violence in America" addressing white fears of urban crime:

The way it strikes people is, there's a statistical probability that I'm going to meet one of these creeps, and the only reason it's going to be me is pure bad luck. . . . The attack will first forcefully remind the average Boston-area citizen that Boston is a violent place, even though most residents may believe New York, Washington and Chicago are more dangerous cities. . . .

In the absence of an explanation, most people will fall back on the notion that this is typical behavior for black men in crime-ridden neighborhoods.

Within days, Chuck Stuart's story was ingrained into the American consciousness. With a few notable exceptions, no one saw reason to doubt it, and those who did, Matthew Stuart prominent among them, were keeping their mouths shut. At Boston City Hospital, where Chuck was still groggy from the anesthesia during his all-night surgery, his family sat silently with him during visiting hours on Thursday night, watching this outpouring of sympathy on the television news programs. On his nightstand, the newspapers were starting to stack up. Reading them over and over, Chuck was beginning to believe the story himself.

In one aspect, at least, the police were watching Chuck Stuart carefully. From the moment the door slammed shut on the ambulance in Mission Hill, interrupting the on-scene interrogation of the wounded man, detectives had been annoyed by the medical authorities who took custody of the victim and moved in quickly to protect him from intrusions in the critical first few days of his hospitalization.

It was especially frustrating to the cops because the guy seemed to be so articulate about the shooting in spite of his terrible wound. Even as Chuck's ambulance sped through the streets toward City Hospital, police were already acting on information they had from him, rattling the cages of the usual suspects in the project to try to shake someone who knew something off his perch.

It wasn't until Thursday, after Chuck was out of intensive care and off the ventilator, that police were allowed in for a formal interview. Two veteran homicide detectives, Robert Ahearn and Robert Tinlin, questioned Chuck at his bedside, and they came away from it feeling that some headway was being made.

Chuck struck the cops as being alert and very cooperative. Chuck's cousin, Patrick Reardon, was in the room when the detectives arrived, and he accepted their invitation to stay for the interview. After apologizing for the interruption, the cops questioned Chuck politely for ninety minutes, and began filling in some missing information on the crime.

For his part, Pat Reardon was not only amazed at Chuck's recall of detail—Chuckie had always been a detail person—but at his ability to overcome the grief and shock that everyone knew was being held tightly in check right under that controlled surface. As he tried to collect his thoughts, Chuck—one cop afterward described him as "inconsolable"—was prompted by the detectives desperate for information. The victim did his best to help, telling the detectives that after being abducted by the gunman, who entered the car at the intersection of Francis Street and Huntington Avenue, he looked over his shoulder at the man in the back seat.

"Turn the fuck around!" the black man told him angrily, according to Chuck. "Drive straight ahead, and don't look in the rear-view mirror!" The police wrote this down carefully.

Chuck said that he noticed the man had on a black baseball cap, and wore gloves with the fingers cut out. He explained that he was forced to drive up Tremont Street and into the narrow streets near the Mission Hill housing project, where the abductor ordered him to stop the car beside an empty lot, across the street from an abandoned tavern, demanding Carol's rings and purse, and Chuck's Seiko Lasalle gold watch.

Chuck said that he and Carol complied, handing over their jewelry. Then the man demanded Chuck's wallet.

"I don't carry a wallet," Chuck said he replied honestly. He seldom carried one when he wasn't at work. According to Chuck, the assailant then spotted the car phone that Chuck had bought for Carol to keep in closer touch.

"You must be Five-O," the assailant shouted, according to Chuck. In the Mission Hill Projects, as the police knew, "Five-O" was the slang term teenaged black males used to refer to a police officer. It was not, however, a term that was in general use among males of the age—late twenties to mid-thirties—that Chuck estimated the man in the car had been. This detail seemed trivial, however.

Chuck told the cops that after apparently deducing that he and Carol were undercover cops, the assailant reached inside his jacket and took out a silver-colored snubnosed .38 revolver. "He shot my wife first," Chuck said, watching the detectives scribble into their notebooks. Then the man turned the gun toward himself, Chuck said, "but I ducked" and the bullet smashed into the visor above the sheering wheel. Chuck said he half turned in an attempt to grab the gun from the assailant; the third shot, fired at almost point-blank range, struck him in the abdomen. Then the shooter grabbed the keys and bolted from the car, running into the night with Carol's purse under his arm.

Choosing his words carefully, pausing sometimes to hold back tears, Chuck managed to describe the gunman in great detail.

According to the report the detectives made from Chuck's descriptions, the Stuarts' assailant was a male "American Negro," aged twenty-eight to thirty-four years, about five-feet-ten in height and weighing between 150 and 160 pounds; "thin and gaunt," with a "black short Afro" haircut, brown eyes. The detective who wrote out the report noted that Chuck described the man as having a "median Nubian" nose, "shaggy, splotchy facial hair," and a "bony structured jaw, high cheekbones." Besides the black baseball cap, he had on a black jogging jacket with "two to three red stripes running down sleeves." Under that, the man wore a dark shirt, was "right-handed, anxious, high-strung," and spoke in a "raspy voice with a sing-song tone."

With Chuck's assistance, the detectives, confused by the meandering ride the taped call to the dispatcher indicated that Chuck had taken, figured out the location of the shooting itself: Mindoro Street between Prentiss and Station streets, alongside a parking lot owned by Northeastern University and a few hundred feet from the Amtrak right-of-way. Across the street, as Chuck had said, was the abandoned Station Cafe. After shooting Carol and himself, Chuck said, the black man ran down Mindoro Street.

"At the time the shooting happened, this place must have been pretty deserted," one homicide detective mused. "Whoever did this must have known to bring them here because it's so empty. You could assume that the killer must have some knowledge of this area."

Chuck thought it over and agreed that must be the case.

The new information gave added impetus to police scouring the Projects to look for well-known criminals who might have been expected to be in that particular area on any given night. Already, some names were starting to rise to the short end of a long list. Willie Bennett's, naturally, was among them. But so far there was nothing besides a general physical description that tied the case to Willie, and hundreds of Mission Hill males fit the same description.

Meanwhile, detectives and other officers were going without sleep to chase down every potential lead in the Mission Hill Projects, as the mayor anxiously awaited results. "We now need people to come forward and provide whatever information they have, whether they saw something or heard something," the mayor declared as the police searched the neighborhood. "Police officers will be combing the public housing development and talking to everyone and anyone."

Armed with the mighty certitude of knowing what they were looking for, the Boston police department stormed through the Mission Hill Projects in the most intensive manhunt in the history of Boston. On their heels came the reporters and television crews whose vans with their eerie microwave antennas soon became fixtures on the street. Somber-faced television reporters used the project as backdrops for their reports on the search for the killer. In very short order, they managed to make Mission Hill a visual synonym for random urban violence.

TWELVE

The Projects

From Huntington Avenue, Tremont Street plunges straight into the heart of Mission Hill, a neighborhood of neat three-story brownstones, brick townhouses, and even some suburban-style split-levels. Though most of its residents don't like to admit it, the neighborhood—once exclusively working-class Irish—is now one of those urban demilitarized zones that often form the buffer between the slums and whatever pocket of white prosperity remains in a city. On one side of Mission Hill sprawls the black bastion of Roxbury; on the other, the Longwood Medical Area and, above that, the urban affluence of the Back Bay clinging to the reclaimed banks of the Charles.

Mission Hill's residents like to point out that they share an entity almost unheard of in the city of Boston: an integrated neighborhood. The statistics certainly support that claim: Of Mission Hill's 15,000 people, about 45 percent are white, 30 percent are Hispanic,

20 percent are black, with the remainder made up of a growing minority of Asians. In addition to rents that are considerably lower than those in the Back Bay, Mission Hill's chief allure is its proximity to public transit and, especially, to the half-dozen colleges that are nearby. Its main landmark is the huge Mission Church, whose twin steeples soar 137 feet each atop a hill that gives the neighborhood its name. But Mission Hill also has another claim that is firmly supported by statistics: relative safety. In the first six months of 1989, the overall crime rate in Mission Hill decreased significantly— by 18 percent. Carol Stuart's murder was only the fourth that had occurred in the neighborhood in the last eighteen months—in a city that was well on its way to averaging more than 125 murders a year.

But as is often the case, statistics are deceptive, and so are Mission Hill's claims to urban harmony. The neighborhood has a border of its own—Tremont Street. On the one side of Tremont are the quiet narrow streets that climb along gentle hills and give the neighborhood its charm. On the other side of Tremont, in the shadow of the church steeples towering 137 feet, on the hill, back behind the brick institutional facade of a building that has the words "Overseers of Public Welfare" chiseled into a stone cornice that is now covered with a new sheet-metal sign that reads "Your Dept. of Public Welfare," in back of all that is a sprawling housing complex officially called the Mission Hill Main but simply known as the Projects.

The Projects, built at the end of the Depression when they housed mostly poor whites, are the bane of Mission Hill. A bleak collection of old, battered, three-story brick buildings with wood window trim that used to be white, the Projects are in a state of obvious disrepair, with blocks of ugly apartment buildings cemented into square plots that have no grass, no sidewalks even—just all-encompassing driveways. Here and there they are dotted with dirt lots that only the most enthusiastic booster on the public payroll would describe as playgrounds. Junked cars take up much of the space on these lots. Elsewhere, alongside the dumpsters that are the only touch of green in the Projects, one way to know which cars are still in service and which are abandoned is that a car in service often has a man bent over the engine under a flipped-up hood, trying to coax it to life.

The other remarkable sight on this bleak landscape is the people—on this side of Tremont, they are black or Hispanic, mostly

Puerto Rican. Except for a few diehards who are widely considered crazy, even by their neighbors, the last whites in the Projects fled a decade ago. On nice afternoons, women gossip on lawn chairs while children dart around the cars and the dumpsters. And in sullen knots on every section of adjoining driveway that could conceivably be thought of as an intersection, young black men pass their lives, watching the scene. And every so often, like vehicles cruising slowly through a safari "natural habitat" theme park, the police glide by in their patrol cars, working hard to match the menacing stares they get from the street.

This is the usual order of life on the streets of the Mission Hill Projects.

But within hours after the ambulances shrieked off, carrying Carol and Chuck Stuart, that uneasy balance of menace and containment had come unglued. Given the mayor's emotional call to arms, given his order to "put every single available detective on this case," the Boston police department hit the streets of the Projects running. By Tuesday afternoon, more than a hundred policemen were on duty in and around the Mission Hill Projects, and it seemed to the people who were unfortunate enough to live there that the cops were on a rampage, using the existing stop-and-search authority to confront, search, and sometimes humiliate and harass any black male they spotted from their cars.

These were good days for black young men in Mission Hill to stay indoors, which was exactly what seventeen-year-old Joey Bennett and a group of his friends were doing on Tuesday, October 23, the day after the Stuart shootings. Excited by the commotion on the streets outside, they were playing Nintendo in Joey's bedroom, and occasionally running to a window to investigate a siren or other disturbance outside. As they played the video game, the teenaged boys were passing a joint around and "talking shit," as one of them would describe it.

Coming back from the window, one of the boys noticed the newspaper clipping that Joey kept in the frame on his bureau, the one with his uncle Willie's picture under the headline: "You'll Never Take Me Alive."

This friend, Dereck Jackson, took the frame off the bureau and sat down on the floor beside the bed to read what the story said about the desperado Willie Bennett, whom all of the boys knew through Joey. The newspaper clipping seemed to ratify his street fame. Even if the clipping said that Willie had signed a three-year contract with the Celtics, Dereck could not have been more impressed.

"Shit," he said admiringly, putting the picture frame back in its place.

"That's my uncle," Joey bragged.

"I know it's your uncle," Dereck replied. "I know your uncle."

"Some shit," Joey said, beaming with pride.

"Yo," said Dereck, who had a thought. "Was your uncle involved in those shootings?" No one had to ask what shootings he meant.

"Yeah," Joey replied impulsively, enjoying the reflected fame.

"Shit!" said Dereck.

The others all laughed derisively and played their Nintendo.

"Shit," Dereck reiterated.

On his way home that afternoon, careful to stay away from any patrol car he saw looming ahead, Dereck stopped to talk with a friend, Eric Whitney, eighteen years old. Everybody in Mission Hill was buzzing about their neighborhood being all over the television news. The noon anchor people were even on the streets outside, standing out there in their suits while the little black kids bobbed and weaved behind them, trying to show their mothers their faces on the news. Dereck was caught up in the scary thrill that pervaded the Projects, where the only media attention usually came from the occasional drug shooting down near the abandoned lots. Dereck told his friend Eric what he knew, what Joey had told him about his uncle. Actually, in his excitement, Dereck told Eric a little more than what Joey had actually said, which consisted only of the word "Yeah." "Joey's Uncle Willie shot that pregnant lady," is what Eric heard.

Eric Whitney could no more wait to share this information than any of the reporters on television could wait to tell their viewers what little they themselves were hearing. Eric positively ran back to his apartment, where he was glad to find his mother at her usual place in front of the television, watching the evening news about the shooting in Mission Hill.

Shouting above the din of the television, he blurted out the news to his mother: "Joey Bennett says his Uncle Willie told him that he shot that lady." Proud to be the first with such a titillating report, Eric saw how he got his mother's rapt attention for once, so he added a little detail to make it a better story. "Willie Bennett even showed Joey the gun and showed him how he shot the lady."

No less caught up in the awful excitement, Eric's mother herself was bursting to share this information that she knew who did it, even if the police and the television people did not. That night, she told her boyfriend, whose name was Trent W. Holland. He was a Boston police officer.

Two cops were routinely assigned to patrol the Mission Hill housing project: Officers William "Billy" Dunn, a veteran of the public housing beats, and Richard Harrington, who had only been on the assignment for a year. Still, he learned fast. Police Superintendent Joseph Saia, Jr., the officer whom Commissioner Roache placed in charge of the Stuart investigation, himself had said that Dunn and Harrington "know everybody and everything in Mission Hill."

Along with scores of other cops, Dunn and Harrington combed the Projects the night of the shooting, questioning people they had arrested before and the usual array of what the *Globe* described as "neighborhood toughs who know most about the crime that goes on around them."

"Somebody in Mission Hill is going to give the guy up," one unnamed cop was reported as saying. "If not to do the right thing, then just to get rid of the heat."

So Officer Holland was pleased to be able to share the interesting information he had gotten from Eric Whitney's mother. It wasn't enough to make a collar by any means, but as the police used everything they had by way of leverage, it was something worth knowing about.

On Thursday, to the mayor's great relief, Commissioner Roache declared that his department had narrowed down the list of potential suspects. "We have reduced our list of suspects to a chosen few," said Roache.

This sounded like good news in Mission Hill, where the residents regarded the police response as a state of siege. None of them could recall anything remotely like it. The cops had never made this kind of an effort to find the killer of a black person, the most recent

victim being Ina Stroud, a thirty-one-year-old mother of five, shot in
the head outside her apartment in the Projects in July. That was
different, many residents were saying. That was a black lady,
involved with crack, a no-account who barely made the six o'clock
news except to show the white folks that the crime was bad. The
message of the response to the Stuart shooting couldn't have been
more clear if the mayor's office had hung a billboard from the church
steeple: "This Is Different. This Was a White Lady."

But this was also decorous Boston, where black people were
not in the habit of putting too fine a point on things. The grocery
stores and front porches of the black neighborhoods were buzzing
with talk—many people there simply did not believe the husband's
story. In places where they knew street crime very well, since they
were so often victims of it, people were saying that this one didn't
ring true. Shooting, yes. Robbery, sure. Drugs all over the place,
especially down by Station Street where they said the white lady got
shot. But the television was saying the man hopped into the Stuart
car down on Huntington Avenue. People in the Projects thought
they'd heard it all, but that was a new one. Crackheads don't act
like that. And then he shot the *pregnant lady* first? Before shooting
the *man*? To people for whom violent crime was something that
sometimes happened to their brother or daughter, that didn't sound
right. People watched their televisions, but shrugged when they discussed it. Something sounded wrong.

And it wasn't just on the street corners that people were wondering out loud. Leslie F. Harris, a black lawyer who works for the
state public defender's office and who would later find himself representing a suspect in the shootings, drove through the neighborhood
every day on his way to work. Something was wrong, he told friends
after hearing excerpts from Chuck's telephone call to the dispatcher.
"I have known a lot of drugged-out addicts—this does not sound like
the act of a drugged-out addict," he said. "Even with them, there
are certain things that are not done. A drugged-out addict would
always shoot the man first. You wouldn't shoot a woman first, especially one who is seven months pregnant and clearly incapable of
hurting you." Besides, he said, "I know that area well. You cannot
drive that route and not pass a thousand people! There are just too
many landmarks . . ." Harris and others were flabbergasted that
Chuck's story was not being challenged. Yet the news media reflected

none of this strong skepticism; few reporters had any contacts with African-American Bostonians whose names did not appear on their Rolodexes under the heading "Black Leaders."

The black leaders reacted defensively.

"What can we do?" an official of the Projects tenants task force told reporters. "We can't go out there and beat the junkies on the corner. We can't do it alone. We need the mayor. We need the police."

Said another, "We don't harbor criminals. We want our neighborhoods safe."

Meanwhile, black men all over the Projects were being stopped and searched, sometimes several times a day. Those unlucky enough to come up in a routine computer check of outstanding court warrants were promptly cuffed and hauled off for questioning. Those whose attitudes cops didn't like soon had cause to regret it. In a tactic first popularized by Philadelphia police in street disputes with Black Panthers in 1970, black males were strip-searched on the streets of Mission Hill. A man who looked the wrong way at a cop who stopped him soon found himself against a wall with his pants down at his knees—often as his girlfriend or even children stood looking on. Nothing that was done on Mission Hill in the aftermath of the Stuart shootings caused the outrage that this did. It was worse than a beating. It was the ultimate sign of disrespect, and a generation of black males from the Mission Hill Projects will never forget it.

A black teenager, Tony Redd, told the *Herald* that week: "They make us pull down our pants and stuff, outside. They talk to us rude, and then you can't say nothing back or else they threaten to punch you in the face." He added, "We're sorry that white lady got killed, but ain't nothing we can do about it. They've been running up on us, searching us every five minutes with their pistols in our faces. They be telling us, 'Give us some information and we'll take care of you.' They'll look out for us, like if you get caught doing something, they'll let you go."

Henry Ash, a twenty-three-year-old black man, said: "They've been harassing us. I get searched every day. Certain people that got little warrants on them, they try to get information out of them. Every day, they mess with everybody—200 to 300 brothers."

On Tuesday night, twenty-one-year-old Terrence Williams was walking with some friends when the police pulled up beside him.

Objecting to what he thought was rude questioning, Williams found himself spread-eagled over a car hood with a police gun at the back of his neck.

"Drop the pants," he was ordered.

William knew enough not to put up a struggle. But he thought: "You want to get my pants down, I ain't helping." He refused, telling the cops flatly: "My pants ain't coming down." The police, weary by the end of a long day, didn't press it. Instead, they cuffed him and took him away on a disorderly conduct charge. After his court hearing the next day, Williams could savor a small victory, telling the arresting officer, a black man: "Sorry, brother, you won the war. But these pants never came down." The officer looked away without replying.

Billy Celester, the police commander of Area B, the district with responsibility for Roxbury and Mission Hill, dismissed the howls of protest that rose from the streets of Mission Hill over the police searches. Celester, a black officer who had grown up in Roxbury and run with a gang as a teenager, scoffed at black leaders who threatened to sue over the search policy: "I just wish they were as much against the perpetrators of violence as they seem to be against the police."

Above Celester, police brass downtown also dismissed the protests. "We've been putting on a lot of pressure up there," Superintendent Saia said when asked about the searches, "and there are a lot of drug dealers that are upset."

Yet after all of the police saturation of Mission Hill, it was embarrassingly clear the leads were flimsy at best, though police said they believed the killer—as if they now had a specific person in mind—was, as an unnamed detective told one newspaper, "still in the area."

"We've got prime suspects—we've got it down to three or four suspects," Saia said on Thursday.

THIRTEEN

'A Steadfast Wife'

In Medford, Carol's parents were not following the news. Incapacitated with grief, they could barely even think about the funeral arrangements. Rosemary and John Leone, the DiMaitis' sister and brother-in-law, came up from the downstairs apartment of the bungalow on Fourth Street to spend Tuesday night, the night after the shooting, with them. At dawn, the Leones awoke to hear them both still weeping softly in their bedroom.

All day Wednesday, the house where Carol had grown up was crowded with relatives and neighbors who had come to do what little they could, offering a hug, a handshake, a tearful nod, making coffee, answering the phone, tending to the doorbell that never stopped ringing. Sometime around ten o'clock, Chuck's parents had come, and were welcomed by Carol's parents with a tearful embrace. The Stuarts didn't stay long; there wasn't much to say. Chuck was out of the woods, at least. The surgery had been successful—he would live.

As the two sets of stunned parents spoke haltingly and stiffly, for they had never been close, Carol's older brother was busy on the phone arranging the funeral.

Carol's old boyfriend Jeff Cataldo, married now and living in a suburb not far from Reading, told friends that the emotionally most difficult moment came when he found her obituary in the *Globe*. It seemed like yesterday that he had held her tiny hand in his as they walked in the mist that drifted in from the sea at Revere Beach. Carol had taught him how to dance. He had believed for many years that she would one day be his wife. Even when they went their separate ways during college, he thought of her frequently and fondly. She was a reference point fixed in his existence. You never really got someone like Carol out of your mind, he thought. And now here was the end for her, on page 38, in this matter-of-fact entry for the historical record, to be tucked away with the yearbooks and the faded prom pictures:

> A funeral mass for Carol Ann (DiMaiti) Stuart will be said at ten A.M. Saturday in St. James Church, Medford, where she was married in 1985.
>
> Mrs. Stuart, tax counsel for Cahners Publishing Co. of Newton, was slain by a gunman who robbed her and her husband Monday night as they were returning to their home in Reading from a childbirth class at the Brigham and Women's Hospital. She was thirty.
>
> She leaves her husband, Charles M., Jr., her infant son, Christopher, her parents, Giusto and Evelyn (Mantia) DiMaiti, a brother, Carl DiMaiti, and her grandmother, Rose (Vesce) Mantia of Medford.

The wake was scheduled to be held over two days, Thursday afternoon from two to four P.M., and the next night, for those who worked days, from seven to nine. On Saturday, there would be a funeral mass, and then she would be buried. Carol was laid out in a closed casket at Della Russo funeral home in her hometown. Atop the casket was a photograph of her in her wedding gown, alone. She was surrounded by flowers and wreaths, more than three hundred arrangements in all, so many that they tumbled out of the parlor and spilled into the vestibule. The simplest of them, a small corsage, lay closest to her. "To Mother," a ribbon tied to the flower said, "From Christopher."

At the hospital, Chuck had little to say after he gave police his initial account. Family members surrounded him protectively, but he didn't have much to say to them either. Reporters trying to phone or cajole their way in found security measures at the hospital more appropriate for a visiting president than a shooting victim, but they respected Chuck's privacy. "He's slipping in and out of consciousness," said Maria Stuart, the wife of Chuck's brother Michael.

On Thursday night, Chuck asked a visitor to hand him a legal pad he kept on the nightstand. In a weak, wobbly script he wrote out a eulogy to be delivered, in his name, at the funeral.

On Saturday morning, the sun shone brightly. The funeral took place at St. James Roman Catholic Church, where Carol and Chuck, and before them Carol's parents, had been married. Four years earlier, the entire neighborhood had turned out for her wedding to Chuck, and they were back so soon to bury her. In all, more than eight hundred people filled the church, among them Governor Michael Dukakis, Mayor Flynn, and the archbishop himself, Bernard Cardinal Law, in full ecclesiastical regalia to assist in the service.

Carl delivered his eulogy, speaking for himself and his parents and thanking mourners for the overwhelming outpouring of sympathy.

"My sister Carol was many things to many people," Carl said, struggling to keep his voice firm. "A loving and caring daughter who called her parents every night just to say 'I love you,' a faithful and sincere friend, an industrious student who excelled at every academic level, a skillful worker, and a steadfast wife.

"My sister really believed in the innate goodness of every one of us," he said softly. "I think the key word to describe her is 'giving.' She spent every day of her life giving of herself to others. She was perhaps the most unselfish person I have ever known. All of us who spent any time with Carol know what a giving and caring person she was. God must be very pleased to have her with him.

"Today we feel a deep sense of loss, and outrage. How could this have happened? What kind of a society tolerates this kind of random and senseless violence? I have no answers. I know, however, that Carol would stand totally against any call for vengeance or retaliation.

"Today we mourn. We suffer the pain of loss. I know that Carol would understand and would help us to heal as quickly as possible—her greatest gift was her ability to reach out and bring happiness into every life she touched.

"Sweet dreams, little sister," Carl concluded. "I know you're in heaven waiting for each and every one of us. We love you. We miss you. We'll never forget you."

The pastor of St. James, Reverend Francis Gallagher, the priest who had married Carol and Chuck, presided over the funeral. Gallagher also was close to the Stuarts—years earlier, while a curate at Immaculate Conception, the Stuarts' parish in Revere, the priest had known young Chuck as an altar boy.

"Many of us were here four short years ago to pray for and with a very happy young bride and groom," Gallagher told the congregation. "This time, we come to pray for Carol Stuart's immortal soul.

"We are naturally overwhelmed by human emotions—anger, resentment, deep sorrow, perhaps revenge. No one can do anything to erase the nightmare that is happening," the priest said, exhorting his listeners to "get rid of all bitterness, passion, anger, malice of every kind and, in place of that, be kind. Compassionate."

But it was Chuck's words that had the most emotional impact on those who had come to mourn Carol. Towering above the pulpit, one close friend from Revere, Brian Parsons, read Chuck's final words to the woman who was his wife:

"Good night, sweet wife, my love."

The words echoed from the vaulted ceiling of the old neighborhood church. "God has called you to his hands, not to take you away from me and all the happiness that God has brought but to bring you away from the cruelty and violence that fill this world.

"He said that for us to truly believe, we must know that his will was done, and that there was some right in this meanest of acts.

"In our souls we must forgive the sinner, because he would too. My life will be more empty without you, as will the lives of your family and friends. You have brought joy and kindness to every life you've touched.

"Now you sleep away from me. I will never again know the feeling of your hand in mine. But I will always feel you. I miss you and I love you.

Your husband, Chuck."

Most of the congregation was crying softly by now. The part about holding Carol's hand brought tears to the eyes even of veterans of tragic funerals such as the police commissioner, the mayor, and the usually impassive Cardinal Law, who brushed away a tear before he made a final blessing. And then it was over. The eight pallbearers, among them Chuck's brothers Matthew, Michael, and Mark, rose in unison from the front pew and arranged themselves by the coffin to wheel it down the aisle. With her mother's sobs punctuating the terrible gloom, the pallbearers carried the coffin into the bright October morning sunlight. "Oh my baby," Evelyn DiMaiti cried, following Carol's coffin to the hearse as if she would climb in beside it. "My sweet baby." Her husband and her son led her to the black car that would take them to the cemetery.

Carol was buried at Holy Cross Cemetery in Malden. On a beautiful, warm autumn morning, she was laid to rest in a family plot at the base of a gravestone that had the names "DiMaiti" and "Mantia" chiseled on it. She was buried beside her maternal grandfather, Salvatore.

The next day, amid all of the media coverage of her funeral and the unfolding story, Carol, a woman whose self-effacing sense of humor always tempered her well-known ideological streak, would have been amused by a headline the *Herald* printed near the story about her funeral. It referred readers to an opinion column on the editorial page: "The Stuart Tragedy: The Problem Is an Oversupply of Liberals."

FOURTEEN

An Arrest

The day after the funeral, as the commotion was finally dying down on the streets of the Mission Hill Projects, Mayor Flynn decided to make a public gesture toward Boston's mortified black community, where decorum was keeping public expressions of outrage over the police searches muted. Undertaking a mission that a top aide called an attempt by the white mayor to take a "healing message throughout the city," Flynn made an unusual foray into the Mattapan Morning Star Baptist Church to give what seemed to be his patronizing assurance that not all blacks were responsible for what happened to the Stuarts. "It is no time for anger or revenge or retaliation," Flynn magnanimously told the congregation. "A tragedy against anybody is a tragedy against all of us. No one group of people, no one community, ought to be singled out because of the actions of a few."

By the time the mayor decided to set off on his healing mission, the police were afraid they had squeezed all the information they could out of the Projects, with nothing good enough to even consider an arrest. Nothing had yet come of the vague information Officer Holland had passed on about Joey Bennett's bragging.

Meanwhile, as the bulk of the extra police presence left the neighborhood, Officer Dunn was working hard on every lead he could drum up from his wide network of contacts in the Projects. He had been around the streets long enough to know that much information that could be squeezed out of them came from people with axes to grind—what better time to settle a personal score than when the police were desperate for some names? Dunn did manage to come up with a name that looked promising enough to call in the detectives—a well-known Projects character named Albie who, Dunn had been told, had robbed a man on Thursday. Dunn and his partner Harrington both knew the guy—Alan Swanson, twenty-nine, a small-time heroin dealer so inept at his trade that he didn't even have his own place to live. Swanson, the officers easily found out, was illegally occupying a vacant apartment at 8 Cornelia Court in the Projects. They decided to pay him a visit. It was worth a check to see what might shake loose.

Together, they went to the second-floor apartment at one-thirty Saturday morning and nabbed Swanson, who offered no resistance, figuring "I hadn't done nothing worth running for." Swanson, who had been convicted nine months earlier of possession of heroin with intent to distribute, told the officers that a friend who said he had a lease on the apartment had given him permission to use it. He had been staying there with his girlfriend for the past three weeks, Swanson said. Proudly he added that they were looking for a place of their own.

By now, a half dozen more cops had arrived. They told a mystified Swanson he was under arrest for breaking and entering. As Harrington snapped on the cuffs, he told Swanson not to worry, that the judge would reduce the charge to simple trespass and he'd be out in a flash. Hearing this, Swanson was nervous—so why bother to arrest me, then? he thought—but not unduly concerned. The police were obviously anxious to find something in the apartment, and if he caused a scene they would certainly get him on something more than B&E—the police can always pile *something* onto the charge, he knew. But he also knew that he hadn't really crossed anyone recently, except another guy from the Projects, and that was only a dispute over some money he had borrowed.

Swanson was already free on bail awaiting trial on an old gun charge. That was trouble enough for a man with a new girlfriend who was insisting on some sign of stability from him before things went much further. The last thing he wanted was any more trouble. He had been keeping his nose clean. Still, he hadn't just come into town on a Greyhound bus. He knew something was up, with all the heat in the Projects lately over the killing of the white lady. *White lady shot in a black neighborhood,* he thought as he stood there with his hands cuffed and waited to see what the cops were up to. He supposed that's what had brought the cops around. He just didn't think it had anything to do with him other than the fact that he was unlucky enough, as usual, to be occupying a place where the police had had reason to show up unexpectedly. Bad luck, but nothing new there.

Standing in the living room with one cop, though, Swanson got plenty worried when he heard one of the officers shouting excitedly from the bathroom. "That's it!" he cried. "We got it!"

Immediately, Swanson felt the younger officer tense beside him.

"He's the one!" The officer boomed triumphantly, walking in from the bathroom carrying a dirty plastic bucket in which Swanson had been soaking his only change of clothing, a lightweight jogging suit. "He did it. He's the one that did it."

"I didn't do nothing," Swanson protested, wondering what it was he was supposed to have done this time.

"You better keep your goddamn mouth shut," he was told. "I don't want to have to tell you twice, asshole."

Swanson didn't have to be told twice.

He was hustled out and taken down to the Area B police headquarters, where the arresting officers trumpeted his arrival: "This is the guy! We got him! He's the one."

Within an hour, they took him downtown to Berkeley Street. Swanson wasn't even sure what time it was, except that it was still the middle of the night. Only when they led him to a door that had the word "Homicide" painted on it did he fully appreciate just how deep was the trouble that he had fallen into.

Homicide as a possible rap had just not occurred to him until then. Until then, he had figured they were just busting his chops. With the degree of naiveté that only a veteran street felon can display when faced with one of those perfectly rare instances when he feels he has absolutely nothing to hide, Swanson decided to cooperate fully. He nodded in understanding as they read him his rights. He said he would answer their questions right away. He didn't need a lawyer present. Getting a lawyer took time, he knew. All he wanted to do was to tell them what he knew—which was absolutely nothing—and get the hell out of there.

As usual, things didn't work out the way he figured they would. For six grueling hours, as detectives relieved each other in shifts, Swanson sat there on the hard wood chair answering variations on the same basic question: "Why did you kill Carol Stuart?" His protests of innocence were hurled back in his face: "Liar!" one detective after another yelled at him.

It was bright outside, well into Sunday morning, by the time Swanson, dazed from lack of sleep and sickened with the fear that he had been set up by someone on the street, decided that he should have a lawyer. He was crying when they finally let him go back to his cell to wait for one.

By then, the police had already obtained a search warrant to go back to the apartment and seize Swanson's jogging suit as evidence. Since police had seen the jogging suit in Swanson's bathroom by the time the search warrant application was filled out, a small adjustment was made. Though Chuck Stuart had clearly told police that the gunman wore a jogging suit with red stripes, the search warrant application that Detective Paul J. Murphy swore out for the apartment where Swanson was arrested routinely listed the evidence being sought in the Stuart shooting—Carol's rings and handbag, Chuck's expensive watch, and the murder weapon itself. At the top of the list on the warrant was: "1 black sweatsuit with white or red stripes."

Detective Murphy alluded to this apparent discrepancy in his affidavit supporting the search warrant application. "The white stripes appeared to have a pinkish color," Murphy stated of the suit observed by the two cops who arrested Swanson. "This jogging suit appeared similar to the suit worn by the man who shot and murdered Carol Stuart." Murphy added, "It is my belief that the black jogging suit observed in the bathroom sink of Apartment 987 located at 8

Cornell Court, Roxbury, is the same suit worn by the person who shot and murdered Carol Stuart on October 23, 1989. It is my belief that the weapon used in the murder of Carol Stuart, a .38-caliber handgun, is concealed inside Apartment 987. . . ."

Hours later, armed with the search warrant, police arrived en masse to search the apartment. Neighbors who came outside to blink at the bright floodlights police had set up on the driveways thought they were searching for a bomb, so intense was the effort.

But the search didn't yield the gun or any of the property stolen from the Stuarts. The subsequent inventory sheet reporting what had in fact been removed during the search, which was supervised by Murphy, listed only one item from the application: "1 black Adidas jogging suit w/ white stripes."

Meanwhile, after being locked up all weekend, the bewildered Swanson was horrified the next day before his court appearance when a jail guard banged on his cell and began a taunt that was soon taken up by the other inmates. They said he had killed a pregnant lady.

The newspapers, alerted by their sources on Sunday to a possible break in the confounding case, didn't have enough of a handle on Swanson even to use his name yet. On Monday morning, the front page of the *Globe* declared that the "police crackdown showed no signs of slowing the pace of the crime wave," while a headline on a related story said, "Stuart Slaying Spurs Death Penalty Calls." Inside the paper, columnist Bella English wrote of suburbanites "scared to death to come into Boston, even on Saturday afternoon." But it was the story atop the *Globe*'s metro page that brought an excited mob of reporters to Roxbury District Court that morning: "Man Probed as Suspect in Stuart Shooting," it said, over an article describing the unnamed man—Swanson—as being on "a list of several suspects developed by police last week following the Stuart shooting. . . . Asked if the apprehension of the breaking and entering suspect was the most encouraging development in the case to date, [Police Commissioner] Roache said, 'Any time you have a suspect who has been on the list earlier in the week, it is encouraging.' "

The next day, the *Globe* quoted police sources who said that Swanson was not considered a "prime suspect" yet in the Stuart case. "Police are investigating three or four individuals a day," the story said, "and are no closer to an arrest than they were the day after the shooting occurred."

Nevertheless, the authorities appeared to be acting as if Swanson was a most important catch. During his court appearance on Monday, October 30, Swanson was held on $5,000 cash bail by Judge Charles T. Spurlock, the same judge who had signed the search warrant the day before. Swanson's court-appointed lawyer, Leslie Harris, objected to the bail as excessive, arguing that his client was initially charged with trespassing, a misdemeanor, and that the charge had been summarily upgraded to unarmed robbery, a felony, to justify holding him in jail while investigators tried to connect him with the Stuart case.

"If they want to hold him [on a homicide charge], then charge him with it," Harris protested. "But don't charge him with something just to hold him."

Swanson's name surfaced publicly in the news on Tuesday, and the clear implication was that a prime suspect in the Stuart shootings was in custody. "Authorities yesterday declined to name Alan Swanson, twenty-nine, as a primary suspect in the murder," said a story on the front page of the *Herald,* under the headline, "Burglary Suspect Linked to Slaying." The story pointed to the police affidavit, parts of which had been read to reporters by sources, and theorized that Swanson "might have been in possession of several pieces of evidence that could tie him to last week's attack on the Stuarts. . . .

"Swanson has been charged with unarmed burglary for allegedly breaking into and occupying the vacant Boston Housing Authority apartment at 8 Cornelia Court on Saturday night," the story said, noting that police had seized from the apartment "a black Adidas jogging suit with white stripes . . . that is believed to be the same worn by the man who terrorized the Stuarts." The story described the other "evidence" seized: "a red baseball cap, a black sweater with a red stain, a blue 'Superman' T-shirt with a red stain, a black 'zip gun,' a live .38 caliber bullet, a sink trap, three copies of the *Boston Herald,* and personal papers and checks written to two individuals, one of them a Cape Cod man."

An accompanying story, written by an enterprising reporter who had himself looked around the vacant apartment after the police had searched it, sounded as if the premises had been the lair of a very dangerous criminal indeed, theorizing that "one or more individuals had illegally used the vacant one-bedroom unit as a heroin shooting gallery and possibly to smoke the powerful cocaine derivative, crack." The article recounted the results of the investigation in exhaustive detail that conspiratorily implied the drug-crazed denizen flushed therefrom: "burnt matches, menthol cigarette butts, crumpled tin-foil wrappers, ashes, a variety of white, green and purple pills and an empty cassette box for *Aretha Franklin's Greatest Hits*" on the kitchen table, and in the bathroom, "a thick brown leather belt, probably used by an addict to expose blood vessels for a heroin injection, was fastened to the end of a broken towel rack" as well as a "toothpaste tube, small bottle of Vicks and a can of aerosol anti-perspirant were visible in the medicine cabinet." Nearby could be found "a three-dimensional portrait of the Last Supper and a package containing light blue rubber tubing, a small vial of chlorine bleach wrapped in a small yellow pamphlet warning of the link between AIDS and intravenous drug use" as well as a "mattress on the bedroom floor . . . a battered old-style stereo [that] was surrounded by debris, including empty cassette cases, cosmetics, feminine hygiene items and a snapshot of a baby girl," not to mention "a variety of toddler and adult clothing, an empty bottle of Wild Irish Rose, a ripped pillow, chicken bones, empty menthol cigarette packs, ashes and empty boxes of Rice-A-Roni and Prince spaghetti." The newspaper article seemed to do nothing other than buttress the general belief that a drug-crazed violent black criminal had shot the Stuarts.

But within days, optimism that things were coming to a head with a suspect faded fast. Lab tests on the clothing taken from the apartment where Swanson was arrested failed to produce any links to the Stuarts. Now, all the police had in custody with any remotely possible link to the murder was a suspect who was at least the right color, black, and a jogging suit that was not. Coming from a neighborhood where jogging suits were practically de rigueur attire, this was not the sort of evidence that the district attorney could take with any confidence to a grand jury.

In fact, Alan Swanson would never be charged with having anything to do with the Stuart case, except in the press and on television—and in jail, where his identification as a suspect caused him to be so reviled that his food was routinely spit in as it was brought to him.

Moreover, in a chilling foreshadowing of things to come soon for another black man who would be accused in the Stuart crime, officials kept Swanson in jail long after it was obvious that he was clear of involvement in the case. On November 6, nine days after Swanson's arrest in the apartment, Roxbury District Court Judge Julian Houston found him not guilty of the original charge. But before Swanson had left the courtroom, the district attorney's office slapped a new charge on him: armed robbery. The district attorney based this on a new complaint filed by the same policemen who had initially arrested Swanson, Officers Dunn and Harrington. The officers cited the account of the informant who led them to Swanson in the first place.

Even though it was increasingly evident that the police were floundering in their attempt to connect Swanson with the Stuart shooting, as late as November 7 the *Globe* was still referring to him as "the focus of the Stuart investigation." However, the new charge against Swanson was unceremoniously dropped on November 20, when the alleged complainant, Antonio Wharton, took the Fifth Amendment and declined to testify against Swanson. Wharton told Swanson's lawyer, Leslie Harris, that police had pressured him to make the armed robbery charge against Swanson.

Harris recalled with some irony that he himself had been wearing a black running suit on the night of the murder—and had not worn it again. He denounced the police conduct as an attempt to "appease the public" with a quick arrest. "Alan Swanson was caught up in the hysteria following the Stuart shooting," he said. "The police felt they had to arrest someone, and Alan Swanson became a convenient scapegoat because of where he lived and who he is."

But the district attorney's office had no apologies for the way the Swanson matter had been handled. For by the time Swanson walked out of court a free man after spending more than three weeks in jail, the district attorney had a much bigger fish to fry. With Swanson ruled out, police sources began to whisper to their friends in the media about a much stronger suspect, this one a "prime suspect," now in custody. His name, the reporters already knew, was Willie Bennett.

FIFTEEN

Recovery

Chuck would spend a total of six weeks at Boston City Hospital, undergoing a series of operations and recovering from each with a speed that amazed the surgeons. Within a few weeks, a patient who had been barely clinging to life was being given a good chance to make a full recovery. Whereas once doctors had thought Chuck would have to use a colostomy bag to empty his lower intestines for the rest of his life, it now was apparent that he would be able to live without the device, which would have been almost debilitating for a vain young man, after a few more months of healing and therapy.

The patient's spirits too were recovering quickly, it seemed. In fact, Chuck's emotional state had been a subject of some speculation almost since he came to Boston City, where from the beginning, hospital authorities made unusual efforts to protect him from the scrutiny not only of the press but of the regular nursing staff as well. In a breach of procedure, regular nurses were actually assigned directly to Chuck, and were told they would be responsible for the patient until he went home.

Not only that, but Chuck's visitors received privileges usually reserved only for relatives of top city officials or the occasional celebrity who might be at City Hospital. They were allowed to park their cars at one of several spaces specifically reserved for them, and once inside the door, they were treated with a kind of deference that caused one baffled friend of the patient's to remark, "I've visited people in hospitals before, but this was the first time I felt like I was a relative of the president of the United States."

Being a working urban hospital on the edge of a high-crime area, Boston City Hospital was no stranger to gunshot wounds. Indeed, it was a standard request among city cops that, if at all possible, they were to be treated for gunshot wounds at City Hospital, so expert and respected was its hardworking trauma staff. Sometimes, a dozen or more patients suffering from serious gunshot wounds lay in its wards. But there hadn't been one quite like Chuck Stuart before.

From the floor nurses all the way down to the security guards who gathered outside to smoke on their breaks in the parking area near the main entrance, a quiet resentment brewed. While there are sixteen private teaching hospitals in the city of Boston, there is only one public hospital, Boston City, an institution that in 1989 provided, according to official data, half of all of the uninsured health care, despite having only 6 percent of the beds, in Boston. Yet in a hospital where poor people were being treated in crowded wards, where the nonprofessional staff was largely black, something rankled about the special treatment accorded to the white man on the fifth floor.

"There was a guard at his door around the clock for the first three weeks," one nurse said. "Okay, maybe that can be justified given the tremendous amount of attention. But he also had a private room, even though he was being billed the regular rates. They allowed him a VCR in that room, too. This is a hospital where many poor people, and I mean black people from Roxbury, are lying in open wards recovering from exactly the same kind of injuries that

Chuck Stuart had, but who gets the private room?" She laughed, but it was clear that among the working staff of Boston City Hospital, at least, Chuck Stuart's vaunted charm was not playing well.

And beyond the special treatment, there was something very odd about the good-looking patient recovering in intensive care. "He seemed, well . . . *cheerful,*" said a female staff member who had occasion to come into Chuck's room on an almost daily basis. "Once, I heard him talking on the phone to someone about plans for spending Christmas. That struck me as so odd. I mean, holiday plans are about the last thing I would have been thinking about under those circumstances. All he seemed to care about was getting out of the hospital and getting on with his life."

Another nurse shared her misgivings with colleagues on the night shift. "He never said a word about his wife," she said, frowning. "His major concern seemed to be whether his intestines would fully heal. He was real worried about having to wear a colostomy bag."

He also made a lot of demands for a person who should have been worried about nothing other than getting back on his feet. Chuck thought nothing of buzzing a nurse from down the hall to fetch him a pencil, for example. And the guy was all business, almost the comic stereotype of the obnoxious yuppie. Here was a guy whose wife had been shot to death at his side, whose baby was losing a struggle for life, who himself had nearly died from a terrible wound, but he'd practically sneer in your face if you said something sympathetic to him. He was always on the phone, making arrangements for one thing or another.

Hospital employees accustomed to seeing grief and sorrow were baffled to detect neither in Chuck.

"Do you know what he says all the time to that friend of his?" one nurse told a colleague. "When this blows over! Like, 'When this blows over, I'm going to do this or we'll do that.' Who the hell talks like that?"

All over Boston City Hospital, where the brass was so protective of its star patient, eyebrows were being raised on the floors and in the cafeteria, and soon the annoyed tone of the whispers had evolved into something else entirely: contempt and skepticism. Hospital workers are like cops—they see life playing out in its elemental forms, and while it may be easy to fool the high-priced administrators and millionaire surgeons, it was hard to get something phony past the grunts. Before the first week was out, some of those who were coming into close contact with Chuck had begun to openly suspect what was usually the case in these things anyway: The husband did it.

While hospital authorities ordered all employees to keep their silence about Chuck, under penalty of dismissal, nurses began expressing serious skepticism among themselves almost from the moment Chuck was wheeled in from the operating room to the trauma unit. Toward the end of the first week, hospital employees on the floor had already had an informal vote on the question of whether Chuck was involved in the murder of his wife. By an overwhelming margin, the employees voted that he was.

The gossip intensified in the weeks after Chuck was moved from intensive care into a private room in an adjacent wing of the hospital. "It was eerie," said one nurse. "After he started getting better and was allowed regular visitors twice a day, you would walk by and look in, and they'd be sitting there—Chuck and his brothers or sisters, parents—absolutely silently, watching the television, not looking at each other until it was time to go, and then they'd sort of file out, sometimes without even a goodbye. It seemed like they had worked out shifts to come and sit there beside him."

Only when his old friend Brian Parsons came by faithfully each night did Chuck show real animation. Chuck always had a list of chores he needed done, and Brian was eager to help. One nurse noticed that Brian had begun wearing a telephone beeper on his belt, and kidded him about it when she saw him by the nurses station in the hall. But she was surprised by his reply: "Oh," he said, "Chuck likes to stay in close touch. He uses it whenever he needs me for something."

Not long after the shootings, Debby Allen, now in her first year of graduate school at Babson College, stopped by on an unannounced visit. Chuck had been calling her home, making Debby's parents, her mother especially, uneasy about how further contact with Chuck would look to outsiders. But Chuck, as usual, persisted. He had a friend call her and ask her to come. He also prevailed upon co-workers at Kakas, who pressured Debby to go see him. In November, accompanied by Beth Madison, a friend with whom she worked after school at the Babson College recreation center, she did, against her parents' wishes.

She and Beth stayed less than five minutes. But it was long enough for Chuck to plumb her sympathy. He went on at some length about his operations, his constant pain, his depression, his need to have visitors. She changed the subject, telling him about graduate school.

"I tried to distract him," she said much later. But he kept at it, wincing in pain and asking her why she wouldn't call him frequently at the hospital.

Her parents, she explained, groping for an explanation.

Why not call me from school? he asked.

School was a long-distance call from a pay phone, awfully expensive for someone on a student's budget, she pointed out.

No problem, said the man who always picked up the check. He had her hand him a writing pad on which he jotted down a number and handed it to her. It was his telephone calling-card credit number. He told her to use it often.

She said she would.

"I knew my mother was uneasy about my contact with someone associated with a highly publicized violent crime," Debby explained later. Afterward, she called Chuck frequently from school, using the credit card number he gave her, she said, because "I wanted to avoid unnecessarily worrying my mother when she received our telephone bills at home."

Carol's parents also came by regularly. They invariably left confused by his uncommunicative manner, even after he was obviously well on his way to recovery. It took a lot of effort to get him to converse beyond the surface pleasantries, but they supposed that might be because of grief, or perhaps lingering pain. They did not speak of Carol, nor did he. As the weeks passed, Giusto DiMaiti, still deep in mourning for his daughter, found it increasingly difficult to sit there for an hour or so with his son-in-law, who always caused him to wince when he called him "Dad" and Carol's mother "Mom." Lying there propped against the neat white pillows, Chuck was such a vivid reminder of who had lived and who had died. It was hard not to demand answers to questions that wanted to force their way through the grief: Why had he taken Carol into that neighborhood that night? Why did he not speak of her now? Why?

Rosemary Leone, Carol's aunt, felt her heart go out to the DiMaitis when she saw them suffer in this silent respect for his pain. "They wanted to ask him about the shooting and what happened that night," she said, and it was all she could do to hold her own tongue when she came along. "But he would just lie there and act like he was dying, and not say anything." When he did talk, he struck her as overly concerned about the way things might be perceived. "Don't say anything to the media," Chuck had instructed them on several occasions. She was ashamed to admit to herself the vague distrust she had always felt toward the young man who had married her goddaughter. She also noticed the way his family seemed to avoid seeing the DiMaitis. When they did happen to meet in the hospital room or the hall, there was a discernible chill.

Once, after going home from a visit to Chuck, Carol's father was asked by a relative whether Chuck had sufficient health insurance to cover the mounting hospital bills.

"Don't worry," Giusto DiMaiti replied in a cool tone that barely concealed his disdain, "Chuck is well provided for."

More frequently than they saw Chuck, the DiMaitis went to Brigham and Women's to see their grandchild, Carol's baby, a tiny little thing who was barely alive. Though the newspapers liked to depict it as a valiant struggle, the fact was that the baby never had a chance. Two months premature, deprived of oxygen during the crucial half-hour interval between the shooting of his mother and the arrival of rescue workers, the baby was already severely brain damaged when he was wrenched from Carol's womb in the hospital several hours later. Wracked with convulsions almost from the moment of birth, Christopher lay at last silent and impassive on a respirator, his lungs undeveloped, his liver nonfunctional, and his brain waves barely registering on the chart. The family knew that it was simply a matter of allowing a decent interval to pass before the inevitable, all the while hoping for a miracle that everyone knew would never occur for this doomed, helpless little shooting victim.

A mile away at Boston City Hospital, Christopher's father was thinking often of his son. Chuck, who liked to anticipate everything, hadn't planned on having a baby linger on into the new life he saw taking shape before him with greater alacrity every day, and a *brain-damaged* child at that. He knew the doctors held out no hope—they had told him, gently but unequivocally, that the infant was not going to pull through—but *what if he did?* What kind of a life could a single man have, saddled with a child, a disabled child? The time and expense of it! What desirable woman would want to share a life with a man who brought such a burden to her?

Chuck asked often about his son.

"Is there any chance at all?" he pleaded to a family member who came to visit.

His question was answered with a sad, slow shake of the head. "They're going to take him off the medication for the convulsions and see if any brain activity registers. They say if they can't find any brain activity—" the relative paused, taken aback by the intensity of the interest on Chuck's face "—well, he should be, you know, removed from the life support."

"To die?" Chuck was sitting up at rapt attention.

"There wouldn't be any reasonable alternative. They would talk it over first with you, of course."

"Well," Chuck said in a businesslike manner, glancing at the clock to see with relief that visiting hours were almost over, "I want to make sure we don't do anything until we're absolutely positive that there's no hope left. Make sure they understand that, okay?"

"Okay, Chuck. We'll just have to wait and see. You get some rest now."

When he was alone, Chuck called a nurse to have a tape put into the VCR. He fired the remote control device at the television set as if it were a pistol, and settled back into the cool white hospital pillows. Afterward, as the nightly dose of painkillers kicked in, he closed his eyes and drifted into dreamless sleep.

On November 9, after a brain scan on the baby failed to pick up enough activity to qualify for the threshold definition of life, Chuck was notified and gave his assent. Hospital authorities arranged for Chuck, his condition upgraded a week earlier from critical to stable, though he had undergone additional abdominal surgery only a few days earlier, to be rushed by ambulance from Boston City Hospital to Brigham and Women's to be at the baby's side. When Christopher, seventeen days old and severely brain damaged for all of his short life, finally was allowed to die, his father was lying on a hospital cot beside him, crying. Outside, Chuck's mother, Dot, and his brothers and sisters waited in the quiet room just off the neonatal intensive care unit until Dr. Stephen Ringer, director of the unit, came in and gave them the word that the baby was gone. The clock on the wall read 4:34 P.M. When he was brought in to the room with them, Chuck joined in their tears.

The hospital would barely acknowledge to interested outsiders that the baby had died, and did so hours later, only after Dr. Ringer secured Chuck's permission to make the announcement.

However, with his new contacts in the news media, who had taken to calling him for updates on Chuck's condition, Michael Stuart was more forthcoming. "The doctors had said if there was no brain activity he should be removed from life support," Mike told a reporter when the baby's death was announced. "We all thought this was the right thing, to let him be with his mother. Chuck sort of had the same feelings, but he was adamant to make sure not to do anything until the doctors were sure." Michael's wife Maria also spoke openly, explaining that doctors had reduced the baby's anticonvulsion medicine a week earlier to get an accurate brain-wave reading. The test, she said, showed things were "not good, not good at all."

Doctors concluded that the baby had died of brain damage caused by the deprivation of oxygen after its mother was shot.

Mayor Flynn lost no time making his feelings known on the latest developments. This was a "sad day," Flynn announced to reporters in his City Hall office, "losing a young baby like that, to go along with the baby's mother." Flynn, decrying the "senseless violence going on in Boston and communities all across this country," added, "This not only affects the Stuart family but affects the entire family of Boston. Those of us who have had the pleasure of seeing young babies born and grow up can personally feel the pain that is taking place in Mr. Stuart, the Stuart family, and all of the people of Boston."

That night, when he heard the mayor refer to him on the eleven o'clock news, Chuck's eyes filled with tears. But the tears dried quickly as the face of Francis O'Meara, chief of homicide investigations for the Suffolk County District Attorney's office, filled the screen. The medical examiner would conduct an autopsy, the homicide chief said, as a matter of routine procedure in the plan to seek a ruling that Christopher's death was a homicide. "If and when he determines it's a homicide, and if and when someone is arrested, they will be charged with two complaints of homicide."

The mayor then added, "The investigation is moving forward at a professional pace. We don't want to see any mistakes made."

Chuck used the remote control device to snap off the television. But before he went to sleep, he had one more phone call to make. He hadn't much liked what he heard when Michael was interviewed. Who knew where this would lead, once a family member started liking seeing himself on the television. So Chuck sent the word out to his family: no more comments to the press. From now on, Chuck decreed, John T. Dawley, a lawyer and old family friend, would be the only one to talk.

Dawley, a few years older than Chuck, had grown up in Revere and knew the Stuart family well. Chuck had hired him, as soon as he began thinking clearly again after his surgery, to handle financial and other details, such as the life insurance claims for his wife, and the complicated paperwork on insurance for the car and for Carol's stolen jewelry. True to form, Chuck had not hired some hometown drudge to handle his affairs: Dawley, after earning his stripes as one of the assistant prosecutors in the office of Suffolk County District Attorney Newman Flanagan, had settled into a prestigious Boston firm, White, Inker & Aronson. He still maintained friendly ties to the DA's office. Indeed, when Chuck Stuart hired him from his hospital bed, Dawley had just finished a stint as campaign treasurer for the unsuccessful bid of John Flanagan, one of the DA's seven children, for a city council seat.

To reporters, Dawley described his role as assisting in "in interpreting things like the significance of what doctors, police, or district attorneys" might tell Chuck or his family. But it soon went further than that. As he recovered, Chuck had amazed Dawley and everyone else with his meticulous attention to detail. Almost as soon as the anesthesia from his first operation wore off, nothing seemed to escape his notice; and realizing that the publicity was not going to disappear, Chuck began to rely more and more on his attorney to follow through on such matters as press relations, as well as particulars such as the inquiries that were coming in from development agents for Hollywood production studios eager to obtain his rights for a hoped-for television movie about the "Camelot couple" gunned down in the prime of their lives. Before Christopher died, he even had Dawley do research on the legal ramifications of removing life support from the baby.

To some of the hospital workers who frequented Chuck's room, it seemed the guy was always either on the phone or giving orders to someone standing at his bedside.

Leslie Harris, the public defender who had represented the first black suspect, Alan Swanson, was one of those who realized with some amazement just how obsessed Chuck had become with what was being said about him. Early in November, Harris was baffled to get a letter signed by Dawley that threatened to sue him for "slander of Charles Stuart and causing pain and suffering to the estate of Carol Stuart."

Harris finally tracked down the apparent source of Chuck's complaint. At a recent community meeting, Harris—whose charges of police scapegoating of Swanson had been widely publicized just a few weeks earlier—happened to be discussing a murder case in New Hampshire in which the victim, coincidentally, was a seven-months pregnant woman who had been killed by her husband. Amid speculation on such a crime, Harris had offered several possible motives, including the possibility that the baby was someone else's.

All Harris could guess was that someone had overheard part of the conversation and somehow it had been relayed to Chuck at Boston City Hospital, where he assumed Harris had been referring to him. After the initial letter, Harris never heard another word on the threatened lawsuit. But in the hospital, Chuck was telling friends that he liked the idea of having a lawyer on duty and thought he could continue it indefinitely once he got out.

SIXTEEN

Matthew

One member of Chuck's family stayed conspicuously away from Chuck's bedside. Matthew.

Wondering if he was ever going to see the $10,000 Chuck had promised him, Matthew went about his daily routine, driving to work each weekday at Eastern Chem-Lac, the paint factory in Malden where he mixed colors and where he had recently received a raise to $10 an hour.

On Friday and Saturday nights, and sometimes on Wednesdays as well, Matthew could usually be found with friends, drinking beer and listening to heavy-metal music at the Atlantic, their favorite rock club on Revere Beach, just as he had most weekends since turning twenty-one. The only real change friends noticed—and they attributed this to shock and grief over what had happened to his older brother (Matthew never mentioned Carol, whom he disliked for putting on "airs")—was that he was drinking more than usual. Like most of the young men and women his age, Matthew was a drinker. But now friends noticed that his mood would turn black and sarcastic after four or five beers, where before it would have been ebullient and playful. And he did not like to hear mention of Chuck.

"Hey, Matt, how's your brother doing?" one acquaintance who hadn't seen him since before the shooting asked him one night about two weeks afterward at the Atlantic.

Matthew fixed him with a sneer. "What brother?" he asked in a tone that dripped with contempt.

The friend, who was aware that while Matthew looked up to Chuck, he also sometimes resented Chuck's superior attitude, stammered, "Chuck, I mean."

Matthew downed a fast swig of beer and banged the bottle on the table. "Chuckie?" he said, wiping his mouth with the back of his hand. "Poor Chuckie? Chuckie's doing just wonderful. Don't worry about Chuckie, okay?"

"Sorry, man. I was just asking."

"Don't worry about poor Chuckie," Matthew repeated sharply. Embarrassed, the interloper turned to walk back to his table. As he did, he could hear Matthew snarl over the din, *"Okay?"*

Such moments were easily brushed aside by those close to Matthew, who believed they would pass as the Stuart family began to put their life back together. But there was another change in Matthew's usually laid-back personality that genuinely puzzled some friends, and that was the way he reacted to the celebrity status the shooting had brought to the Stuarts. In the immediate aftermath of the shooting, until Chuck hired the lawyer, Michael Stuart had emerged as the family spokesman; Michael's number was fixed on reporters' Rolodexes along with that of Steve Reardon, the cousin who owned Reardon's tavern on Broadway in Revere and who could always be counted on for a quote.

Largely ignored by the news media, Matthew often complained about the intense press attention on the case. But the fact was, few people outside his immediate circle of friends were paying attention to Matthew, the most gregarious of the Stuarts—and, he knew secretly, snickering in his beer, the one with a real story to tell, if he ever chose to tell it.

"I know Chuckie better than anyone," Matthew boasted a little over a week after the shooting. And then Matthew did something that amazed his listener. He laughed uproariously and continued laughing to the point where he was obviously forcing it.

Aside from such instances, however, few friends thought enough of Matthew's sullen behavior to remark much on it, even though it was very unusual for him not simply to let others know what was on his mind. "Things are tough all over," as the young men of Matt's age in Revere had begun to say sarcastically to each other. Unlike their older brothers, Matt's peers had no realistic visions of a future that was appreciably different from the droning present—not in the Revere of the late 1980s, where even the Wonderland dog-racetrack out on the highway wasn't hiring, where even laborers' jobs were becoming hard to find and then to keep, as the New England economy soured. Like Matt, many of them still lived at home with their parents, holed up in their boyhood bedrooms with a VCR on the bureau beside an amplifier pumping Arrowsmith CD's through bookshelf speakers at fifty watts a channel. By the time they were approaching their mid-twenties, all that some of them could point to as a solid improvement in their living conditions was that at least they had their bedrooms to themselves finally. Night school and a twenty-thousand-dollar car danced in these young men's pipe dreams, not split levels in the far suburbs with swimming pools in the yard.

Beyond that, it was well known that Matt shouldered, along with his brother Mark, the next youngest, who also lived at home, the burden of caring for their father, who had been diagnosed a few years earlier with Parkinson's disease. Recently, the senior Charles Stuart's health had deteriorated to the point where he needed help to dress and even to get up in the night to go to the bathroom. Then, early in the fall, Dorothy Stuart, Matthew's mother, was in the hospital with an operation for breast cancer—and this happened right around the time his girlfriend dumped him. Then his sister-in-law was blown away and his brother shot in October. Things were tough all over, all right, but the young men who knew Matt Stuart in Revere realized that things were especially tough for him. So, few of them were unduly surprised when he announced in November that he was going to California for a while to "think things over." Janet had a relative who lived near Los Angeles and had a spare bedroom. With Mark at home to take care of their father, Matt fled with his troubles to California.

*   *   *

Back in Boston, the news media had run out of steam on the Stuart case as the police failed to come up with a suspect. But they hadn't lost interest. The story was one of those that made the competitive juices flow—at the *Herald*, the publisher, Patrick Purcell, a tabloid veteran who had once run the *New York Post*, said that the Son of Sam murder case of the late 1970s was the only thing he had experienced that remotely approached it in competitive intensity. Purcell, who liked to tweak his daintier colleagues at the *Globe*, was already inordinately pleased that fall as the *Herald*'s once anemic circulation edged up to the 370,000 level, especially since he attributed some of the recent growth not to the usual staples of tabloid journalism, crime and sports, but to beefed-up coverage of political and international news, such as the collapse of communism in Eastern Europe. So when the Stuart story broke, Purcell was amused, and not a little worried, when the *Globe* jumped on it with both feet. "We're the tabloid—it was supposed to be our kind of story," he said. "But the *Globe* was as aggressive as at any time in their history on this story. They saw it as their opportunity to reestablish their presence in local hard news."

But by the second week of November, with no break in the investigation, there was little to report besides rumors. And, as editors in print and broadcast newsrooms would later find themselves saying, quite defensively, rumors are not news. Especially not the famous rumor that everyone was now starting to hear—the rumor that Chuck Stuart's story stank.

The rumor was pervasive on the sometimes overlapping news media and law enforcement grapevines, and flashes of it were even traveling on the circuits out of town. No one had hard information, of course. No one really could point to anything solid. It was more in the form of gossip that began to sound compelling, and sometimes it was just in the way people snickered cynically over those stories about the "Camelot couple." Everyone knew there was no such thing, and never had been. There were these persistent whispers of Chuck's cocaine use, intimations of a girlfriend in the shadows, not to mention all that clucking from the hospital rumor mill about the way the guy was behaving, like a tinhorn Mafia don instead of a crime victim. A cop's wink-and-a-nod after three late-night beers with a reporter took on significance in the light of day. Everybody, it seemed, was in on the gossip except the readers of Boston newspapers and the viewers of television news.

At the *Globe*'s headquarters out along the freeway, a contingent of reporters, united in their concern about that worrisome irony, marched into a top editor's office to demand action, but they soon marched out again in disarray, with the admonition "We don't print rumors" ringing sharply in their ears. At the *Herald* building a few blocks from the combat zone in downtown Boston, the editor, an Australian named Ken Chandler, went into the corner office of his boss, Purcell, to confide: "There's something wrong with this story."

Chandler had been the recipient of the loudest complaints of all, which were coming from a corner of the *Herald*'s congested city room where thirty-four-year-old Michelle Caruso, who had taught English before deciding to become a reporter, and who prided herself on having "street smarts," was telling anyone who would listen exactly what she thought of Chuck Stuart's story. Like other reporters and cops, Caruso (whose name would nevertheless appear on many subsequent stories that would name Willie Bennett as the chief suspect) had been troubled by the odd tone of Chuck's taped conversation with the state police dispatcher on the night of the shooting. She had even enlisted a colleague, reporter L. Kim Tan, to accompany her on a drive retracing the path Chuck supposedly took on the night he and Carol were shot. Like others, she could not understand how he could have failed to find help sooner. None of the news accounts after the shooting had pointed out what was patently obvious to anyone taking Chuck's alleged route: Except for a few isolated areas that had to be actually sought out, the area was teeming with people and traffic. A gravely wounded man seeking attention for his dying wife would have had to hide to avoid encountering it.

Pressed to come up with facts to support her hunch, Caruso got on the phone to a good source in the past, assistant district attorney Francis O'Meara.

"Something's wrong," she insisted.

But O'Meara told her she was barking up the wrong tree. Everyone with an ounce of brains had first considered the husband as the suspect, but it just wasn't in the cards on this one, not with the way that guy had been wounded.

"You have got to understand," O'Meara said, discussing Chuck's wounds, "seven vital organs have been damaged. This was no surface nick."

"But Franny, if it was a shot in the leg or foot, no one would have believed him. He had to do *some* damage." She became insistent. "Well, are you going to do anything about it?"

She heard O'Meara laughing on the other end. "I might be inclined to agree with you, if we didn't have another lead in another direction," the assistant district attorney confided.

"You got a suspect?" she demanded.

"I'm not talking suspects. I'm talking about a lead in another direction."

This was clearly bullshit. The name of Willie Bennett had already leapt to the reporter's mind. It was one of the names police sources had been tossing around for days. It was one of the names you heard from the people on the street in Mission Hill. She had already looked up the clips on the guy, the legless cab driver shooting, the shooting at the cops. She knew Willie had been out of Walpole for a year.

So she tried her luck. "You don't mean Willie Bennett, do you?"

O'Meara wasn't laughing now. "I'm not going to comment on any names you throw at me," he told her.

He didn't have to. He could have told her she was nuts, that he never heard of any Willie Bennett. He could have told her that. She interpreted the fact that he did not as a sign that she had hit the nail on the head.

For a while, for too long as it turned out, she failed to pursue her hunch about Chuck.

Neither she nor the few other reporters who were expressing doubts were aware of other disquieting matters that would have had them pounding on their editors' desks had they known, particularly one piece of gossip traveling along the area's elaborate police grapevines about Chuck's love life, for one thing.

Suburban police in Willis had already officially alerted their counterparts in Boston to the talk about Chuck's close friendship with Debby Allen; a routine check with Chuck's friends and co-workers quickly confirmed the existence, if not exact nature, of that relationship. Certainly, the two had been seen together after work on occasion. In fact, police talked to Debby herself a week after the murder. She told them it had been an innocent friendship. Debby said she was convinced that Chuck was deeply in love with Carol.

But by the second week of November, a much more troublesome bit of gossip was being traded among the cops and their friends. On November 11, only a little over three weeks after Carol's murder, a suburban cop passed on to Boston some amazing scuttlebutt: Apparently someone was going around openly saying that Chuck Stuart had been looking for a hit man to kill his wife. The suburban cops had tracked down the rumor to a suburban man who knew David MacLean, the Lowell truck driver whom Chuck had approached at the end of the summer. Yes, said the man, MacLean had told him, and other people too, about the conversation in which Chuck had asked if he knew someone who could "take care of . . . you know, kill" his wife.

A Boston detective, skeptical of such incredible information from a suburban cop, looked up MacLean's number and phoned him, but the flustered trucker immediately denied ever saying such a thing, and the detective let the matter drop without a follow-up call— or without leaving a number in case MacLean wanted to phone back with a change of mind.

The information was discounted and routinely filed away, lost in the excitement: The same day they checked out the MacLean rumor, Boston police believed they had finally found their man.

SEVENTEEN

The Detectives

By now, cops had eliminated every other suspect on their short list and Willie Bennett stood alone at the top. However, even under the typically minimal standards required by a grand jury to accede to a prosecutor's request for a criminal indictment, claiming what the police and district attorney's office knew to be so—that it was perfectly obvious Willie did it—would not suffice. The media and the public expected an arrest any day. Any case with this much publicity starts to smell bad after weeks gone by without an arrest. But it wasn't that easy. Evidence, of course, was necessary.

So when the information about what Officer Holland had heard from Maralynda Whitney, Eric's mother, found its way to the ears of homicide detectives, coming as it did with the magic name of Willie Bennett attached, they uttered the word "Bingo." Responding to the alarm, some of them rushed to the smoke and started fanning the flames.

The week after the teenage boys had gathered to play Nintendo in Joey Bennett's room, Dereck Jackson got a phone call from the friend he had told about it. Eric Whitney was calling to warn that homicide detectives wanted to question him about Willie's involvement.

"I don't know nothing about it," Dereck insisted.

But the process had moved well along in the homicide unit. The cops were out looking for Dereck. On Friday, November 3, the boy was called out of class at McKinley Technical High School. When he walked into the principal's office, two Boston police officers were sitting there along with his principal and guidance counselor. The school authorities had the presence of mind to advise the frightened boy that he did not have to answer questions if he chose not to do so. The officers suggested that Dereck come along with them. Dereck said he would rather not.

Shrugging, one of them, Officer William Dunn, the cop well known in the Mission Hill projects, asked to use the phone.

Standing at the principal's desk as the teenager sat stiffly nearby, Dunn spoke quietly for a minute to Lt. Peter J. O'Malley, the homicide detective who was in charge of the Stuart investigation. Dunn then cupped his palm over the mouthpiece and looked directly at Dereck. "Peter says you can come now, or you can come down later and you won't have a choice," the policeman informed the boy.

Dereck declined politely. Without a warrant, there was little more the cops could do. They left.

After school, Dereck ran into seventeen-year-old Leroy Cox, one of the boys who had been there when Joey Bennett supposedly implicated his uncle Willie. By now, the boys who had been in Joey's room fooling around knew that they faced a very tricky jam, and what Leroy had to say didn't make Dereck breathe any easier: The cops had already hauled Leroy down to homicide headquarters, where Detective O'Malley gave him something to think about, coldly informing the boy that he would be sent to prison for twenty years, as an accessory to murder, if he lied about what he knew of Willie Bennett's involvement. On the other hand, O'Malley had suggested, he would "get off easy" if he told the truth.

In a panic after talking to Leroy, Dereck found Eric Whitney, and was dismayed to learn that Eric had already met with police. Eric knew what the cops wanted, and pleaded with his friend to cooperate when he was brought in for questioning. "Dereck, you got to say this, or you're not leaving—tell them Willie came in high with a .38 in his hand and told how he shot the Stuarts."

Dereck, dreading the inevitable, did not have to wait long. That night, the cops picked up both him and Eric and drove them down to homicide in South Boston. They took Eric into a separate room. In the adjoining room, Dereck sat facing five officers, among them Dunn and Trent Holland. Detective O'Malley did most of the talking.

It became sickeningly clear to Dereck that the gathering in Joey's room right after the Stuart shooting had assumed a bizarre life of its own. According to what the police evidently had heard from various people, not only had Joey Bennett bragged about his uncle doing the shooting, but Willie himself had come into the room to actually show the boys how he pointed the gun. Yet, Dereck knew, it was pure fiction.

Astonished that the pot-addled joshing in Joey's room had come to this, Dereck insisted to the cops that all he had heard Joey do was mumble something and laugh when asked about the shooting. "I never heard Willie say nothing," the frightened youth added as he faced the detective across a table in the harsh fluorescent glare of the interrogation room.

O'Malley snorted. *Nobody never knows nothing*. To police, that was always the way with "these people," as the residents of the housing projects were routinely called. But of course, with a little prompting, all of a sudden the truth usually would finally spill out.

Dereck said he wanted a lawyer, but O'Malley scoffed at the request. "You don't need no lawyer," he said. "You're not under arrest."

As the questions went on incessantly, Dereck kept insisting that he knew nothing about Willie Bennett being linked to the Stuart shooting. All he and the others had been doing in Joey's room was playing Nintendo and bullshitting, he insisted. Furious, O'Malley put on the pressure. "I'm going to pin your fucking ass for twenty years in Walpole—you'll *never* get out," the detective shouted.

At that moment, Dereck turned nervously to watch Officer Dunn, with whom he remembered several unpleasant street encounters in the past, push back his chair and leave the room. Dereck was terrified that they were going to put him alone in a dark room with Dunn, a former Marine in his late thirties who, at six feet two and over 250 pounds, had the build and, as the teenagers in the projects well knew, the temperament of a grizzly bear.

But in a few minutes, Dunn thumped back through the door with a badly shaken Eric Whitney in tow. Dunn had already made sure the teenager had seen the pair of brass knuckles the cops liked to flash to young suspects. This had had its effect—stammering, Eric had blurted out that he had been in the apartment and heard Willie Bennett confess, in detail, that he had, as Eric told it, "busted" the Stuarts.

Aware of Eric's story, O'Malley didn't miss a beat when the two boys were sitting together warily at the table. "You're fucking lying," he snarled at Dereck. "What you said happened doesn't sound right. What Eric said happened sounds like the truth," the detective said. Dereck, who was not sure he knew *what* Eric had said, insisted that his story was the truth. He even offered to take a lie detector test, which only made O'Malley laugh.

"The only lie detector I have is right here," the detective said, pointing to a smiling Officer Dunn. Both boys gulped.

O'Malley sat back in his chair and reiterated what would happen to someone who did not tell the "truth" in such a serious matter: "Walpole for twenty years," he repeated, and then added to Dereck: "You listen good to what Eric has to say."

Taking the cue, Eric stammered: "Don't you remember you told me what Willie Bennett said?"

Frightened as he was, Dereck had been managing to stand his ground. But now, with the cops glowering at him and threatening to send him away until he was thirty-seven years old, and with his friend quaking beside him practically in tears, Dereck decided with trepidation to take the path of least resistance.

Yes, he conceded with a weary sigh, Willie Bennett had admitted the Stuart shootings that day in front of the boys.

It was clearly the answer the cops wanted. Briskly, O'Malley began asking formal questions, and had both teenagers speak their answers into a tape recorder. When he was through, O'Malley asked Dereck one more time for the record, "Is that the truth now, Dereck?" Nodding, the teenager swore it was.

Just before they were told they could leave, O'Malley flipped a twenty-dollar bill across and said, "Here, go buy yourself something at McDonald's."

That night, Dereck kept seeing that twenty-dollar bill and the smug satisfaction on the face of the cop who had tossed it casually over to him. Over and over, his mind replayed the scene as if it were from a old movie—and in fact it was, only in the movies it was something on the order of "Here, go buy yourself a cup of coffee." Like everyone else in the projects, Dereck spent a lot of time, day and night, in front of the television. He had probably seen more movies than most film critics, and he knew this line always meant that its recipient was scum. Twenty-buck scum.

Troubled and ashamed, Dereck decided at last that he had to do the right thing. He phoned Eric, who seemed equally upset, and told him, "The bottom line is, we got to tell the truth. I don't feel right." Eric agreed. The next morning, Saturday, Eric phoned Officer Holland, his mother's friend, and told the patrolman that he and Dereck wanted to come in to make another statement. "We want to come back and tell the truth," he said.

Later in the morning, Holland brought Eric and Dereck back in to homicide headquarters. Holland took Dereck into one room while a very angry O'Malley fixed a contemptuous stare at Eric in the next.

As they tried to retract their statements, the boys were acutely aware of just how tangled the lies had become. The cops kept up their disquieting allusions to Walpole for lying in a homicide case. To teenagers from the Boston projects, "Walpole" was one of those words like "Sing-Sing" in the old movies—as a threat, it did not need much elaboration. But the cops kept at it.

"They don't play around at Walpole," one of them told Dereck while O'Malley questioned Eric in the adjoining room. Another officer laughed and said a good-looking boy like him would need to be especially careful in the prison showers. Gleefully, he warned the aghast teenager, "Don't drop your soap in jail!"

In the next room, O'Malley was disgusted with Eric having second thoughts about his story. "I'm tired of fucking with you," the detective told the boy, who watched in horror as he began filling out an arrest sheet.

This had the desired effect. "Stop!" Eric cried, certain that he was headed straight for prison. "Stop! I'm lying again! The tape is true!"

With that, O'Malley had Dereck hustled in to confront his sweating friend. Obviously, many lies had been told. Retracting their

stories of the previous day would be conceding making false statements. The cops noted that the criminal code had a term for such
an action: *perjury*.

Eric pointed to a police booking sheet that O'Malley had put
on the table and told Dereck, "If we don't stick with the story,
they're going to arrest us. They are not playing. We're not leaving
here. They are going to book us right now. They're saying twenty
years. Man, I want to leave here."

More intimidated than ever, now that he was back inside police
headquarters, where sometimes the only way to leave was in cuffs
riding in the back of a sheriff's van, Dereck felt his resolve disappear. Chagrined, desperate only to see the outside of the police
station once more, he capitulated. Anxiously, both boys agreed to
stay with the stories they had sworn to the day before implicating
Willie Bennett. When they were through, Officer Holland gave them
a ride back to Mission Hill.

A week later, the homicide detectives believed they had accu-
mulated enough preliminary evidence to make their move with search
warrants for the residences where they believed Willie Bennett spent
most of his time: his mother's and his sister's apartments in Mission
Hill, and his girlfriend's house in suburban Burlington. The task of
actually compiling the evidence on Bennett had fallen to O'Malley,
a detective for the past ten years and a police officer for twenty-eight
years in all. To get court approval for the searches, a routine matter
once a reasonably clear suspect had come into focus, O'Malley
needed to specify in an affidavit what the police expected to find,
and why they were looking for it.

On Friday, November 10, O'Malley sat down at the IBM
Selectric typewriter on his desk at the homicide unit and began
pecking away, first describing the undisputed facts of how the murder
was discovered after Chuck Stuart's frantic call to the dispatcher,
and then adding everything that had been learned from interrogations
of the teenage boys and other Mission Hill residents:

> . . . it was determined that the exact location of the robbery
> and shooting was on Mindoro Street, adjacent to an aban-
> doned building, formerly known to Boston police and area
> residents as the Station Cafe, a short distance from Station
> Street.
>
> On November 3, 1989, at 9:29 P.M. your affiant inter-

viewed Dereck Jackson of 185 Cabot Street, Roxbury. Jackson is 17 years old and is a student at McKinley Tech. This interview was tape recorded. Jackson told me that on Tuesday, October 24, 1989, he went to visit his friend Joey Bennett at 7 Alton Court, Roxbury. . . . Joey Bennett is the nephew of Willie Bennett.

Jackson stated that he was in Joey Bennett's room with David Brimage, Mike Williams, and Joey Bennett, when Joey Bennett showed the group a newspaper article that stated Willie Bennett had kidnapped a M.D.C. officer and did a number of robberies and killings. He said that the article quoted Willie Bennett as saying he wasn't going to be taken alive. Jackson remembered seeing Willie (in newspaper article) being taken away by undercover officers. My own investigation had uncovered what I believe to be one of the newspaper articles described above (a copy of which is attached and incorporated herein by reference).

The next day, Wednesday afternoon, October 25, 1989, Jackson stated he was at Joey Bennett's apartment with David Brimage, Michael Williams, Leroy Cox, and Ronald Ferguson and Joey Bennett. The group was in Joey Bennett's room when Willie came in. Willie Bennett said that he shot the Stuarts. He told the group that he was wearing a black Adidas jumpsuit and got in the car and told the Stuarts not to look at him and *not to look in the rear-view mirror.* He made them drive straight to the Station Cafe and took their money. The guy made a motion and Willie Bennett said you're 5-0 and he shot them. Jackson also stated that Willie Bennett then demonstrated with the gun in his hand how he had shot them . . .

O'Malley went on to describe the evidence police had obtained from a Mission Hill woman who had told them of encountering Willie bragging about a shooting:

On November 1, 1989, at about 9:20 P.M., your affiant, at the Homicide Office, had a conversation with Tony Jackson, b/f, dob 5/26/69, of 50 Tobin Court. . . . Also present at the time were Detectives Thomas and Halstead.

Jackson states that on Thursday, October 26, 1989, or Friday, October 27, 1989, at about 7:00, 7:30 P.M., at 50 Tobin Court, her brother Bruce Jackson and Willie Bennett were drinking in the front hallway of the building. They were drinking 40 oz. "Private Stock." They had two bottles. Bruce Jackson left to meet his girlfriend and Tony Jackson was outside with her child and the dog. Willie Bennett started to pound the door and walls. Jackson asked him what was the matter. Bennett stated that he wanted her to promise not to tell anyone what he was about to tell her and she stated that she would not make the promise. Bennett stated, forget it.

Bennett remained quiet for about 15 minutes and she was playing with her child and the dog. Bennett came and started talking to her. Jackson told Bennett that she would not tell anyone and Bennett stated that the bullet was not meant for the lady, it was meant for the man. The man owed him some money and the man was not willing to pay Bennett, but still wanted to buy a bundle of heroin. (A bundle costs $150).

Jackson stated that she had known Willie Bennett for about 8 years. She stated that she has seen Bennett wearing a black and red running suit. Wears the running suit 3 or 4 times a week and has seen him wear a variety of different hats. She stated that she did not notice if he wore gloves. Jackson stated that she has lived in the area for 15 years.

On November 4, 1989, your affiant interviewed David Brimage, of 300 Ruggles Street, Roxbury. Brimage is a student at Madison Park High School. The interview took place at the Homicide Division of the Boston Police Department. Brimage stated that on October 24, 1989, while at Joey Bennett's apartment he recalls Joey Bennett saying his uncle did the shooting. Joey Bennett tried to convince Mike, Dereck, and Junior that his uncle, Willie Bennett, did it. He showed them articles from old newspapers about his Uncle Willie. He showed them an older silver-colored gun with 3 empty and 3 full chambers. Joey tried hard to convince the three of them that Willie did it. Joey told them that Willie has a red and black jogging suit. Willie came into the room and saw Dereck reading his news clippings. He started to say something, left the room, and called Joey out. The three of them could hear Willie talking to Joey and mentioning the gun. Joey came back and put the gun and clippings away. . . .

The police fully expected to find what they would be looking for while searching the Bennett residences: physical evidence linking Willie Bennett to the crime—specifically the running suit, the murder weapon, and the things that Chuck told the police the murderer had stolen (Carol's wallet, her purse, her ruby ring, and her engagement ring, as well as Chuck's gold watch). With the volume of witness testimony he had outlined in the supporting affidavit, O'Malley had no problem getting a judge to issue the warrants. Within hours, O'Malley's affidavit was being avidly passed around among police involved in the Stuart case. Before long, the affidavit would be the foundation on which the police "sources" would inform reporters that Willie Bennett was the man. Talking to reporters, the sources would quote directly from O'Malley's words summarizing the statements of the witnesses.

To the news media, hungry for a break in a sensational case that had the competitive juices flowing as nothing before in recent memory, the affidavit presented a impressive amount of circumstantial evidence from a number of witnesses, all pointing the finger right at Willie Bennett. Furthermore, it was all on official documents, all duly filed with the search warrants in Superior Court. The only trouble was, none of it was true.

E I G H T E E N

The Suspect

Since he was so well known to the police, who are understandably alert to the whereabouts of a self-described cop-hater with an established propensity for violent behavior, it was no surprise to anyone that Willie Bennett's name had been on a list of potential suspects in a shooting that occurred right on his own turf. "If he wasn't currently behind bars, Willie was just one of those guys who automatically made the list any time you had a good crime in the neighborhood," one cop noted.

But Willie was surprised by the unholy vengeance with which his well-deserved reputation suddenly caught up with him. On parole, trying hard to keep his head down in the heat that roared into the projects after the Stuart shooting, Willie learned just how visible he had become. Like any other denizen who routinely runs afoul of the law in a place where running afoul of the law in one way or another is a fairly ordinary activity, Willie found out he couldn't hide from his past. On four separate occasions during the last week of October, he was stopped, searched, and questioned. But they never had enough to go beyond that.

On Halloween, Officer Dunn, accompanied by a parole officer, Paul Hartford, went back to Bennett's mother's apartment with more questions. According to police, Pauline sat in the kitchen and told her son's parole officer that Willie had lived with her since getting out of Walpole the year before, and usually hung around the Projects. As Pauline was speaking, Willie's girlfriend, Faye, entered the room. Under questioning, Faye told the officers that Willie had spent the previous week with her at her home in suburban Burlington. She said it was ridiculous to think that Willie had anything to do with the shooting of Carol Stuart. Furthermore, she said, Willie did not even own a jogging suit like the one they were looking for.

The next day, clearly worried by the intensity that his mother and girlfriend told him the police were showing in their questioning, Willie managed to flag down his parole officer on Parker Street, a few blocks from where Carol Stuart had been murdered. He tried to explain the situation, saying that he had been hoping to get his life together while living in Burlington with Faye and looking for a job. They were expecting their own child in four months, Willie said, insisting he had absolutely nothing to do with the murder.

The police clearly believed otherwise by that point. Even as Willie was seeking reassurance from his parole officer, a net was starting to descend over him.

On the morning of November 11, just before three o'clock, Willie's sister, Paula, woke up to a loud banging in her second-floor apartment at 26 Tobin Court in the Projects. About a half dozen police rushed in when she opened the door.

"Willie ain't here," she hollered, knowing that was who they were after.

"We know where Willie is, don't worry about that," an officer replied, holding up a search warrant. "What we want is the shit Willie took from the Stuarts."

Paula, with one of her children cowering behind her nightgown, stepped aside to let the police in to search. They spent forty-five minutes rummaging through closets and drawers, but took nothing with them when they left.

After searching Paula's apartment, the police officers joined up with a larger group of cops and raided the apartment of Willie's mother, Pauline, at 7 Alton Court, which is only a few minutes' walk from the spot where Carol and Chuck Stuart were found shot.

At first, the officers feared that Willie might be there, but they relaxed after thoroughly searching the large apartment, which had rooms on the first, second, and third floors connected by a stairwell. As Pauline Bennett tried to quiet an autistic grandchild who was terrified at the disorder in the middle of the night, police banged their way through the things in her apartment. They pulled out drawers and dumped them on the floor, overturned boxes, and knocked racks of clothes from closet hangers.

By the time they were through, officers could be seen in the dim light of dawn hauling out to their cars big plastic trash bags full of things from Willie's mother's apartment. Among them were bundles of letters addressed to Pauline from a relative; letters to Willie, who seemed to have a sentimental attachment to his prison correspondence; batches of family photographs; stacks of personal papers belonging to Willie and other members of the household; an appointment book; a woman's wallet and purse (neither of which remotely resembled the description of the ones taken from Carol Stuart); and, from the bedroom of Joey Bennett, among the letters and expired motor vehicle registrations and other claptrap a teenager tends to accumulate, a newspaper clipping from the 1981 arrest of Willie Bennett, with the headline proclaiming Willie's vow not to be taken alive. The officer who found it on top of Joey's bureau was appalled to see that the boy was so proud of his uncle that he displayed the clipping in a picture frame.

From Joey's dresser, police also took a yellow slip of paper with the word *Willie* scrawled at the top, listing two phone numbers: one for Faye, who police knew was Willie's current girlfriend, and the other for Dolly, who police would discover was another.

At about the same time, there was another raid going on in Burlington, a town with a large population of working-class blacks northwest of Boston. A task force of local and Boston cops descended on the white split-level home of Faye Nelson on Winn Street, where they expected they would find Willie himself. A few days earlier, looking for any reason to arrest Bennett, detectives were delighted to discover during a routine computer search that he had recently defaulted on a warrant issued for a simple motor vehicle violation.

They knew that would be sufficient reason to put the cuffs on him and take him to jail when they found him—an encounter that, the police hoped, given the man's record at responding to surprises from the cops, would occur when Willie was fast asleep.

It did. At three o'clock in the morning, Willie's girlfriend, five months pregnant, answered the pounding on the door. Though she had anticipated a visit by police looking for Willie, she was astonished and terrified by the sheer force of their arrival. About a dozen cops in riot gear, all with their guns drawn, noisily rushed into the house the moment she cracked open the door. Outside, on the two-lane street, a swarm of police cars sat with their emergency lights flashing red and blue. She counted at least ten cars in all. Already, neighbors in their night clothes were sticking out their heads onto nearby front porches to investigate the commotion.

"Where is he? Where the fuck is he?" a couple of officers were demanding, making Faye feel as if they thought she was trying to hide him. Actually, all she was doing was trying to avoid being trampled as they barged around her. One of them displayed what she supposed was a search warrant, and snatched it away before she could read it.

The cops seemed to know their way around. Given Willie's reputation, they had come prepared for a fight. A group of them ran for the lower-level bedroom, where half of them crouched outside the partially shut door with their guns ready while the others stomped inside. In a few seconds, there were so many cops crammed in the door frame that they could barely push the groggy, handcuffed Willie Bennett into the hall. Faye, in tears at the time, would later think that the cops falling over each other to get Willie through the bedroom door resembled a Three Stooges routine.

As at the two other addresses, police rummaged through the house. But Willie hadn't really moved in—in fact, he and Faye were spending more time at his mother's place in Mission Hill than they were in Burlington—and besides the infamous Willie himself, now under escort by a grim phalanx of armed riot policemen on the charge of driving in Charlestown while his license was revoked, the cops didn't come away with much. The inventory of the property taken as a result of the search of the Burlington home had hardly made it worthwhile for so many officers to get out of bed on overtime that morning. It listed but a single item, which could have belonged to

Willie, who had no gun with him, or could have as easily been dropped in the commotion by one of the officers: "1 (one) 38-cal live round of ammunition."

With Swanson already virtually eliminated as a possible suspect, even though *he* was still languishing in jail on a frivolous charge, the commotion in the Mission Hill Projects that accompanied the arrest of Willie Bennett sent major alarms into the news media, and the Sunday papers brimmed with it.

The *Herald* treated the arrest with a blaring front-page headline: "Police Nab #1 Suspect in Stuart-Killing Case." The story began: "A convicted cop-shooter and armed robber from Roxbury—who is considered a 'prime' suspect in the shootings of Charles and Carol Ann Stuart—was apprehended by police yesterday after a series of dramatic search raids, sources said."

The story made a point to note that Assistant District Attorney O'Meara refused to confirm or deny that Bennett had been arrested. It quoted Bennett's mother, Pauline, as saying she had been told by police that her son was believed to have been involved in the Stuart murders.

"They say he's a suspect. He's been in trouble before. He knew he was a suspect. He was nervous and upset about it," Willie's distraught mother told a *Herald* reporter. "I guess they feel he's capable of doing it. The least little thing that happens, they're going to blame it on him."

The *Globe* treatment, which nevertheless ran at the top of the front page on Sunday, began: "A paroled convict who is the primary suspect in the slaying of Carol Stuart . . . was arrested by police on an unrelated charge early yesterday." Said the Globe account, "police would not comment for the record on Bennett's connection with the Stuart case."

Although they conceded that police hadn't found any evidence linking Willie to the Stuart murders, the accounts of his arrest in the papers and on television went on at some length. They described the violent criminal past of the newly identified "prime suspect," for example, quoting Thomas Horgan, an assistant district attorney who had prosecuted him in the 1981 armed robbery and assault on a police officer: "He is a danger to all law enforcement."

Even the people closest to Willie had to go along with that one, though. "He doesn't like cops," his sister Diane conceded with a shrug. But he wasn't being accused of disliking cops, she had to point out. He was being accused of shooting the pregnant lady and her husband.

All at once, and virtually without attribution other than an occasional fleeting allusion to "sources familiar with the case," Willie Bennett was designated as the primary suspect in the murders by a news media that suddenly found the Stuart story had come alive once again, and the chase was on. The next day, they advanced the scenario by quoting "sources close to the investigation" who said that Bennett would be charged with an unrelated robbery when he appeared in court that day. But the *Globe* also noted:

> According to sources familiar with the investigation, witnesses who are cooperating with the police assert that Bennett admitted his involvement in the shooting of the Stuarts during conversations with them. Witnesses have also told police they had seen Bennett wearing a black sweatsuit similar to the one described by Stuart as being worn by the man who shot him and his wife. . . . Sources familiar with the investigation say the witnesses have attributed to Bennett statements that only the gunman and Stuart would know had taken place.

The *Herald*, meanwhile, found a woman whose statements apparently were the source of some police suspicions about Bennett—a woman who "allegedly told police she saw Bennett . . . holding a silver gun on the night the Stuarts were shot." However, the account went on, "in an interview with the *Herald*, the woman denied that she has implicated Bennett in the Stuart case. The woman claims she told police she had seen Bennett with a gun one night about a week prior to the shootings, but she denied seeing him on the night of the shootings.

"The woman said police are pressuring her to implicate Bennett. 'They said I seen Willie Bennett running the night of the killing. I know one thing. I didn't see him no night of no murder. I only told police the truth. They think I know more.' "

This assertion seemed to knock out a major underpinning of the police case against Bennett as the reporters knew it so far. But it was soon lost in the chase.

On Monday, a real charge was lodged against Willie, who was

arraigned in district court in suburban Brookline on an outstanding complaint of stealing $642 at gunpoint from a video store there on October 2. He pleaded not guilty.

Referring to Willie as a "mad dog running amok," Louis Sabadini, an assistant district attorney of Norfolk County, where Brookline is located, demanded that the defendant be held on cash bail of $50,000. The prosecutor said witnesses had identified Willie as the robber from a photograph. Joel Goodman, Willie's lawyer at the proceeding, protested that $5,000 was typical bail for the charge. Judge Henry P. Crowley came closer to the district attorney's position than the defense: He set bail at $35,000 cash. Willie was taken back to jail. As had Swanson's attorney, Willie's said that his client really was being held without charge on the Stuart murders.

The next day, in a front-page story headlined "Prime Stuart Shooting Suspect Jailed," the *Herald*'s Caruso and Tan seemed to have found new support to buttress anonymous allegations that Bennett was involved in the Stuart shooting. The *Herald*'s unnamed source explained the previous discrepancy of the woman witness's statement that she hadn't in fact seen him with a gun on the night of the shootings: The woman and other witnesses were backing off their stories because they were "fearful of making statements to incriminate Bennett in the Stuart case while he was out on the streets. They were afraid of him because he's the type who'll come back and shoot you up," a source said. "He's a shooter. He'd blow your head off in a second. That was the word on the street."

The *Herald* took the occasion to note: "A source said investigators believe Stuart may be able to pick out his assailant by his voice. Bennett is said to have the same raspy 'sing-song' voice as the man who robbed and shot the Stuarts, sources have said." The same day, the *Globe*, which didn't have the problem of having earlier exhibited any second thoughts on the witnesses' statements, noted with approval that the Brookline robbery charge afforded Boston authorities an opportunity to keep Willie under lock and key until they could firmly link him to the Stuart case. "Investigators, meanwhile, plan to use the time while Bennett is held to build a stronger case against him in the Stuart shootings," the *Globe* said. "Suffolk County prosecutors and detectives probing the shootings met yesterday to map strategy for an investigative grand jury into the shootings."

*   *   *

One of the things the police learned, soon after Willie was behind bars, was that their suspect in fact had two concurrent girlfriends: Faye, and Yvonne "Dolly" Jenkins, the mother of one of his children. Faye, questioned again, told the officers that Willie, while trying to get back on his feet after prison, spent most nights at his mother's, and the rest of the time with her. But occasionally, she said, he stayed with Dolly at her apartment above a real-estate office in Roxbury.

At dinnertime on November 22, after noting a mailbox in the lobby on which the names Jenkins and Bennett appeared jointly, police raided Dolly's apartment. Among the things they removed were ten recent newspaper clippings in which Willie was mentioned as a suspect in the Stuart shootings, seven photographs of Willie and Dolly together, and a single, recent photograph of Willie by himself.

Things seemed to be moving smoothly at last for District Attorney Flanagan. In fact, the district attorney's office was now hoping to go before the grand jury within a week to bring evidence seeking an indictment of Willie Bennett for the murders of Carol and Christopher Stuart and the shooting of Charles Stuart.

But there was one vexing snag. Despite what sources were telling reporters, the witnesses upon whom investigators had built their case against Willie were not falling into line as expected. Unfortunately, one by one, they were either recanting or denying what they were said to have told police. Dereck Jackson and Eric Whitney, the two teenagers whose statements were the bedrock of the search-warrant affidavit that had led to the arrest of Willie Bennett, were among those who changed their stories, saying the police had used coercion and threats to force them to affirm their false statements.

Nevertheless, the eight ball was in place, with Willie in his accustomed place behind it. During the third week in November, police took a selection of eight color photographs of black males to Chuck Stuart's bedside. Chuck studied the pictures carefully before selecting two—one of which was a photo of Willie Bennett—as the ones who "most resembled" the gunman.

"But I would have to see the guy in person to be sure," Chuck told his visitors.

On November 22, detectives brought another batch of photos, which included the recent picture of Willie that had been taken from Yvonne's place in the raid, and sat beside Chuck's bed to ask him if any one of these looked like the man who had shot him and Carol. The police perked up when Chuck held Willie's picture and his hand began shaking.

"What's the matter, Chuck?" one officer asked.

"This," Chuck replied, handing the photograph back. "This is the best picture I've seen so far." The detectives could see that he was crying. They decided Chuck was too emotional to continue with the photo session. They left without asking him specifically if the picture that so disturbed him was of the man who did the shooting.

The latest bedside session was leaked to the press immediately. "Stuart 'Reacts' Seeing Pix of Slaying Suspect," the *Herald* declared the next morning. While noting that Chuck had not formally identified Bennett as the assailant, the story, by Michelle Caruso and L. Kim Tan, indicated that momentum was gathering against the prime suspect:

> Meanwhile, yesterday, Suffolk County prosecutors brought several witnesses who are acquainted with Bennett before a grand jury probing the Stuart shootings. About a dozen other witnesses, including Bennett's girlfriend and residents of the Mission Hill housing project where Bennett lived, also have appeared before the grand jury since last Wednesday, sources said.
>
> Sources said some of the testimony given has been harmful to Bennett. One witness testified to seeing Bennett lurking in the Mission Hill housing project with a silver gun in his right hand the night the Stuarts were robbed and shot in an abandoned area near the project. The witness allegedly saw Bennett around 10 P.M.—an hour and a half after the Stuart shootings. Stuart told police his assailant used a "silver snub-nosed revolver." Police have determined that the Stuarts were shot with a .38-caliber gun.

Unaccountably, the story failed to note what the same newspaper had reported only days earlier—that this witness had since recanted her testimony. Yet by the week before Thanksgiving, Flanagan's office still hadn't managed to compile a cogent enough case against Bennett to ask the grand jury to vote on an indictment. Meanwhile, in Superior Court in Dedham, Willie pleaded not guilty to the robbery at the Brookline video shop. Unable to meet the bail, he was taken to Norfolk County Jail to await trial.

N I N E T E E N

Lineup

At the end of November, Judith J. Lindahl, one of the court-appointed lawyers then representing Willie, asked O'Meara at Flanagan's office to give her some guidelines for getting her client into a lineup, which she expected any day. He declined, she said.

Actually, Flanagan's office had made preliminary inquiries to hospital authorities about holding a lineup at Boston City, perhaps using the auditorium, but the response wasn't even lukewarm. The hospital refused to consider it. Besides, Chuck's lawyer and spokesman Dawley told Flanagan's office that his client wasn't yet "emotionally able" to deal with confronting the suspect in person.

At Boston City, Chuck was itching to get home and busy attending to his business affairs, including the necessary forms for the insurance payments that were coming due over Carol's death. Even though he apparently had regained his spirits and overcome his shock, Chuck still surprised hospital workers who knew him. No one ever heard him mention Carol or the baby. But one nurse did hear him talking a lot about "the new car he said he was planning to buy as soon as he got out."

The day came sooner than anyone who had seen the young man on the operating table the night of the shooting could have imagined. On Tuesday morning, December 5, just two weeks before his thirtieth birthday, fifty pounds lighter than when he went in, Chuck was released from Boston City Hospital. It had been six weeks since he and his wife were shot in Mission Hill. Chuck's mother accompanied him to the front entrance. Outside, his father waited in the back seat of the car. Smiling wanly, walking slowly, the weakness from the hospital stay and the surgery readily apparent, favoring his side where he now was wearing a colostomy bag that he would have to keep on for months until his lower intestine fully healed, Chuck got gingerly into his parents' car and his mother drove him back to the house in Revere where he had grown up.

"The doctors say his condition is stable but progressive," Dawley announced to reporters when they heard Chuck was out. "The outlook is very positive. He's mobile, but he's resting. He's able to walk, but his movements are delicate. It's clear his marching orders are to take it easy."

As to the future, the lawyer said Chuck had no definite plans yet about returning to work at Kakas, or about anything else. "Plans are premature at this time," he said. "He has some soul-searching to do—he needs time to sort things out."

That was made a little less difficult, because Matthew was still in California and wasn't due back until Christmas week.

By the time he left City Hospital, his bank account was healthier than it had been in years. On December 1, Chuck had an associate deposit a check for $82,000 from John Hancock Mutual Life Insurance Co.—the proceeds from Carol's life-insurance policy at Cahners, which paid double her annual salary in the event of her accidental death. By then, he had been assured, other insurance claims were well along in the processing stage, including one he had filed on a $100,000 policy he took out on Carol after she became pregnant. There were several other claims being processed as well.

The Monday before Christmas was his thirtieth birthday. Chuck felt pretty good, and eager to start looking that way, so he phoned Bill Zecco, his downtown hairstylist, to make an appointment. Bill hadn't seen him since before the shooting; on the phone, he started offering his sympathy; Chuck was in his usual rush. Well, Bill said, he was tightly booked with the holidays ahead, but he could make some quick adjustments and squeeze him in on Thursday, if the morning was okay. Chuck said he would be there.

Acutely aware of the milestone his life was passing at the age of thirty, worried about the time he had wasted since the shooting, Chuck was fretting about his appearance—the sunken cheeks and dark circles under the eyes and the sickly pallor, but not the weight loss. Before the shooting, his weight had ballooned up almost in tandem with Carol's, but without the excuse of pregnancy. He could have stood to lose thirty of the fifty pounds he did drop in the hospital, and a man with Chuck's hearty appreciation of good food wasn't going to start complaining about the need to gain twenty pounds. Still, he could think of a lot better ways to go on a diet.

He needed cheering up. On his birthday, he headed up from Revere to a jewelry store he knew in Danvers, Ostalkiewicz Diamond Importers, where he asked to look at diamond earrings. There he acted oddly enough that the two clerks in the store remembered it months later. He asked for a magnifying glass to examine the tray of earrings, the way someone in the industry would. What's more, he had a companion, a tall, younger man in a dark leather jacket, who seemed to be even more expert about jewelry. Chuck, explaining he had recently had surgery, asked to sit down to inspect the earrings. Only after the companion nodded his assent did Chuck agree to make the purchase, a set of half-carat diamond earrings set in gold.

"How's business?" Chuck asked as a clerk, Renee French, wrote up the sales slip for the purchase price, $999.

"A little slow," she said.

"It's that way all over Massachusetts. I'm in the fur business, and it's pretty slow."

He paid with a check drawn on his and Carol's joint account. Immediately recognizing the name and address on the check, the salesclerk later recalled thinking that Chuck did not strike her as someone in a stage of mourning, even a late one. Her second thought was to wonder who the earrings were for. A girlfriend already?

On Wednesday of that week, Chuck had a little more cheering news, this time from his employers. A letter had gone out from Kakas to all of Chuck's customers, announcing that the commissions on any purchase they made while Chuck was recuperating would be credited to Chuck. His friend Pete Jaworski, the assistant general manager, signed the letter.

The next morning, it was snowing lightly in downtown Boston, just enough to dust the branches of the trees white in the Public Garden across the street when Chuck sauntered into the Spa salon for his haircut appointment. A spray of bells on the door jingled lightly as he arrived.

"Charles!" Bill Zecco was delighted to see him, but shocked by his gaunt appearance. Still, Chuck's handshake was as firm as ever.

Since several customers already were waiting in the lounge, and Bill wanted Chuck to be as comfortable as possible for a man still in the glare of publicity, he led him immediately into a small room that was used for the privacy of those men who wished to have their hair dyed. Bill wasn't sure what to say at first, but he noticed that Chuck was all business, as usual, checking his watch as he settled into the chair.

"Actually, I want to color my hair," Chuck said, looking over his shoulder at the hairstylist. "It's starting to show gray. But I don't want to change my appearance, you understand? How long will it take?"

Bill blinked. "With a trim and a coloring? Fifty minutes."

Chuck nodded. It was impressive to Bill that the man had such a firm grip on himself already, but then he supposed his relaxed manner might well be the result of medication. He had read every word in the papers about the Stuart case. The man had been through hell. Still, it seemed odd to be worrying about gray hairs at this stage of things—and he could see that Chuck only had about ten gray hairs anyway. It would be a lot simpler to yank them out than to dye them.

As he set to work on his customer's wavy brown hair, he caught Chuck's disconcerting stare in the mirror.

"Oh, by the way, I want to thank you for the card you sent me in the hospital."

Bill felt a surge of empathy that almost brought tears to his eyes. "Charles," he said, pausing with his scissors in his hand. "I just want you to know that ever since this whole awful thing happened, I have been thinking of you. I don't know if it's because I have a wife and a daughter, and I know how I would feel if something happened to them." Bill realized he was practically blubbering, but pressed nevertheless. "And I can almost imagine how you must feel, what you must be going through, and I just want you to know that you're . . . you know . . . in my thoughts, and in my prayers."

In the mirror, he saw Chuck with one eyebrow raised, studying him.

Unnerved, Bill prattled more. "And if there is anything I can ever do—"

"Thank you very much," Chuck said, cutting him off firmly.

Bill tried another tack, this time with more success. "Well, how are *you* feeling?"

At this, Chuck brightened, launching into a discourse on his bouts of surgery and on the interminable length of his hospital stay. In detail, he described his operations and the pain that still hadn't gone away. He joked about needing to gain weight, and wondered if Bill knew of a good diet to do so. People had been "incredible" to him in the hospital and afterward, Chuck said. Not only was he on full salary but he could take his good old time about coming back to work.

"What a great time of the year to be off," Chuck said with a satisfied sigh.

"I suppose," Bill replied tentatively, thinking, the man is obviously on heavy medication. He is in deep mourning and still under awful stress. That explains this behavior, which under other circumstances might be described as elation. With that thought, Bill couldn't hold back a new surge of real sympathy. "Well, as I said, Charles, I am terribly, terribly sorry for what happened to your wife."

"Thank you. Can I see the back of my hair, please?"

Flustered, Bill positioned the mirror so Chuck could inspect the trim.

Later, after Bill had colored the gray hairs, Chuck remained fixed on his appearance. "Good," he said, inspecting the dye job. "How long does it last? When should I come back?"

"Well, you should probably come back in four or five weeks."

Chuck muttered his thanks and went out to pay the receptionist the bill, which came to seventy-five dollars. Then he approached Bill with a smile, holding out his hand.

"Merry Christmas," he said, shaking it firmly and pressing cash into Bill's palm, as if tipping a maitre d'.

When Chuck went out into the snow, Bill looked down and saw that he had a fifty-dollar bill in his hand.

The day after Christmas, over the objections of Bennett's court-appointed lawyer Robert Sheketoff, who continued to insist that police had to date produced not a shred of evidence linking his client to the murder of Carol Stuart and her baby, Flanagan's office got an order from Superior Court directing Bennett to appear in a police lineup.

Two days later, a city car picked up Chuck in Revere early in the afternoon and brought him to police headquarters on Berkeley Street. There, he was taken to a the dimly lit lineup viewing room and invited to sit in front of a long one-way mirror that looked into the adjoining room where eight black males—seven of them employees of the police department and the other Willie Bennett—were brought silently in front of him.

"Chuck, what we need from you is to tell us which of these guys looks most like the guy who did it," one of the district attorney's assistants told him when the men came out on the other side.

"Okay."

"I know it was dark and you didn't get a good look at the guy. So you tell me which one is the closest, okay?"

"Right," Chuck murmured. He looked intently at the group of black males, nervously studying each face through the glass as the men stepped forward in turn. When all eight had done this, Chuck still hadn't picked one out. The detectives were worried. It was one of the problems with a lineup in such situations. A victim who hadn't had a good look at the guy usually tended to be extremely cautious. Too cautious, some cops believed. On the other hand, Bennett's lawyer was painfully aware that of the eight males in the lineup, seven of them had the well-behaved look of municipal employees. Among them, his client tended to stand out. He was reminded of a routine that comedian Richard Pryor had about a black man in a lineup with a nun and a duck.

"One more time?"

"Please," Chuck said.

Again, he studied the faces, one by one. They all looked like schoolboys in a spelling bee—all except this one guy. Number three resembled the others in approximate weight, general age, and height. But there was a meanness about the man, a menace that Chuck, alert to nuance, could detect by the hint of a sneer as the suspect stood mutely gazing into his own reflection in the glass.

Chuck said, "That one."

"Which guy? Number three?"

"Yes."

"He's the guy?"

From somewhere deep in his psyche, a weak sally of fairness fought through to the surface; instead of making a positive identification, Chuck backed off a little and said, "I can't say for sure, but—"

"He looks most like the guy? Most like him, Chuck?"

"Yeah."

"You're sure?"

"Yes."

"Number three looks most like the guy who did it, who shot you and your wife, Chuck?"

Chuck nodded.

"Say yes or no, Chuckie."

"Number three most resembles the person who shot my wife and I," Chuck said.

The assistant district attorney stood up and stretched. "Okay," he said into the intercom to the officer in charge of the lineup on the other side of the glass. "That's it."

The men filed out silently. Number three was the only one who had the walk, the ghetto roll in his stride. Number three, shoulders squared, head high, was Willie Bennett.

Finally, ten weeks after the ambush in Mission Hill, Chuck had come face to face with the man he knew police believed murdered his wife and child. Word raced through the sophisticated grapevine in police headquarters: We got him. Willie was barely in the wagon headed back to Norfolk County Jail before the reporters got phone calls from their sources: Chuck had identified the guy. No doubt about it.

The next day's account in the *Globe* had the headline "Stuart Is Said to Pick Out Suspect" and quoted a source as saying that Chuck had made a "positive identification. It was absolutely crystal clear. That's the guy."

The *Herald* seemed ecstatic. Under a big front-page headline, it reported:

"Charles Stuart positively identified William 'Willie' Bennett in a police lineup yesterday as the gunman who wounded him and killed his pregnant wife, sources said.

" 'It was as positive an ID as I've ever seen,' said one source. 'He didn't hesitate.' "

The district attorney, Newman Flanagan, knew better than that. It had not been by any means a positive identification, but all things considered, it had been an acceptable one. And that alone was good news, because what the press had not chosen to emphasize, although reporters had certainly begun ferreting out the facts well enough, was that the case against Willie Bennett had begun to wobble a bit lately. Indeed, if they were not so completely certain that Bennett had done the crime, investigators might have had good reason to despair as 1989 drew to a close. One after the other, witnesses cited in the police affidavits, Dereck Jackson among them, were either repudiating or changing their statements—sometimes more than once. Some of them, like Jackson, were now openly claiming the police had coerced them into falsely implicating Bennett. Because they were so completely certain that Willie was guilty, and that it was just a matter of time before they had gathered enough reliable information to prove it, investigators weren't unduly worried about the shaky witnesses from Mission Hill, where it was believed that everyone lied all the time to cops anyway. Still, with people asking to change their testimony, it was getting to the point where the grand jury had begun to show some signs of confusion as investigators prepared the path for an indictment. So it didn't hurt to have it get around that Chuck had fingered the guy for certain. Sometimes, it was simply a slow and careful process, to build a case good enough for an indictment, and there was no point in spinning it out day by day in the newspapers and on television. In fact, neither Flanagan nor any of his aides had as yet publicly identified Willie Bennett as the prime suspect. That had all been done anonymously, with much help from the press.

As the chief investigator on the case, but dependent largely on the spade work of the police department, which did not officially report to him, Flanagan had been alternately amazed, amused, and annoyed at what he read in the newspapers. Sometimes, for the thirty-five-cent price of a paper, he was astounded to read important new information that the high-priced, high-pressure, months-long investigation by the Boston police homicide unit had somehow failed to uncover. But other times, the information in the press was so bad that it became something of a game to try to guess which anonymous detective was whispering which half-baked theory to a gullible and desperate reporter—and why.

Flanagan himself had been careful to stay above it all. There would be time to take credit later. With an election coming up in less than a year, even a Democratic incumbent virtually assured of victory savored the importance of timing.

From his earliest days as a politically ambitious prosecutor, Newman Flanagan knew how to play the press. In 1975, he had first gained an avid following among voters in white enclaves of Boston when, as an assistant district attorney, he prosecuted a Boston City Hospital physician for manslaughter in the death of a fetus during a legal second-trimester abortion. Even though the state's Supreme Judicial Court overturned the conviction, Flanagan, whose father had been a city treasurer, came out of it a folk hero in a city where almost two out of every three citizens are Roman Catholic. Attacks against him by the usual liberals quoted in the media only put the icing on the cake. With his shock of white hair and his hearty bonhomous bluster, tirelessly working the communion breakfasts and Knights of Columbus banquets, Flanagan handily won the district attorney's job in 1978.

Reelected twice without serious opposition, by 1989 Flanagan was a sturdy fixture at the helm of the Suffolk County District Attorney's office, a grand and florid raconteur, a politician defined by his friends no less than his enemies, some of whom complained that his tenure as the chief prosecutor had been marked chiefly by slipshod investigations and a chronic inability to attract to his large staff any but a relatively few assistant prosecutors who were not white Irish males like himself.

Flanagan prided himself on his roots in West Roxbury, then an Irish stronghold. The boys in the neighborhood who prospered as adults, and many of them did, became cops and firemen and civil-service bureaucrats, and the most motivated turned out as priests and lawyers. Two of his brothers, in fact, were priests. Newman had followed his father into the law and brought to the district attorney's office a disposition that reflected the West Roxbury he had grown up in—a no-nonsense, keep-your-nose-clean attitude that valued loyalty to friends, obedience to the rules, and deference toward authority, even when it was unfair. One reminder Flanagan was fond of repeating was that, in his day, if a boy came home from school and complained to his mother that he had been unjustly "whacked" in class by the nun, he could expect to be told, 'Well, that was for the time you did something else that the Sister didn't know about,' and promptly "whacked" again, for good measure.

"Consciously or not," a Dorchester District Court judge, James Dolan, once said, Flanagan's office seemed to reflect "the notion that since the minority community generates a disproportionate amount of crime, they should bear the consequences." The district attorney professed not to be bothered by such criticism, reiterating his firm belief in the basic franchise of the district attorney's office. Each step right up the line, the procedure of justice was magnificent in its clear simplicity, Flanagan believed: After a crime, the victim complained, the police investigated, the district attorney prosecuted, the grand jury evaluated, and the trial jury decided. When necessary, the judge interpeted, subject to review by higher authority. That was how it worked; each step along the route had checks and balances; justice routinely prevailed. Even when the occasional mistake was made, it all came out in the wash. Under this system, a prosecutor functioned primarily as a conduit; his prosecutors were not the primary investigators, Flanagan often pointed out. This was the beauty of the system.

As such, a suspect such as Willie Bennett would have his day in court. Coming as they did on the last business day of 1989, the newspaper stories about Chuck Stuart positively identifying Willie Bennett sounded an appropriate coda to the year. By the time the business of government stirred back to life after the holidays, the process would move along to its next step. Within a week or so, the district attorney's office was planning finally to indict Willie Bennett for the murder of Carol and Christopher, and the attempted murder of Chuck.

TWENTY

A New Year

"Chuck Stuart is encouraged at the direction the case has taken regarding recent developments," Dawley told reporters the Friday before New Year's. "He wants to go back to work as quickly as possible."

Actually, Dawley's statement was only half accurate. While Chuck was indeed pleased to have the grand jury clearly focused on Willie Bennett, he had no plans at all about getting back to work any time soon. In fact, he planned to take it easy for a while. Kakas had kept him on the payroll—he appreciated that, but had also pointed out to friends that he knew Kakas sensed there would be a public outcry if he were not being paid. With that sweet arrangement, and with the insurance money waiting like a fat cushion, Chuck saw no reason to get back to the rat race before he was good and ready—if at all.

But Chuck's well-being wasn't the only thing Dawley was asked about on Friday. That night, a local television reporter was the first to broach publicly the unpleasant rumors that had begun to come back to life. Interviewing the compliant Dawley, reporter Karen Marinara alluded very discreetly to the questions being asked in whispers about the possibility that Chuck's story wasn't all that it seemed. Dawley, slightly taken aback, replied politely if abstrusely, "I honestly think that if one could know the intimate details as those of us who are in this case know them, one could look you right in the eye and tell you there's absolutely no scintilla of compliance—this tragedy is nothing more than a random act of violence."

Chuck was still mending from the surgery more quickly than anticipated, and faced only one more relatively minor operation. If all progressed as expected, he could lose the hated colostomy bag in six weeks or so.

To kick off the year on the right note, he and Brian Parsons were planning a weekend getaway to Quebec, toasting the future amid the gustatory delights of French restaurants. At Chuck's request, Brian had already gone to the travel agency and picked up the plane tickets. They were due to leave January 5.

For Chuck, free at last from the pressures of answering questions and pointing fingers, a truly awful year was about to end. As if to mark his new freedom, he decided to move back to the empty house in Reading. The Christmas wreath Carol had put on the door, with baby-blue bears on the bottom, was still up. Across the street, his and Carol's friends, the Vajdics, had been minding the two Labradors, Max and Midnight. When Chuck stopped in to see them, Maureen Vajdic thought it very odd how the dogs abruptly turned away from him.

Late in the afternoon of New Year's Eve, tired of the endless entreaties to "take it easy," Chuck asked a friend to drive him into Boston to take in some of the city's annual "First Night" festival. That day, even the weather seemed to change with a portent of better times to come. A morning of freezing rain gave way to a balmy afternoon that coated the big ice sculptures erected on Boston Common for the festival with a glistening patina. By the time they parked downtown and made their way slowly up the hill with the crowds converging on the Common, it looked more like the Fourth of July on the Esplanade than December 31 on Boyleston Street. Chuck took it all in with delight, the Common with its lawn thronged with tens of thousands of people in swirls of bright winter clothing, a million tree branches sparkling with melting ice, all of it aglow with the ruddy wintery face of prosperity.

In the evening, a parade marched up crowded Boyleston Street past elegant shops twinkling with their Christmas lights. In furs and parkas, with strollers and lawn chairs, festooned with brand names that spoke of good taste, the crowd swelled into the night, marking the end of the 1980s in the glow of the shops and cafes of the Back Bay, from Prudential Center to the Ritz-Carlton at the foot of the Public Garden, where many thousands more spilled onto the lawns all the way to the head of the Common.

By midnight, it was a truly massive crowd of more than a quarter-million well-heeled people, gathered in well-mannered if raucous celebration of the end of the 1980s in the bracing open air of a place, their place, that had helped to define their decade. As midnight approached, the crowd, pressed around the big clock on the Common, took up a chant that rippled across the lawns, down through the Public Garden to those crowded against one another on Newbury Street: *Ten! . . . Nine! . . . Eight!—Take* that *Times Square!—Seven! . . . Six! . . . Five!* The last seconds were smothered in a deafening roar that bellowed from the throng, and then the air thundered with gunpowder; booming starbursts of fireworks streaked the night and caught in freeze-frame the hills and the downtown glass towers, the granite hulk of the Bunker Hill monument across the river and beyond, etched in the lightening, the iron hulk of the Tobin Bridge high over the vast black harbor.

Matthew partied grimly until early New Year's morning and awoke with a sense of dread that was worse than any hangover. In the baleful light of New Year's day, he knew that the excuses had expired; no one's holidays could be ruined now. He knew it was time to do what he had been promising since returning from California just before Christmas.

Actually, Chuck had made it a little easier for his kid brother. Chuckie always pushed his luck, but in the weeks after he got out of the hospital, Chuck was pushing it a little harder than usual, at least as regards his youngest brother—hassling him more than usual, nailing him with snide comments, getting on his case. Chuckie, of all people, who was supposed to be so smart, was starting to piss off the wrong person.

Family loyalty weighed heavily. For a while, it had looked like Chuckie wasn't even going to make it. And then the guy was struggling to get back on his feet and pull his life together. What kind of a kid brother would drop a bomb on him after all that? But this was not a case of telling the old man who had banged the Chevy into a fireplug with a load on. This wasn't some Revere cop busting stones over an open can of beer, or a phony homeowners' insurance claim over a stolen tape deck, or a fur coat that fell off the back of the proverbial truck in Chelsea. This was a case of *murder*—premeditated, first-degree, spend-the-rest-of-your-sorryass-life-in-Walpole murder, pure and simple.

This was heavy shit indeed. Matt had seen enough police shows to know what the word "accessory" could mean. From day one, the thought caused a shudder; after brooding for three days after the shooting, a terrified Matt had finally gone up the family chain of command, to the link just under Chuckie. He told Michael what he knew. And together, they had gone to an uncle, a former Revere tax assessor who had a law degree but no longer practiced. Hushed inquiries went out. Caution prevailed. Wagons were circled. Time passed.

Outside the tiny loop, few people knew for some time. But it wasn't the kind of secret a young man could manage to keep from the woman he loved, and Janet Monteforte had long since pulled it out of him, of course. And the loop widened when she told her parents. Aghast, they hustled their daughter to the family lawyer, John Perenyi, who practiced in suburban Brockton. Before long, Matt was pouring out his story to his girlfriend's family lawyer. No, he told the lawyer, he did not know who had killed Carol. No, he said, he had not seen her body on the front seat when Chuck tossed the bag into his car. No, he did not know Chuck himself had been shot, nor was he aware that there was a gun in the bag until he got back to Revere that night. Nervously, Matt explained the insurance scheme Chuck had laid out for him. That was all he knew for sure. No, he had never got the money Chuck had promised. The rest was conjecture.

The lawyer realized that Matt had agonized over the situation, especially over such matters as duty and loyalty. Peering at Matt over his half-rimmed eyeglasses, aware that "there wasn't a lot of support in the family for going to authorities," Perenyi did not put on any overt pressure. "I figured it was his decision to make," Perenyi said. Only Matt could decide what to do, and when.

Anyway, by the end of 1989, it was clear to the few people who knew the truth that time was running out. The rumors were now spreading out from Revere like rings on a pool of water: Chuck Stuart's story stank. Some people made phone calls. Well before Christmas, every newsroom in Boston was trying to check out anonymous calls saying Chuck's story was a lie.

Those who knew the truth sensed that inertia had been overcome. Opinions were sought. Legally, it was a complicated situation. But it looked like Matt might be in the clear, if he was telling the truth. A quirky Massachusetts law that had been on the books since colonial times stated clearly that a person could not be prosecuted for harboring a blood relative accused of a crime, or even for helping that relative to conceal a crime. The law defined "blood relative" as a parent, spouse, child, sibling, grandparent, or grandchild. So long as he had no part as an accessory in the commission of that crime, Matthew did not appear to be legally culpable for the murder of Carol and the baby.

Ethically, it was not complicated, at least for a lawyer operating under the firm principle of attorney-client privilege. Unless a person with knowledge of a crime decided to come forward voluntarily, there was nothing a lawyer could do, given the constraints of client confidentiality. It was strictly up to Matthew himself, Perenyi knew. If he was telling the absolute truth—that is, if he really had been naive enough to believe that Chuck was going to pay him ten thousand dollars for an insurance scam involving jewelry that was worth about half that; if he really had no part whatsoever in the murder of Carol; if all he had done was what he said, which was wait in the dark and drive away, blind and quick as a bat out of hell; *if he really had not known that Carol was shot when he accepted that bag*—if that was the truth, if no one could ever prove otherwise, then with luck, he might get out of it with merely a bad reputation.

At the end of December, when Matt read in the newspaper about Chuck making a positive identification of a suspect, he told Perenyi that he decided he had to go through with it. But he did not want to ruin what was left of the family holidays. With a sense of consideration and dreadful resolve, he chose the day after New Year's.

The afternoon before, Matt told Michael that he and Janet were going to see Perenyi, and then they were going to the district attorney. It was now time to tell the whole story to the others, to Mark, Neysa, and Shelley. And then it would have to be done. United, the children would have to tell their parents that Chuck, the fabulous Chuckie, was a liar and probably a murderer.

Late Tuesday afternoon, with Janet holding his hand, Matthew arrived at Perenyi's office. The meeting was excruciating for the young man from Revere. "It's not easy to turn state's evidence on your brother," Perenyi said. But momentum had overcome resistance. There would be no stopping now. Satisfied that he could find no holes in a story he had walked Matthew through again and again, Perenyi phoned the district attorney's office with a message that brought the district attorney, Newman Flanagan, right out of his chair: Matthew Stuart had a crucial statement to make about the role of his brother in the shooting of Carol and Christopher Stuart—but first certain reassurances had to be in place, primary among them that it was understood that Matthew was immune from prosecution under the state "blood relative" law if his story was true. Given that assurance, everything was ready. Perenyi and his client were told to come downtown the next day, after regular business hours, so as to not attract attention from the reporters who kept an eye on the comings and goings at the district attorney's office.

Meanwhile, as the tearful preparations were being made in Perenyi's office, the remaining siblings in Revere prepared themselves for what was obviously going to be a long ordeal. The oldest of them, Shelley, took charge.

"This is going to kill Dad," she said. The elder Stuart and his wife, who doted on Chuckie, had to be told the truth.

At dinnertime on Tuesday, as Matthew was at Perenyi's office going over his statement, there was a gathering at Shelley's house. Michael didn't come; he had the afternoon shift at the firehouse. But Shelley wanted everybody in line before they headed over to Lowe Street to tell their parents.

Impatient, adamant that he not use an excuse like work to get out of it, Shelley picked up the phone and called her half-brother at the firehouse a little after six o'clock.

"We're all meeting here right now," Shelley told him in a no-nonsense tone. "We're going to Mom's." She waited.

Michael sounded very nervous. He was aware that all calls to and from the firehouse were automatically recorded. "Well, I can't leave here until I talk to the deputy," he said.

"When will that be?" There was a cold edge to her voice.

"Well, he's on the road right now. I couldn't even begin to tell you—"

Shelley interrupted: "Can't it be an emergency crisis at home?"

"I suppose I could say that . . ."

"*Say it*, Mike! That's what it is!"

Mike didn't like being pressured by his sister, his *half*-sister, but he felt backed into a corner. "What's going to happen?" he asked meekly.

He knew damned well what was going to happen. "We're going to tell Mom and Dad," she said.

"What are you going to tell them?"

There was a pause, as if she couldn't believe he had asked such a question. "We're going to tell them we know Chuck was involved," she said finally, in a tone that showed she had taken charge of the situation. "We're not going to say he killed her."

Mike felt numb. "Yeah, right," he mumbled. "Wow."

"I know, Mike. Get ready."

He didn't reply.

"Okay? We're all together, Mike," she said.

It was anybody's guess what "all together" meant by this point. "Who's there?" Mike asked.

Mark and Shelley's husband, Steve, were already on hand. Matt and Janet were due back from the lawyer's any minute. Neysa was on the way.

"Neysa doesn't know?" Mike asked.

"Neysa doesn't know . . . yet."

He thought this all had taken care of already. "Oh Christ," he said. Neysa still had to be told.

"Okay?" Shelley said, waiting.

Mike sighed with resignation. "All right," he said. "I'll get out, I guess."

Shelley was glad to hear that. "All right," she said.

"Maria wants to go too," Mike added, volunteering his wife.

"Tell her to come. But you guys have to be here soon, though."

"All right."

"Like within ten minutes," Shelley said firmly.

"All right," Mike said.

As soon as he put down the phone, he picked it up again to call Maria.

"They want me to go," he told his wife.

"Where?"

"To my mother's."

"With who?"

"Mark, Shelley, and Neysa and—"

"Does Neysa know yet?"

"I don't think so."

"Is she going to find out at the same time?"

Mike wished he had asked Shelley this. He felt foolish having to reply only, "I guess."

"Are you getting out of work for the night?"

Mike looked around for someone with the authority to sign him out, and saw no one. "I don't know," he said. "I don't know what to do."

His wife pressed on, "You never know how your mother . . . You might have to stay there a long time and talk."

"I know," he said, feeling miserable.

"Now listen—"

"What?"

"Do you want it to just be the immediate family?"

"No, no! Steven's going, I guess—"

"Steven's going," she said evenly.

"I think so," he said, sighing again and hoping he wouldn't have to ask her. "It's up to you," he said. "I mean, I don't envy it. Believe me, *I* don't want to be there."

She came through for him. "Well, I'll be there for you," she said.

"I know Matt and Janet are going to be there," he added helpfully.

"Matt and Janet?" she asked.

He backed off a bit. "I guess," he said.

"All right," she said. "I'll go. Come and get me."

He was elated. The last thing he wanted was to go there without moral support. "All right," he said.

"I love you," Maria whispered before she hung up.

When Matthew and Janet got back from Perenyi's office, they all went together to Lowe Street. For Matthew, the lowest point of his life to date came when he had to tell his mother that he was going the next day to the authorities with a story that would lead them to accuse her eldest son of murdering his wife and baby.

"Why?" she said over and over through her sobs as her grown sons stood awkwardly beside her and her stepdaughters looked on with tears and pity from their place at their father's shoulder. "Why? My God, my God, why?"

The reply her children now felt was not uttered aloud: *For the money, Mom. He did it for the money.*

Free at last, Chuck knew none of this over the holiday. On Tuesday, he went to a Nissan dealer near Reading and bought a new Maxima for $22,000, trading in the Toyota in which Carol had been killed and presenting a $10,000 cashier's check—from Carol's insurance money—for the difference.

On Wednesday afternoon, when he came to Revere to show off his car, he learned what Matthew was about to do.

At eight o'clock on Wednesday night, with Perenyi at his side, Matthew gave his statement to Thomas J. Mundy, the assistant district attorney who was in charge of the grand jury investigation: how Chuck had offered him five thousand dollars, and then doubled it, to help him in an insurance scam. How they had done a dry run in Mission Hill the night before. How he had met Chuck near the projects, received the bag, drove off without knowing what had happened. How he and McMahon had walked down the railroad tracks in the dark and thrown the bag into the swirling Pines River. Everything except the ring, Matthew said. Moving to answer the obvious question, Matthew reached into his pocket and brought out Carol's diamond engagement ring. He placed it on the table, where it sparkled in the neon light.

Flanagan ordered the immediate arrest of Chuck Stuart. Detectives went to the house on Lowe Street and searched it. Others hurried up to Reading.

But when two Boston detectives, accompanied by a Reading cop, went to the Stuart house on Harvest Road that night, he was gone. A neighbor told them she had looked out the window and seen him pulling into his driveway sometime late in the afternoon, though. The only reason she thought anything of it was because he was in a huge hurry. He had slammed the car door, trotted up the little path from the drive to the front door, and was inside for only a few minutes before he rushed out again carrying a bag and was gone, backing out so fast that he obviously hadn't even bothered to check behind to see if there was a kid on a bike, which annoyed the neighbor.

"Nobody should be in that much of a hurry," she said.

But Chuck knew that time was running out. By the time he found out what Matt was doing, the day was more than half gone. After tearing up to Reading, there was barely enough time to get back down to the city, where his lawyer Dawley had been expecting him after a frantic phone call earlier in the afternoon.

Dawley did not have any reassurance for his longtime friend who had been his client for two months. The day before, Dawley himself had been stunned when Matt walked into his office and told him of an "elaborate plot" concocted by Chuck to cover up the truth about how Carol died. And who had been Chuck's official spokesman during that hoax? The lawyer to whom he was now running for protection.

Dawley would have no more of it. For two hours, he sat in his downtown office early that evening and listened to Chuck's whining excuses and his pleas for help. Implacably, he said there was nothing more he could do. First of all, he represented the Stuart *family*, not just Chuck, and it was clear, from what Matthew had told him, that there were certain conflicts inherent in any defense of Chuck. Second, Chuck didn't seem to quite get it: It was well past the time where a spokesman was going to be able to bail him out. Public image was not his problem; his problem was certain criminal indictment on two charges of first-degree murder. At this point, Chuck needed a good criminal defense lawyer, and Dawley gave him some names. Then he wished him luck and showed him to the door.

A little after nine-thirty, Chuck edged his new Nissan into a parking space at the Sheraton Tara hotel just off the interstate in

Braintree. The night was cold and he pulled up the collar on his lightweight jacket as he walked across the lot to the brightly lit lobby.

He told the desk clerk that he was staying for only one night and paid for the room with his American Express card. Running the credit card through the scanner, the clerk noticed that the young man didn't have any luggage. Not that it was all that unusual. Lots of people checked in without luggage. She slid the key for Room 231 across the counter, and told him how to find it. Later, filing the credit card slip with the night receipts, she thought the name on it was familiar. So was the man's face. *Charles Stuart. Chuck Stuart? Of course. The guy whose wife was murdered.*

Once settled in his room, Chuck had a night ahead with nothing to do. At least the television had cable. He studied the selections, which included Home Box Office and ESPN, the sports channel. But the game Chuck was most interested in—on his car radio, the Celtics had been using clutch shooting to protect an early lead against the Washington Bullets at the Garden—wasn't on. And listening to the radio by yourself in a motel room was too depressing. He flipped through the channels listlessly. "Quantum Leap" on channel 4. "China Beach" on 5. "Candid Camera" on 7, plus the usual cable claptrap.

He picked up the phone and dialed the front desk.

"This is Mr. Stuart in 231."

"Yes sir?"

"I'd like to have a wakeup call for the morning, okay?"

"Yes sir, what time?"

"Four-thirty."

"Four-thirty A.M. Fine, sir."

"Thank you."

Satisfied that his schedule was in order, Chuck emptied the coins from his pocket, dropping the change into a clean ashtray on the desk. Disconsolately, he watched the television for a while but couldn't get interested. Finally, he undressed and crawled in between the cool motel sheets and snapped off the light.

Miles away, the doorbell rang just after midnight at the DiMaiti house in Medford. Wondering who it could be at that hour, Giusto DiMaiti opened the door and saw three men who identified themselves as Boston police detectives. Puzzled, he invited them in, asking "What is this all about?"

One of the detectives showed him a diamond ring in a plastic zip bag, and asked if he had ever seen it before. The old man stiffened. He knew immediately. As he studied the ring that he had last seen on his daughter's finger, one of the detectives edged casually into the living room and seemed to be looking around.

"Yes," Giusto said, moving to the couch to sit down shakily. "That's Carol's ring." He handed the bag back.

"You identify this as Carol Stuart's engagement ring?"

"Absolutely. But why didn't you have her husband identify the ring? Where did you get it?"

The detectives looked at the floor. "I'm sorry, Mr. DiMaiti. We can't give you any information at this time," one of them said as they left.

After agitated snatches of sleep, Chuck was wide awake at two o'clock in the morning in a room so dark he could barely see its outline. With those thirty-pound motel curtains pulled across, if you wanted dark at night, you got dark. A motel beside an interstate was one of the few places left where anyone could be dependably alone, unplugged from the grid. For Chuck, this particular anonymous room offered the additional comfort of sanctuary; it was a hideout, cool and protected as a cave. He lay in bed breathing evenly while his eyes adjusted to the darkness. Besides the digits that glowed red from the clock on the nightstand, the only light in the room came from a two-inch gap at the edge of the curtain, from which the streaking headlights of cars and trucks on the interstate flung shadows that swept the wall.

Chuck realized that in his desperation he had forgotten about dinner, an oversight that was virtually without precedent in his life. "Call me anything but late for dinner," was one of the affectionate family jests that had always attached itself to Chuckie, who seldom missed a meal for any reason. He got out of bed and pulled on a black wool sweater over dark trousers, and took the stairs down to the lobby, which was deserted except for the night clerk watching listlessly from behind the gleaming brass-railed registration desk. Nodding to her, Chuck looked around for vending machines, but the hotel did not keep such things in sight. In a big, well-furnished public lounge just off the lobby, an old black man worked polishing the marble floor with a buffing machine that he maneuvered like a lawnmower. The old man hummed quietly as he worked in the glow of a wood fire that roared in the fieldstone hearth.

The hotel was a sprawling building designed in an English Tudor style except for its most curious physical features, which were soaring brick towers that leapt back additional centuries through architectural history to affect the appearance of a medieval castle. Chuck stood outside in the cold, with the ersatz battlements of the castle walls looming against the lightening predawn sky behind him, and squinted across the darkened parking lot. Over the roofs of parked automobiles, he noticed the blue and white logo of a service-station sign down the hill, beside the highway. Hungrily he made his way through the dark to the bright lights ahead.

There were two employees on the all-night shift at the store, and both of them were always alert to anyone coming through the door during the dangerous hours, the ones between two o'clock and dawn. Usually it was only some guy—you didn't see a lot of women this hour of the night—paying for gas or looking for the bathroom, or some kid with glazed eyes and the munchies, but you never knew. Chuck didn't rate the kind of attention a black man might have received—a black male wandering the little aisles in search of a box of aspirin or a candy bar could depend on one of the clerks taking just that moment to have something to do in the same aisle. All a white man usually was confronted with was a craned neck from behind the cash register. But Chuck merited more than the routine attention that night. For one thing, he was dressed unusually, all in dark clothing. And for another, he was acting in a manner that both clerks decided, without discussion, was odd. Here was this tall customer coming in unannounced—that is, there had been no head-lights bouncing into the lot, the guy was apparently on foot—with this tight little grin on his face as he approached the cash register.

"How you guys doing tonight?" Chuck asked, looking from one face to the other.

The response was one slight nod and one cold stare.

"Looking for something to eat," Chuck explained, glancing around. He acted distracted, as if expecting someone to burst in on him. His eyes darted here and there. Anyone accustomed to dealing with the public would have pegged him as the sort of guy who, given an opening, would trap you in a situation involving at least an uncomfortable conversation, if not worse.

The clerks watched silently. Framed in the concave mirror on the wall above the milk cooler, Chuck went to a narrow aisle and studied the packaged baked goods before choosing a small box of chocolate chip cookies. Then he took a sixteen-ounce Diet Coke from the cooler, shutting the insulated door with a thump. Paying for the snacks, he thumbed two dollars from his wallet and groped in his pocket for change. But he realized with annoyance that he had left his coins in the room.

Chuck hated the clutter of small change in his pocket, especially pennies, and always made an attempt to get rid of his change when he paid for something. It was one of those quirks he had. Often, to the consternation of cashiers and any customers waiting behind, he would fumble in his wallet and pocket for whatever combination of bills and coins he could come up with to end up with larger bills or fewer coins in change. A purchase of $4.89, for example, might prompt Chuck to search out and hand over a ten-dollar bill, two nickles, and four pennies, in order to receive a five-dollar bill and a quarter in return.,

But not now. "No change," Chuck said with a shrug, sliding over another dollar bill.

At the door, Chuck turned as if he forgot something. But he only wanted to ask a question. "You guys are open all night, right?"

"Open twenty-four hours," one of the clerks replied. "Why?"

"Nothing," Chuck said with a wink. "I just might get hungry again, that's all."

After the customer was gone, the clerk who had spoken turned to the silent one and said, "What a weirdo."

The telephone trilled quietly. Chuck opened his eyes and squinted at the digital clock. It was exactly four-thirty. He lifted the receiver, mumbled "Yeah" into it, and pushed it back in its cradle. *Rise and shine*, as his mother always called on school days when he wanted to stay home sick. *Rise and shine.*

In his underwear, he went to the little desk and found some hotel stationery in the center drawer, next to the Gideon Bible, which was opened to a page titled "John," as motel-room Bibles often seemed to be. At the desk, he began writing on the pad, struggling to get the wording right. Unlike the eulogy for Carol that had been so well received at her funeral, this was just a few sentences. But he labored to achieve the right accusatory implication—some of those who read it should infer that they bore a certain *responsibility* for things. It was not Chuck's fault that he had ultimately failed to fulfill great expectations.

An hour later, after tearing up several sheets of paper with false starts, he was satisfied with what he had written. The note conveyed no remorse because he felt none. It simply conveyed surrender.

By the time he took a shower and dressed in blue jeans with the same black sweater he had worn to go to the store during the night, it was six o'clock. On schedule, he slipped on his parka and went down to his car carrying the letter. Everything else he left in the room, including his spare change on the desk and a clean colostomy bag on the dresser.

He drove north on Route 93 toward the skyscrapers of Boston outlined against a dawn-gray sky. At the Tobin Bridge, the Bunker Hill monument rose in the light that had started to fall on Charlestown to the left.

As he knew from all of the traffic jams he had endured on the way to Revere, the bridge had one lane on each level that seemed to be under permanent construction. Given the hour, it was easy to pull off and park the Maxima in the clear on the right, behind the barricades. It was only a little before seven, and not many vehicles were coming across on this level yet. But he knew he had no time to dawdle. Even though he was on the lower, outbound level, he knew that traffic would be fairly heavy soon with commuters bound for the day shift at the oil terminals along the banks of the harbor in Everett and Chelsea and Revere. From experience, Chuck knew the Tobin was carefully patrolled. Given the possibilities of the huge traffic snarls that could ensue, a stalled vehicle didn't stay stationary on the Tobin for long. The bridge's breakdown crew prided itself on getting a lane unblocked within minutes.

He waited until a tanker truck lumbered over the hump of the center span and rumbled by, and then he sprung the release lever under the dashboard. Getting out, he bent over the engine for a moment until a car passed and the roadway was empty. The smell of the winter ocean blew up from the harbor. Gulls coasted and squawked on brisk updrafts that tousled Chuck's expensive haircut as he turned on his heel and suddenly dashed fifteen feet to the chest-high guardrail, vaulting it in an instant. A hundred and fifty feet below, the icy currents of the Mystic River rushed to the sea.

In a warm office near the toll booths on the upper level of the bridge, Arthur Suckney had settled into the morning's routine. A longtime member of the bridge's breakdown crew, it was Suckney's job to monitor the television screens that showed pictures being transmitted from cameras fixed above critical points on the double-decked bridge that rises in two great soot-dark cantilevers high above the stubby piers and choppy waters of the inner harbor. The bridge carries historic Route 1 between Charlestown and the North Shore at Chelsea, and because of its formidable height and imposing location over the juncture of two rivers at the aperture to the sea, it attracts the occasional person determined to commit suicide in a manner that is both effective and dramatic. Each year, an average of seven people plunge to their deaths from the Tobin, but as Suckney scanned his monitors an hour after his shift had begun on the morning of January 4 he was especially alert. Not only was the roadway saddled with even more construction than usual but there had been a spate of what the bridge employees referred to as "incidents" lately.

On Christmas night, a sailor, attached to the museum-piece USS *Constitution* at the Charlestown Navy Yard, had managed to walk along the bridge without being noticed. He perched on a railing until police and crewmen arrived. Drunk, despondent because his wife had left him, the sailor listened politely to the entreaties of his would-be rescuers for five minutes. The man then said "See you later" and jumped to his death. The incident traumatized those who had come to the man's aid, and bridge employees were further shaken a week later when there was another "incident." A twenty-year-old man from Revere had simply bolted from a taxicab at the tollbrooth's upper level and, as the driver and bridge workers watched aghast, flung himself over the side to his death. To see a human being kill himself in front of your eyes is to be assaulted; some workers who had witnessed both incidents were already scheduled for counseling. Everyone, Suckney included, was coming to work wondering if the next one would happen on their watch.

At seven o'clock, routinely scanning the monitors, Suckney

noticed an automobile that must have just pulled into a construction area on the center span. The hood was up. There was no one around. Quickly checking other monitors, Suckney could see no sign of a pedestrian anywhere in the vicinity of the breakdown. The car hadn't been there a minute or so earlier, when he last had checked the screen, so he knew its driver couldn't have gone far on foot.

Following routine standard procedure, Suckney notified the sergeant on duty and took an elevator down to the lower deck, below the tollbooths, where he got into a truck and drove the quarter mile to the spot where he had seen the breakdown. Routinely, Jerome Cronin, a state police officer on patrol at the bridge, also responded to Suckney's report of a breakdown.

Suckney looked worried when the state police car pulled up behind the parked Nissan Maxima.

As Cronin bent into the car to investigate, Suckney went over to the guard rail and looked down. It wasn't quite sunrise yet; the light on the harbor wasn't very good. But for an instant, he thought he saw something floating on the water. When he blinked and looked again, it was gone. Cronin came over and looked down, and he, too, thought he saw something that was gone in a flash.

There was no thought of hesitation. The standing order was clear: If in doubt, err on the side of caution.

"We might have a situation here," Suckney told the policeman.

Cronin nodded. "Jumper?"

"Not sure."

Cronin passed over the note he had found on the front seat of the car. "Look at this," he told Suckney. It was written on a sheet of Sheraton Tara hotel stationery. "I don't have the strength to go on," the note said. "I love my family and the last four months have been hell. I am sorry for all the trouble." It was signed, "Chuck."

On the river, responding to the alarm, rescue boats put out from their piers.

TWENTY-ONE

The District Attorney

Ashen-faced, with dark bags under his eyes attesting to a sleepless night, the district attorney slouched in front of a jumble of microphones at the center of a long banquet table in the press room at Logan Airport. To his left sat Francis "Mickey" Roache, the police commissioner, and beside him a very unhappy Mayor Flynn, who had spent much of the Christmas and New Year's holidays trying to decide whether to make a run for the hotly contested Democratic nomination for governor in the September primary. That possibility went into Boston Harbor right along with Chuck Stuart, Flynn sensed.

As Flanagan spoke, divers were still dragging the bottom of the Mystic River looking for Chuck's body. Flanagan was stunned by the sudden twist in the case. "During the course of the evening," the district attorney said, "several members of the Stuart family, and friends, gave statements." As the reporters edged closer, Flanagan looked around sharply like a teacher alert for cheating in the back row. But everyone was at attention, straining to hear how he was going to explain himself out of this one. "These statements clearly exculpated Willie Bennett," Flanagan said, practically spitting out the words, "and inculpated Charles Stuart in the murder of his wife and infant son."

A commotion arose, a chorus of rapid questions, but the district attorney raised his hand for silence. He fumbled on the table and held up the plastic freezer bag containing Carol Stuart's engagement ring. Camera shutters chattered as he displayed the bag and frowned through his glasses to read from a statement. "Also at the time, a ring, ID'd as Carol Stuart's engagement ring, was turned over to police at the district attorney's office." He looked around again, as if awaiting a challenge. But all he saw was the glassy eyes of the television cameras focused on him. The reporters had their heads down, scribbling into notebooks. "After a careful review of this new evidence," Flanagan said, flinching almost imperceptibly when he heard someone snort loudly at the words *careful review*, "I instructed Boston police homicide detectives to arrest Charles Stuart for the murder."

That much the reporters had known since early morning, when they first learned of Matthew's action the night before. The $64,000 question now was: Where was Chuck? On the bottom of the Inner Harbor, as expected—or somewhere else? There being no body so far, some were wondering about the possibility that Chuck had managed to fake a suicide and escape, perhaps making a monkey of the district attorney's office once again. Even at that moment, was he sipping his chardonnay on some plane over their heads, en route from Logan to sunny Mexico? It was almost noon, and all anyone knew for sure was that Chuck's car had been found on the bridge with a suicide note on the seat, and that the cops wanted to arrest him. Chuck himself was conspicuously absent, living or dead, despite the intense efforts all morning of divers from the combined maritime rescue units of the police, the Coast Guard, and MassPort. The press conference was being aired live by every broadcast outlet in town, all of whom would follow it with special reports that had to begin with that one big unknown: was Chuck Stuart dead?

The answer came even as Flanagan faced the reporters. On the cold, wind-whipped river, a grisly competition had developed among the various dive teams working the search grid downstream from the

Tobin Bridge. On and off for almost four hours, three separate teams of divers had been trudging the murky bottom, each man holding onto a long tow bar for guidance, each hoping to be the one to stumble across a body in the muck. At about twelve-fifteen, a Red Cross boat was chugging from the MassPort pier at Logan with stacks of sandwiches and jugs of fresh coffee when shouts rose from the stern of the *Sentinel,* the state police boat whose crew had pulled up the most recent previous Tobin jumper a week earlier.

"Coming up!" the crew chief yelled, and the call was taken up by exhausted, wet, shivering rescue workers on the other boats, which bobbed and jockeyed to close in against the strong midstream current.

"Got him!"

A blur of international distress orange swirled to the surface as two divers bobbed up, struggling on the surface with a body. All around, others who had been resting on adjoining boats jumped back into the river to assist the two state police divers in bulky insulated drysuits hauling the body to the surface. Chuck's exposed skin was frozen stiff in the salt water, whose temperature was a degree below what would freeze fresh water. With great effort, the divers, who by now numbered more than a half dozen, edged the body over to the boat like tugs at work against a sluggish barge. Finally they managed to push and haul the sodden bulk across the *Sentinel*'s heaving stern gunwale. Coughing and grunting, two divers clamored on board and pulled the body all the way across. Spewing water, it slithered heavily to the deck, where it lay lifeless and sopping. One of the divers was crying quietly. His partner went into the cabin and collapsed on a bench in front of an electric heater, spitting the stink of the river from his mouth. In the water, the others bobbed quietly back to their own vessels, impervious to the surface gas slick from the engines that lapped at their frozen lips.

On the banks, on the piers, television and still cameras, professional and amateur, took it all in. Overhead, helicopters clattered and swooped. It was a sunny, brisk day, and hundreds of spectators had gathered along the ice-choked banks of the harbor and on the stubby piers. With the boats clustered in the river and all of the activity on the banks and in the air, the scene had the look of a winter regatta. Some of the spectators cheered and applauded as the rescue boats began churning across the choppy river toward the south bank, in formation like a determined flock of ducks.

At Logan, where he had just wrapped up his press conference, the district attorney was walking to his car when a policeman approached and told him. Flanagan listened with his head down.

"That's the end of it, then," Flanagan muttered as he got into the back seat of his car and the door shut softly behind him.

On Saturday, Chuck Stuart, who liked so much to be the center of attention, went furtively to his grave on a cold and dismal morning.

Under the watchful eye of police detectives, family members and a handful of friends gathered at the old wood-frame Immaculate Conception Church in Revere for the service. Across the street, a new Immaculate Conception church had begun to rise above the rubble of a construction site, and the hundred-year-old church where Chuck had been an altar boy was now decrepit-looking, with the paint peeling on the outside and the cold winter draft seeping past sills that no one bothered to caulk anymore. Yet the altar had an oddly festive look; bursts of orange poinsettias and fragrant green balsam wreaths left over from Christmas brightened the surroundings, impervious to the despair that pressed down on the hearts of relatives, people who had always been taught to value propriety, even in its absence, and who now sensed that even the honest act of mourning would appear to be impertinent.

In their misery, Chuck's family had been denied even the joyous dignity of a proper public wake the previous night. Only those closest to the family had known about it. To others, to the press as well as to any casual acquaintance who might have wished to pay respects, the man in the coffin had an alias. Tight-lipped workers at Verducci Funeral Home in downtown Revere were under strict instructions: No, the undertaker's employees swore to any outsider who asked, the wake was not for a Mr. Stuart. It was for a Mr. Pizzaro.

Before the funeral mass, the Reverend Richard Messina, the pastor of Immaculate Conception, had struggled to decide what was appropriate to say over the body of this young man who, like his father and great-grandfather before him, had seldom been at a loss for words himself. After all, the deceased had not admitted to his alleged crime, either in a court of law or in a confessional; nor had he even been formally accused of a crime by the authorities. Wherever his soul might be, his legal status reposited in purgatory, and delivering a homily under such circumstances was not the sort of challenge a priest welcomed. Messina hadn't even known Chuck, and barely even knew his parents. Though the Stuarts lived around the corner from Immaculate Conception, and their kids had gone to the parish school, Charlie and Dot Stuart actually had been attending Sunday mass at Saint Anthony's on the other side of town for many years, because Saint Anthony's had fewer steps out front for Chuck's disabled father to climb.

Messina decided on a vague homily that offered hope and adroitly skirted a matter that usually was of some interest in a church: sin. "We cannot explain the events of the past, and we certainly can never understand them," the priest told the grim-faced mourners, and looked directly at Chuck's parents, who sat stiffly in the front pew, weeping.

> Memories can help to heal. Memories of early childhood, innocence and boyhood pranks, of achievement, successes, and of all the good that was done. We are not judged on one moment of our lives, not just on the moments of sin and violence. . . . We can do nothing but trust in the Lord and believe that his mercy will take care of us all, and that includes Chuck. . . . I believe in the afterlife we are given the opportunity to make amends for our sins. For some, it may take longer than others—but in the end, we all return to God.

Matthew, sitting beside Janet Monteforte, also cried openly throughout the thirty-minute service. As a woman in the choir loft sang the lilting strains of the Schubert "Ave Maria," Matthew rose with the others and walked to the altar, where his receiving of Communion was taken by the congregation as a sign that he was without grievous sin.

Afterward, Chuck Stuart, always punctual in life, was late going to his grave. To thwart the media cameras, the family decided to have the casket kept behind for a while after the funeral. A few hours later, it was brought quietly to a flat, tree-bare expanse of well-tended ground at Woodlawn Cemetery, which sprawls through Everett along the border between Middlesex and Suffolk counties, a little south of Holy Cross Cemetery, where Carol was buried. The cemetery, founded in 1850, distributes a brochure that describes it as "one of the oldest nonsectarian rural and garden-type cemeteries in America" and "one of the most beautiful cemeteries in the country." Visitors are advised: "Dignified behavior is expected and will be required." Among some of the mourners, who were after all Irish and thus could find a certain grim irony even in the meanest of deaths, it did not go without notice that Chuck finally had found peace in a neighborhood he would have approved of.

Chuck Stuart is buried in a grave marked only by a brass plate with a number on it, 1444. At its head, there often can be found a single pot of geraniums, placed there from time to time by someone who had loved him, his oldest sister, Shelley, who searched for a long time through the pity and the sadness and anger and finally found far back in her mind the image of a little boy, anxious to please, who never forgot the flowers.

Epilogue

The Grand Jury

In all, four Mission Hill residents, including Dereck Jackson and Eric Whitney, testified before a grand jury in November, 1989, about Willie Bennett's alleged role in the shooting. Each one subsequently recanted their statements, saying they had been pressured by police into making them. Each one subsequently denied having any information whatsoever that would link Willie Bennett to the crime.

A new grand jury was impaneled shortly after Chuck killed himself. Called to testify, Matthew Stuart and his friend John McMahon declined to answer most questions, citing their rights under the Fifth Amendment. That grand jury quickly stalled in its proceedings when Chuck's mother and legal heir, Dot Stuart, refused to waive the attorney-client privilege that Chuck's lawyer, John Dawley, invoked when asked to testify about what Chuck had told him the night before he died.

By the first anniversary of Carol's death, state and federal investigative panels were looking into the actions of the Boston police and district attorney's office in the Willie Bennett matter; meanwhile, the Suffolk County grand jury had not met for over eight months. It had not been able to issue a report, pending the district attorney's request—then being considered by the state's highest court—that Dawley be forced to break the privilege and tell what Chuck had confided to him, if anything, on the night of January 3.

Said Paul K. Leary, the first assistant district attorney: "It's baffling to us why the Stuart family doesn't want this to be told, unless they are protecting somebody. Our whole theory has been that the Stuart family wanted to get to the bottom of this. But if they won't waive the privilege and become a roadblock, the public will be enraged."

In November 1990, the state's highest court upheld the Stuart family's position. The grand jury continued on inconclusively well into 1991.

Mayor Flynn

The night after Chuck Stuart jumped off the bridge, a beleaguered Ray Flynn stood in the cold outside the State House defending himself, a posture he would come to find familiar as outrage mounted over the way his police department had handled the Stuart case. The mayor, who prided himself on a reputation for wading right in to take charge of crises, was bewildered and angry at the way this one had taken control of him. That night, he lashed out at the only villain he could think of: the late Chuck Stuart. "There's the person that started this whole thing," Flynn declared bitterly. "There's the person that came up with the most sinister, devious proposal that has had more of a disruptive influence on this city in my time as mayor of Boston." Flynn called Chuck's hoax "such a devious scheme, such a terrible plan."

Asked if he would apologize to the residents of Mission Hill, the mayor dodged. "Everybody owes an apology to the Mission Hill neighborhood," he said, adding that he was offering his own personal regrets for "whatever it is" that had offended black residents.

With a police escort, Flynn then was driven down to Mission

Hill to meet with Willie's mother and offer the city's regrets for what the mayor's press secretary called "the disruption caused when the police came into her house with guns drawn, frightening Mrs. Bennett and an autistic child." But nothing seemed to be going well for the embattled mayor, not even this simple gesture. Despite his best intentions, the mayor's stiff demeanor and rushed manner insulted rather than mollified Willie's mother and other relatives, and they made no bones about it when the microphones were held in front of them afterward.

"The mayor came in and spent one hot second in my mother's home, and then flew out the door," scoffed Ronald Bennett, one of Willie's brothers, who had been with his mother when Flynn and his entourage showed up in a bluster of walkie-talkies and flashing lights. Flynn, who had been on duty almost around the clock since he got the late-night phone call saying that Chuck was suddenly the suspect, struck the Bennetts as being horrified at the prospect of having to accept their hospitality. "My mother offered him a chair to sit in, but he didn't want to sit down," Willie's brother said. "He acted like my mother's house wasn't good enough for him." Willie's sister Linda added, "He came in and rushed back out. He didn't want to come here, you could tell. He was so nervous he was shaking. I thought he was going to have a heart attack."

A year after Chuck's death, Flynn still had not managed to regain the momentum that had characterized the early years of his administration. Battered by the regional recession, Boston's finances were tottering, the school system was acknowledged to be in shambles, and crime in fact had begun to soar, with a murder rate that reached an all-time high in 1990.

"Boston got hoodwinked," was all the mayor would ultimately concede of the Stuart case.

Willie Bennett

Willie's new lawyer, Robert George, an attorney well known for defending suspects in high-profile criminal cases, had expected to spend the week after New Year's 1990 preparing for the indictment of his client, not the sudden exoneration. As Chuck Stuart's body was being hauled out of Boston Harbor, George was already on his

way to the Norfolk County Jail, where he helped the dumbfounded
Willie draft a statement that said, in part:

> Although the prosecution in this case cleared me as a sus-
> pect, this is not enough. My life and my family's life has
> been ruined, and no one is willing to take responsibility. I
> have always maintained that I was innocent of the terrible
> crime which caused the death of Carol and Christopher Stu-
> art, and now I have been proven right. It is a shame that it
> took the suicide of the real killer to open people's eyes. . . .

George stated the following:

> Flanagan would like to blame the news media, but it was ob-
> vious the police and the prosecutor were ready to indict and
> convict Bennett, an innocent man. It took a man jumping off
> the Tobin Bridge to his death to make the prosecutors even
> acknowledge that Bennett was not a suspect. I feel sad for the
> man who jumped off the bridge today, but that's the same man
> that would have sat there and watched Willie Bennett go on
> trial, and testified against him, if things had gone his way.

He called the actions of the police and district attorney in the case
a "travesty of justice."

From the day he was arrested in November, Willie remained in
jail awaiting trial on the unrelated charge of robbing the Brookline
video store. "My record is what put me here," Willie said of his
latest sojourn in jail. "My past—it follows me everywhere I go." On
October 5, 1990, a jury found him guilty of armed robbery of the
video store; he was sentenced to a term of twelve to twenty-five years.
By the first anniversary of the shooting of Carol Stuart, Willie was
back in Walpole prison.

Matthew Stuart

The day Chuck jumped to his death, Matthew's lawyer, John Perenyi,
made the only public statement about Matthew's role.

> What he told the authorities was that he had been in an
> automobile in the Mission Hill area and had met his brother.
> That his brother had given him something and he transported

it back to the house, and later discovered that the bag he had been given contained some of the things that were originally reported as robbed from Carol and Chuck Stuart by the alleged assailant.

Matthew really doesn't know what happened. It's just a lot of conjecture and surmise. He does not know who shot his brother. He does know he was up there (on Mission Hill) by prearrangement with his brother and was going to receive something, which he in fact received, tossed from one car to the other. But he did not see Carol in the car with his brother at the time, and he saw no gun. He told me his brother was very cryptic about everything that had been discussed beforehand, and for that matter was cryptic when Matthew tried to speak to him about it when Chuck was in Boston City Hospital.

Matthew did not know that Chuck had been shot when the bag was tossed into his car, Perenyi said. Nor did he know what was in the bag until he got back to Revere, the lawyer said, according to what Matthew told him. Why had it taken so long for Matthew to tell the truth?

Matthew is considerably younger than his brother Chuck, and looked up to him. He made an initial attempt to come forward through a family member who is a member of the bar, although not actively so, and there was apparently a certain division in the family as to what he ought to do. He was caught in a situation that was really beyond his power to completely understand and react to in an adult manner, and he was torn—and understandably so—between what he maybe thought was a duty to come forward and tell what he knew, and on the other hand, an understandable reluctance to cause problems for his brother, who was recuperating from a gunshot wound. He agonized over it for a considerable period of time. . . . Things sort of came to a head when he read in the newspaper that his brother had identified Mr. Bennett.

Perenyi's statement, based as it was on what his client had told him, created a hubbub in legal circles. Shortly afterward, Matthew hired a noted Boston defense attorney, Nancy Gertner, who had first made her reputation defending the antiwar activist Susan Saxe on a homicide charge in 1975. Gertner said of her client's potential liability: "I don't see any responsibility for the murder of Carol Stuart here."

On the first anniversary of Carol's murder, Matthew was still living at home. By February of 1991, authorities had not been able to present any evidence before the grand jury to challenge Matt's account of the night of October 23, 1989.

Michael Stuart

On January 11, 1990, amid the furor that followed Chuck's suicide, Richard Clayman, a lawyer hired by Michael, suggested that the siblings call a press conference to clear the air. Before a mob of reporters and photographers, Clayman introduced Michael, Mark, Shelley, and Neysa—Matthew was conspicuously absent—and confirmed what everyone already knew by then—that Chuck had approached Michael about murdering Carol in a "disjointed, vague conversation" weeks before her death, and that subsequently Michael knew about Chuck's involvement in the murder itself *three full days* before he helped carry Carol's casket past the grief-paralyzed DiMaiti family at St. James Church. And, Clayman confirmed, Michael maintained his silence outside the family about what he knew until after Chuck was dead.

"This man is clean," Clayman shouted, marching up behind Michael and planting his palms on his shoulders. It had been a time of "agony" for the Stuarts, the lawyer said, because "they loved Carol DiMaiti. They are on Carol's side. It is important . . . to understand that there has been no charade here."

The conversation with Chuck "had no significance to Michael," Clayman insisted. "I reviewed it with him and it doesn't have a hell of a lot of significance now," either. Of course, he conceded, other people could well argue that such a conversation might in fact be significant. "I am comfortable that after an examination of this entire scenario, and talking to my client, that there is no violation of the law, that he did not violate any statute whatsoever, that his hands are legally clean."

By the anniversary of Carol's shooting, Michael was reported to have separated from his wife and was living quietly in an apartment in Revere.

The Boston Media

To a great extent, it had been a textbook case of bad journalism. But it wasn't over with the printing of Willie's statement on the day after Chuck died. The next day, the *Herald* seemed to go out of its way to discredit Willie's lawyer, who was referred to in one story as "a highly visible attorney attracted to cases generating media attention." The *Herald* account also quoted unnamed "critics" who "suggest George is more interested in promoting himself than he is interested in his clients," and found reason to point out that George "is well known for his defense of convicted cop-killer Ted Jeffrey, and Terrence Taylor, who was accused of participating in the murder of twelve-year-old Tiffany Moore."

By the end of the week, Flanagan's grudging "exculpation" of Willie Bennett aside, the newspapers were still hammering away at the former suspect, almost as if to say that he deserved what he got because of the other things he had done. In the process, rumors that Willie was still somehow involved—perhaps in a drug deal with Chuck gone bad—were actively fanned. One particularly glaring instance came in the *Globe*, in an article by Mike Barnicle that ran at the top of the front page, quoting sources who reviewed Willie's criminal background. The column even offered up Willie's seventh-grade report card, saying, in part:

> When this incredibly bizarre story finally comes to an end, it will be shown that detectives from the homicide unit merely covered themselves with glory. Despite having a suspect, Bennett, who had, in a moment of ignorant street swagger, actually claimed carrying out a crime he did not commit— shooting Carol Stuart—and despite testimony from several black residents of the project one day after the crime occurred that they had seen Bennett with a gun and jewelry on the evening Carol Stuart was shot, the police balked at charging him with murder.
>
> Perhaps reluctance came because they knew him and understood that Bennett did not finish the seventh grade. He dropped out of the Timilty School in 1964. Then, the Boston public school system listed his verbal IQ at 64, performance IQ at 65, and a full-scale IQ of 62. Stamped on his academic

record is the following term: Mental Defective. Here are the marks of his last report card issued that November:

Conduct: E
Effort: E
English: E
Math: E
History: E
Science: D
Geography: D

The E does not stand for excellent. The man's pathetic, violent history is so much a part of the unyielding issues of race, crime and drugs tearing daily at America that it is amazing how any black minister or black politician could ever stand up and howl in public that his arrest was a product of police bigotry and a volley of discrimination aimed at all black residents of Boston. Where, after everything they had been told, would they expect the cops to start looking? The Myopia Hunt Club? Willie Bennett is a sociopath. . . .

Two days later, another Barnicle column printed by the *Globe* said:

As a matter of fact, the greatly relieved Bennett issued a statement through his self-promoting attorney claiming that his life had "been ruined" because his name and photograph, linking him to a shabby crime, had appeared in the papers and on television more often than Manuel Noriega's.

Naturally, a pack of publicity hounds within the black community—a few ministers and headline-hunting politicians now passing themselves off as skilled homicide investigators—jumped on Bennett's arrest as proof of a racist plot by the white power structure to make every black man, woman and child in Boston out as ruthless, bloodthirsty criminals. I guess they are upset because nobody thought to beat the truth out of Stuart that night in the hospital after he had shot and very nearly killed himself. . . .

Debby Allen

The headline that she had dreaded appeared on the front page of the *Globe* the Sunday after Chuck's suicide: "Probers Link Stuart, Woman," it said over an article reporting:

> The woman, a graduate student, had worked at Kakas for the last two summers, according to neighbors and friends. She graduated from Brown University last year, they said.
>
> The woman, described as striking and blonde, had been questioned by police in late October and had told police she and her boyfriend had socialized with Stuart and his wife once or twice before.
>
> Police questioned the woman again yesterday after police searched Stuart's Reading home on Friday and found telephone bills that indicate she had been calling Stuart at the hospital by using his credit card.

The next day, the paper ratcheted the story up a little, reporting that

> Investigators, now postulating that money may not have been Stuart's only motive, are considering a romantic angle as well. . . .
>
> Sources said police believe that Stuart, dissatisfied with his wife, particularly at her pregnancy, had a romantic relationship with Allen that began in July. Allen has continued to deny to authorities that she had such a relationship with Stuart, and investigators said they do not believe she had any involvement in the conspiracy to kill Carol Stuart.

Debby was prepared for it, however. Her lawyer, Thomas Dwyer, Jr., denounced the stories about Debby in the newspapers and on television. "I am extremely concerned on behalf of my client that the Boston media has failed to learn any lesson out of this experience since October," Dwyer said. "I think the question should be asked whether the media is in fact acting as an accessory to Charles Stuart's wrongful intent."

Debby also issued a statement, through Dwyer, which said in part:

> I was never romantically involved with Charles Stuart. He was one of a group of friends at Kakas Furs where I worked

during the summers of 1988–1989. I also got to know his wife, Carol Stuart, at that time. On more than one occasion, both Stuarts described their marriage to me in warm and loving terms. I was shocked when I learned that Carol Stuart was murdered and Charles Stuart critically wounded. I believed Mr. Stuart's statements that they were the victims of a violent robbery. My belief was reinforced in December when Mr. Stuart told me that he had recognized the murderer in the lineup at the police department. During my entire friendship with Mr. Stuart, I was dating Brian Heffernan, whom I met while studying at Brown University. Brian met Mr. Stuart on several occasions and Brian was well aware of our friendship and my efforts to help him after the murder. . . . At some point in late December it became apparent to me that Mr. Stuart no longer needed my support. I firmly told Mr. Stuart that as a friend there was nothing more that I could do for him. This was my last conversation with him.

My friendship with Mr. Stuart was not romantic. I socialized with him both alone and with others on a few occasions. The only presents I received from Mr. Stuart were a pair of sneakers, a sweatshirt and a joke gift. He gave me a card— not jewelry—for my birthday. This is simply a sad and tragic case. The real tragedy is the death of Carol Stuart and her baby. In comparison to the DiMaiti family's loss, the unjustified injury to my reputation is of little consequence.

The DiMaitis

Three weeks after Chuck's suicide, Carol's parents made their first public statement since the shootings and the last they would make for another ten months, when they would express "distress" that a television movie on the case had aired before the grand jury could complete its report. On January 25, the DiMaitis announced that they had set up a scholarship foundation, in Carol's name, to give financial aid to deserving students from the inner-city streets where their daughter had died.

His voice trembling, Giusto DiMaiti called his daughter "truly the brightest of lights in our lives, a light that will never go out in our minds," and added:

Her mother and I were filled with pride for the way she lived
her life. She brought joy and comfort, not only to us, but to
all she knew. Carol was a loving, caring person who always
thought of the other person first. She loved to help those less
fortunate than herself, and she was constantly trying to
improve their place in this world by donating her legal skills
to them. . . . Mere words cannot express the terrible empti-
ness we feel, or how much we miss her now and will miss
her for the rest of our lives. All she ever wanted was to be
a good daughter, wife, mother, and be happy in her life. She
was not given the opportunity to fulfill all of those wishes,
but as far as we were concerned she succeeded in every way
possible as a pure, loving human being.

By the anniversary of Carol's death, the Carol DiMaiti foundation had raised $500,000 for scholarships.

The Estate

By the time the various life and property insurance claims had been
sorted out, the estates of Chuck and Carol Stuart had a value that
appeared to approach a half-million dollars, all of it tied up in a
complicated Probate Court dispute between the DiMaitis and the
Stuarts. Among the assets were $7,000 in a bank account in Carol's
name, $5,000 in a bank trust fund for Chuck to which people had
contributed in the months after Carol's murder, and the Nissan
Chuck had bought the day after New Year's.

The major complication tying up probate was the same legal
uncertainty that kept the grand jury in knots. Upon Carol's death,
in the absence of a will, her estate was divided between her husband
and her infant son. Upon the baby's death, seventeen days later, his
share of his mother's estate went to Chuck. And upon Chuck's death,
all of the assets went to his own parents. But if criminal or civil
proceedings were to officially determine what already was obvious,
that Chuck had murdered his wife and son, the DiMaitis could lay
claim to much of his estate by arguing that he had illegally gained
control of the assets of his wife and son by murdering them.

In May, a Reading realty firm was advertising the Stuart house,
empty since Chuck hurried off on the afternoon of January 3, as "an

immaculate home on quiet street. Seven rooms, three bedrooms, two baths, big country kitchen. Heated sunroom overlooking inground pool and hot tub. A must see, and the price is $219,000."

Ten months after Chuck's death, the house, which the Stuarts had bought for $239,000 in 1987 was still on the market, though its price had been reduced to $209,000. In an appropriate summation of the era, the local real estate agent handling the listing said that people who came to look at the house frequently cited the notoriety surrounding the Stuart case and were demanding a bargain.

The house was sold not long after that, for $188,590.

Early in 1991, almost a year to the day after Chuck Stuart's death, the DiMaiti family filed a wrongful-death civil suit against his estate, alleging that on October 23, 1989, "Charles M. Stuart, Jr., shot Carol DiMaiti Stuart in the head." The suit, which sought in excess of $500,000 in damages, was quietly settled out of court a few weeks later. Lawyers wouldn't disclose the terms of the settlement.

The Police

On December 18, 1990, the office of the Massachusetts Attorney General, James M. Shannon, issued a detailed report on allegations of civil-rights abuses by the Boston police department in the Stuart case and other instances, in which black suspects were questioned.

Noting that Boston police refused to cooperate in the investigation, the report documented a pattern of "improper and unconstitutional conduct" by city police officers in stopping and searching black citizens. Specifically addressing the Stuart case, it said: "Repeatedly, the police appear to have threatened, coerced, and offered favors to obtain testimony that would implicate Willie Bennet."

A separate federal grand jury investigation into police conduct in the Stuart case was continuing in the winter of 1991.